THE SHAPE OF THE PAST

FRANKLIN D. MURPHY

THE SHAPE OF THE PAST
Studies in Honor of Franklin D. Murphy

Giorgio Buccellati & Charles Speroni, Editors

Institute of Archaeology and Office of the Chancellor, University of California, Los Angeles

Institute of Archaeolgy and Office of the Chancellor
University of California, Los Angeles
Copyright © 1981 by The Regents of the University
of California
All rights reserved
Library of Congress Catalog Card Number 81-83849
ISBN: 0-917956-31-1
Printed in the United States of America

Contents

Foreword

FOR SOME TIME UCLA has been planning to sponsor the publication of significant contributions of interest to the world of scholars and also to the general community.

It is meaningful that the first such publication was sparked by the desire of several distinguished art historians, archaeologists and anthropologists to pay tribute to former UCLA Chancellor Franklin D. Murphy on the occasion of his sixty-fifth birthday.

Just as these scholars, and many others throughout the United States and Europe, owe a debt of gratitude to Dr. Murphy for help received through his good offices, we at UCLA owe an even greater debt for his wise, strong and skilled leadership during his memorable tenure from 1960 to 1968.

Dr. Murphy was deeply involved, with his characteristic élan, in all aspects of our multifaceted campus, an involvement gratefully acknowledged by the naming of Murphy Hall and the splendid Franklin D. Murphy Sculpture Garden.

Charles E. Young
Chancellor
University of California, Los Angeles

Preface

THERE ARE NAMES of individuals in the history of the Western World that are quickly associated with the great works for which they were directly or indirectly responsible. Indeed, through repeated usage, some of these names have become common nouns. One such noun is "Maecenas," which, as everybody knows, is used to designate a munificent patron of art and literature. Gaius Maecenas, it will be recalled, who was a contemporary of the Roman emperor Caesar Augustus, was a statesman and a patron of literature in particular, but also of the arts.

From Classical Antiquity to the present time, one could easily assemble a list of "maecenases" to whom the world owes a great debt of gratitude, for, without their commitment and far-sightedness many works of art and literature which enrich our lives never would have been created, and many more would have perished through neglect.

In our century the traditional maecenas has largely been replaced by government subventions or by foundation grants. This is as it should be in a changed world, but one must not forget that, in ideal circumstances, funds are not distributed blindly, but rather only after careful scrutiny and approval by a body of discriminating individuals. It is fortunate indeed when foundations are guided by individuals of broad knowledge and vision, who are committed to the highest standards of taste and scholarship. In our estimation, such a "rara avis" is Franklin D. Murphy, to whom this volume is dedicated.

Dr. Franklin D. Murphy was born in Kansas City on January 29, 1916. He received his B.A. degree from the University of Kansas, and the M.D. degree from the University of Pennsylvania. Although he was trained in medicine, and in fact he taught medicine for a few years at the University of Kansas, Dr. Murphy has been an administrator since 1948, first as the Dean of the School of Medicine at the University of Kansas, then as Chancellor of the same University between 1951 and 1960, and subsequently as Chancellor of the University of California, Los Angeles, between 1960 and 1968.

Many American universities have bestowed honorary degrees on Dr. Murphy, and the Republic of Italy has honored him with the title of "Commendatore." Until recently, he was the Chairman and Chief Executive Officer of the Times Mirror Corporation, and at present he is Chairman of its Executive Committee. Further, he is serving on the Board of Directors of Ford Motor Company, of Hallmark Cards Inc. and of the BankAmerica Corporation, and on the Board of Trustees of the Ahmanson Foundation, the National Gallery of Art, the Carnegie Institution of Washington, the Eisenhower Exchange Scholarship Program, the J. Paul Getty Museum, and of the Los Angeles County Museum of Art, of which he was formerly President. In past years he has served in similar capacities on an equally large number of boards, councils, and foundations. Of particular significance in the present context is his presidency of the Samuel H. Kress Foundation, a post he has held since 1963, and his trusteeship of the Ahmanson Foundation.

Those of us who have had the distinct pleasure of working with Dr. Murphy have all along been astounded by his energy, his innovative ideas, his seriousness of purpose, and his complete dedication to whatever he undertakes. His love for learning, with a penchant for the arts, anthropology, archaeology and the humanities, is deep seated and of long standing. Thanks to his appreciation for the accomplishments of "homo sapiens," and to his love for knowledge and beauty, many scholars and educational institutions have been benefited, and much has been done that would not have been possible otherwise. Bearing in mind that "omne trinum est perfectum," I will mention only three of his numerous contributions to the areas mentioned above: the Chair in Art History, which he was instrumental in establishing at the University of Kansas; the beautiful Franklin D. Murphy Sculpture Garden on the UCLA campus, which he conceived and has been guiding with taste and discrimination; and the prestigious Ahmanson-Murphy Aldine Collection, housed in the Department of Special Collections of the UCLA Library, which owes its existence to his absorbing and active interest in books and to his continued support of the UCLA libraries.

This volume of essays is offered to Dr. Franklin D. Murphy on the occasion of his sixty-fifth birthday, and it is intended as a collective expression of esteem and appreciation for the depth and range of his interest in the arts, the humanities, archaeology and anthropology through the years, and also for having supported the scholarly projects of the contributors to this volume, and of others who were unable to meet our deadline.

Professor Giorgio Buccellati and I wish to thank all those who have contributed so willingly to this volume.

A particular expression of gratitude is owed to Chancellor Charles E. Young of the University of California, Los Angeles, who has made this publication possible, to Mrs. Teresa Ruggieri Joseph, UCLA Latin American Center, for coordinating the project, and to Ms. Carol Leyba, UCLA Institute of Archaeology, for editorial assistance.

Charles Speroni
Dean Emeritus
College of Fine Arts
University of California, Los Angeles

THE ORIGIN OF WRITING AND THE BEGINNING OF HISTORY

Giorgio Buccellati

University of California, Los Angeles

PERHAPS AS A FORM of intellectual shorthand, most scholars would readily associate the beginning of history with the introduction of writing. The problems raised by this accepted cliché are rather formidable if one begins to probe them even superficially. What is the value and meaning of periodization, that is, of categorizing cultural process? What are the criteria that can be used in implementing periodization? How legitimately can a single cultural trait be used to divide in two the entire development of human culture? And how are we to define exactly the phenomenon of writing and to document its inception in the archaeological record?

Of these questions, the last one—about description and typology—has been dealt with more specifically and at length in the literature, largely because the study of individual writing systems has led to a generalization, even on the theoretical level, of the conceptual, technical, and historical underpinnings of the phenomenon, as evidenced, for instance, by the studies on grammatology by I. J. Gelb. In recent years, the discovery of the Tartaria tablets and the growing interest in a variety of marking systems (from the Balkans to the Indus basin) has renewed the interest for the diachronic aspect of the question. Little can one find, however, with regard to historical and historiographic evaluation of the data: "historical" in the sense of an assessment of the phenomenon of writing in its wider institutional implications, and "historiographic" in the sense of an explanation of its importance as an ordering criterion in the analysis of the human past. It is to these dimensions of the problem that the following reflections are devoted.

Let me start by saying that I argue in favor of the essential validity of the cliché that writing *is* the hallmark of history. In so doing I am perhaps only articulating what is *implicit* in the communis opinio but, it seems, is far from obvious. When reasons for the importance of writing are stated in the literature, they cluster around two poles, history and historiography. Historically, the introduction of writing is considered as a flag referring to some

Author's Note. A first draft of this paper was read at a meeting of the Pacific Branch of the American Oriental Society in Tucson, Arizona in April 1977. It has since benefited from comments by I. J. Gelb and Norman Yoffee, which are gratefully acknowledged. The concept developed here benefited also from a lively conversation with Franklin D. Murphy, to whom this version of the paper is dedicated, with admiration and gratitude: admiration for his unique intellectual posture vis-à-vis questions that affect the heart of our cultural growth, and gratitude for the confidence he has exhibited over the years toward my research.

other system, a symbol for a larger set of changes which took place at the same point in the course of human development, the so-called urban revolution. In this sense writing is both the result and the target of a complex social structure, which is intrinsically conditioned in its growth by the availability, or lack, of an effective communication system. Historiographically, one notes, first, how writing allows for a high degree of *specificity* in conveying information, and, second, how it increases dramatically the *amount* of information that can be transmitted among members of a given society and, beyond them, to us as historians.

ENERGY AS THE MEASURE OF EFFECTIVENESS

The key question, if we are to strive for a more explicit evaluation of the phenomenon, is to determine how to measure the effectiveness of writing. Only then can we compare literate and preliterate stages within the development of a given society and assess the degree of variation between the two. I cannot offer a formula for a quantitative measurement and consequent comparison, but I wish to propose a criterion that seems to allow for a fairly differentiated type of analysis. It may be stated as follows:

> The degree of effectiveness of writing is proportional to the *amount of energy expended* in obtaining a given level of communication.

Even without precise quantification, it is readily apparent that for a wide range of cases writing provides a much greater degree of communication in relationship to the amount of energy given as input.

Let us consider, for example, the case in which an intended message includes a reference to a specified number of animals, for example, two cows. If the message is to be fixed in a permanent medium (i.e., it is not simply oral), it may be conveyed representationally: the animals will then have to be rendered to scale and with pertinent details as to genus (bovines rather than any other quadruped), sex, age, and so on; the total number of animals intended will have to be matched by the total number of animals represented—the same figure will have to be repeated several times; compositional problems will have to be solved, with regard to coordination of the figures, framing, background. The energy spent in coping with these aspects of a representational effort may be measured in terms of hours or even days, depending on the training of the "artists," the nature of the medium chosen (e.g., stone or clay), the quality of the end product. By contrast, the notation "two cows" in writing takes but a few minutes. If minutes and hours are taken as units of energy, we come close to approximating the quantitative measure of the energy expended.

The disparity between the two approaches, representational and graphemic, becomes even wider if we look at some other aspect of the communication effort. In the representational sphere, the identification of an individual out of a genus, a specific man, for instance, requires a consummated craftsman: only a masterly rendering of physiognomic traits can differentiate one man from another, so much so that effectiveness in conveying the message can no longer be measured in terms of time, but must take into consideration the imponderable of artistic talent. In other words, not only will it take longer, it will also be much rarer that a man be identified representationally as a specific individual. Graphemically, on the other hand, the energy output remains constant as in the previous example of the two cows: the proper name and other ancillary features (filiation, place of origin, occupation, age) will univocally identify an individual for the same time expenditure of a few minutes.

It is important to note that the graphemic renderings to which I have alluded ("two cows," a proper name) presuppose other symbolic systems as intervening between the actual objects and the message embodied in the writing system, i.e. a counting system in the first example and a naming system in the second. A representational message, on the other hand, presupposes no particular convention other than generic attunement to a given stylistic mode. Writing, in other words, is a symbolic convention which builds necessarily on a number of other symbolic conventions—of which language is the most important one.

It is further important to note that writing as a communication medium is not simply a surrogate of a representational type of expression. Rather, it may be said that the two develop to some extent along mutually exclusive lines. While writing, for instance, thrives on the existence of complex symbolic identifiers, representational art will develop in the direction of rendering naturalistic traits. This means that in representational art an intended detail cannot easily be abstracted from the entire situation, whereas writing provides exactly the means for such an abstraction. The written message about "two cows" abstracts the features of count and genus and omits a host of details which in representational art must instead be rendered (relative size, color, etc.) even when they are irrelevant to the intended message. Hence we may say that energy saving as found in writing is also the result of an intellectual ability to segment our perception of reality into such portions as may be selected depending on circumstances.

INTELLECTUAL PRESUPPOSITIONS

We can assume as certain that language is a condition sine qua non for writing, and that it in fact developed much earlier in time. While perhaps obvious at first, a study of the relationship between the two serves to highlight, unsuspectedly, important aspects of writing as an intellectual innovation. To this end, we must first compare writing with tools and mechanical devices such as we see them develop in prehistoric times. As with writing, tools provide means for extending energy, and mechanical devices means for storing it, although writing is different in that energy is stored not as extrasomatic mechanical power, but rather as a set of abstract conventions. Where the comparison with tools becomes illuminating is in the observation of the mental processes underlying their use.

The process of making tools and mechanical devices, and the corresponding development of suitable skills and techniques, is universally recognized as a distinctive feature of human culture from earliest times. It is typical of this cultural trait that it entails a modification of natural data for purposes of use which are specific and repetitive. The tool is an extrasomatic extension of muscular energy ready for man to use at will; it creates a potential on which man can draw as the need arises. This situation may be described by saying that *the sequence of steps between manufacturing and use is not necessarily contiguous:* a tool is manufactured at one point in time and space for its potential use at an unlimited number of other points which differ, temporally and spatially, from the point of origin. In fact, even the steps to be followed during the manufacturing need not be contiguous: chipping of a stone tool need not take place all at once; it can be interrupted and resumed, even by different toolmakers, because there is an established procedure which controls manufacturing. This procedure is cultural in the specific sense that the connection between its steps is symbolic, and it is as such typically and exclusively human.

The advance in the evolution of symbolic procedures was one whereby certain procedures came to be articulated for which the sequential steps were *by necessity non-contiguous*. A typical example of this is agriculture. Perceiving the relationship between sowing, irrigation/fertilization, and harvesting implies the ability to subsume within a symbolic overarching procedure a set of activities which are by necessity separate one from the other in time and, to some extent, in space. The intellectual background of agriculture as a technological process may thus be understood as the ability for connecting among themselves procedural steps that are essentially noncontiguous. To say that this procedure was symbolic implies the ability to conceptualize the steps and to relate them logically; it implies, in other words, language as a symboling tool. It is, in fact, so important to be able to view the world symbolically through effective linguistic communication that it has been suggested that slowness of progress in the Palaeolithic may be linked with the inadequacy of language in that period (Oakley). Indeed, anatomical observations have been made which help to explain on a physiological level how language must in effect have been less articulate before the full development of the pharynx took place (Lieberman). In any case, we may say, to use the terms introduced above, that language is a mechanism designed to make it possible to represent as symbolically contiguous procedural steps which are not physically contiguous. The connection between sowing and harvesting is temporally noncontiguous in the physical world, but is made logically contiguous by means of linguistic devices. Alternatively, the symbolic representations of the procedural steps are made contiguous by means of symbolic configurations: if words are used as the symbols for the procedural steps ("sowing," "harvesting"), they can be brought together within a sentence ("sowing leads to harvesting"), whereby the contiguity of the symbols is real even on the physical level (of the phonological utterance). Thus, language may be understood as a means to make symbolically contiguous procedural steps which are essentially discontiguous, as the physical embodiment for the capturing of logical connections. However, it is an embodiment which is not permanent. And that is precisely the innovation brought about by writing. Writing transfers what is essentially a somatic procedure (language) to an extrasomatic level, thereby fixing onto a permanent medium the logical connections which language can express but fleetingly. It is an evolutionary step which seems almost predictable. But in order to explain more closely the innovation, it will be well to apply truly evolutionary models to this process. Thus the question which needs to be asked, in terms of the so-called Romer's principle, is: What was the *conservative* factor which posited the need for the innovation? We will be able to give an answer after a brief detour, which will allow us to explore first the techniques that were already available and served as the breeding ground for the development of writing.

TECHNICAL ANTECEDENTS

That writing as a working system (i.e., as we first find it in Mesopotamia) did not spring full blown from a vacuum is obvious. That earlier steps have to be postulated in the specific line of development which eventually led to the Uruk tables and Sumerian writing has always been assumed logically on the basis of an internal analysis of these tablets. That even more remote antecedents may be found in a variety of notations known to us from prehistoric cultures from beyond Mesopotamia seems increasingly possible. What has perhaps not yet been argued is the link between such antecedents and writing proper on the basis of the intellectual presuppositions they both share.

The technical antecedents of writing may be divided into two broad categories, depending on whether or not they are *syntactical* in nature. To the nonsyntactical category belong such items as markings on objects; whether incised, painted, or stamped with a seal. To the syntactical category belong calendrical sequences and other numerical notations. The distinction between the two categories is one of essence and it should not be underestimated. Nonsyntactical notations are symbolic in terms of their correlation to individual entities, that is, they act as direct pointers to a given element of reality, for example, the owner of a given object. The direction of such pointing is given by the context, much as in a representational setting. That is to say, the link between the symbol and reality is not in itself symbolic, rather it is situational: there is, in other words, no written syntactical relationship between symbols. If we look instead at calendrical notations and numerical reckonings, we find a juxtaposition of symbols where it is the juxtaposition as such that determines the reading criterion; the written sequence acts therefore itself as a notation—a syntactical notation—in such a way that the very link between symbols is symbolical. The importance of the syntactical notation lies in the fact that here the nature of symboling is elevated to the second power, introducing one further degree of abstraction in the process: individual symbols become endowed with a positional symbolic value. This leads to the distinctive autonomy of writing as an expressive medium, that is, autonomy from the contextual or situational.

Calendric notations have long since been stressed in the literature as key traits of early cultures, for instance by Gordon Childe and Leslie White. In recent years, very specific claims for calendric documents, dating as far back as 35,000 years ago, have been advanced and argued in considerable detail by Alexander Marshack. While controversial, his theories have the distinct merit of providing a consistent syntactical explanation for complex and recurrent sets of markings, which is as close an approximation to decipherment as one can expect to have. As for numerical reckonings of another type, many tablets with numerical markings have been found, especially in recent years, at protohistoric levels from a variety of sites in the Near East. According to an intriguing hypothesis advanced by Denise Schmandt-Besserat, these tablets fix in a writing medium a different procedure which had been in practice long before the time of the first tablets—a procedure whereby small clay objects of different sizes and shapes (especially spheres, cylinders, and cones) had been used as counters: the objects may have been standardized in such a way as to make shapes and sizes correspond to given numerical items so that clusters of counters could be used to refer to the desired totals. The early numerical notations on tablets, which actually have the same shape as these counters, might very possibly be the result of these counters having been impressed on wet clay. If the theory is proven correct, and all indications are that it will, we would have here a specific locus for the transition from a concrete correlation between physical items (counting based on the clustering of counters) to a syntactical correlation between logical units (counting based on the relative position of symbols).

If calendrical and numerical notations provided the model for that essential feature of true writing which is syntactic symboling, it must be recognized that nonsyntactic symboling, of the type referred to above, also played an important role, in that it provided a rich inventory of symbolic items which were suitable for pictographic categorization of man's growing mental universe. It may be said that nonsyntactic symboling provided the static elements, and syntactic symboling the dynamic principle which together made true pictographic writing possible.

The intellectual presuppositions and the technical antecedents we have described go back at least to the beginning of the Neolithic and most likely beyond as far as the Upper Palaeolithic. But it took in any case several millennia before writing was actually introduced as a regular routine, and that was only after the maturing of specific social preconditions: the growth of the state was the catalyst which brought together syntactic symboling and noncontiguous logical linkages. The merging of the two was called forth by the need for an effective handling of *social* constructs which were more varied in content than the items of the calendar, and less regular in sequence than the steps of, for instance, the agricultural cycle. A full reckoning of staples as they were being distributed to classes of people, for instance, was only possible, especially on a large scale, if expressed by permanent symbolic syntax, that is, by writing.

THE NEW EXTRASOMATIC EXTENSION

Against the developmental background we have been outlining, and with effectiveness as a measuring criterion, we can now attempt to define, as we said at the beginning we would set out to do, the range of newness, and the resulting significance, of the introduction of writing. I will proceed along two lines of inquiry, both of them having to do with the nature of mental processes: first, the extension and, second, the restructuring of brain functions.

Comparable only to language, in terms of previous cultural evolution, writing played a unique role in crystallizing consciousness. Individual data and, through syntactic symboling, elements of thought processes, became susceptible of a formulation in a permanent medium. This allowed for a quick and safe retrieval of information, thereby enhancing the power of memory. This, then, brings us back to the notion of energy as formulated at the beginning. Against the background of human evolution from the origins of the species on, and with a terminology derived from it, we can provide a new and very specific formulation to describe the innovation represented by writing. The growth of human culture had been characterized from the beginning by the successful development of extrasomatic features which extended the range of human capabilities beyond the inherent limitations of genetic evolution. Thus tools provided such an extension of muscular energy that the effectiveness of human performance became multiplied by a higher and higher factor: tools and mechanical devices were an extrasomatic extension of muscular energy, which developed through a cumulative process of increased complexity. This process depended on human control, and therefore indirectly on human genetic evolution, but did not itself develop according to the patterns of genetic evolution. It is as part of this sequence that the meaning of the introduction of writing can best be understood. Much as tools did for muscles, so writing did for the brain: writing can therefore be defined as *the first extrasomatic extension of logical brain functions.* The data that were previously accessible only through a somatic function, that is, that of memory as provided by the brain, came to be transferred onto such an extrasomatic medium as provided by writing.

We can now ask again the question which was left unanswered above: What was the conservative factor which posited the need for the innovation of writing? The observation of two concomitant factors provides the basis for an answer. First, the growth of cultural and social institutions was such that it bombarded human consciousness with an ever increasing amount of information. What is more, the relevance of this information for the successful performance of normal human activities came to be greater and greater. As a result, there developed perhaps for the first time the consciousness about forgetting. Such conscious forgetfulness entails by necessity a specific element of memory, that is, the memory that once one knew something which has become unknown at the moment when that knowledge has become relevant. Hence the need to increase the power of memory if retrieval of pertinent data is to be ensured at the moment of relevance.

But such increase could not be based on indefinite physiological growth—and this is the second factor in our argumentation. Even if there is no one-to-one correspondence between cranial capacity and brain functions, the two are nevertheless clearly related. Now it has been shown that by Upper Palaeolithic times, between 100,000 and 40,000 years ago, the previously constant growth of brain size had come to an end, as a result of a variety of factors, such as fully achieved bipedalism. Increase in memory could thus no longer be supported by any sustained growth of brain size and correlative (to some extent) brain functions. If Marshack's conclusions are accepted, it is precisely at this juncture, around 35,000 years ago, that the earliest syntactic notations appeared, marking the first true antecedents of writing. But even if this date is pushed to a later point in time, a logical connection between the two thresholds (physiological limitations on further growth of the brain and the introduction of writing) seems plausible. The conservative dimension of the innovation is thus to be found in the need to provide a suppletive function for a genetic limitation which did not allow man to cope with the increased demands on his memory.

THE NEW CATEGORIZATION SYSTEM

The impact of the innovation I have been describing was such that it led to an effective restructuring of certain aspects of man's mental categories. Writing came to serve as an additional memory bank, but—and this is a crucial difference with respect to human memory—a bank from which individuals could draw what they had not contributed personally. This is the essentially *impersonal* aspect of the phenomenon of writing: the communication of information, the transmission of knowledge came to be possible without personal contact, without face-to-face communication. Hence knowledge came to have an identity, a hypostasis of its own. It was a way for man to crystallize almost outside of time what were and are, otherwise, essentially fleeting moments of consciousness. A victory over time, perhaps, even if at the expense of the fully human and personal conditions of communication. And yet the immensely greater *range* of communication which became possible enlarged to an awesome degree the horizon of man's awareness of his mental universe.

Writing, then, was an extension of logical brain functions but, we may add in conclusion, an extension obtained through a *passive* medium. The data stored could be manipulated only when they were extracted from the medium and reinserted within active brain processes. In this perspective we may perhaps better understand the innovation of electronic data processing, which is providing precisely the next stage along that line of development, namely an *active* extrasomatic extension of logical brain functions, whereby information can be not only stored, but also manipulated extrasomatically. The consequent human anguish many feel in front of the computer is then in line with the element of impersonality which writing introduced long ago into man's relationship to his universe.

Whether the cybernetic revolution is ushering in a wholly new phase of human development, some sort of "post-history" after "prehistory" and "history," it will be for some future, in fact some very future, paper to tell.

These titles are referred to, by author's name, in the body of the text. An analogous theory, though from a different point of view, was published, also in 1977, by Carl Sagan.

BIBLIOGRAPHY

Childe, G.
  1951   *Man Makes Himself.* New York.

Gelb, I. J.
  1952   *A Study of Writing.* Chicago.

Goody, J.
  1977   *The Domestication of the Savage Mind.* Cambridge.

Lieberman, P.
  1971   "On the Speech of Neanderthal Man," *Linguistic Inquiry,* 11,2, 203-222.

Marshack, A.
  1972   *The Roots of Civilization.* New York.

Sagan, C.
  1977   *The Dragons of Eden.* New York.

Schmandt-Besserat, D.
  1977   "An Archaic Recording System and the Origin of Writing," *Syro-Mesopotamian Studies* 1,2, 1-32.

White, L.
  1959   *The Evolution of Culture.* New York.

VULVAS, BREASTS, AND BUTTOCKS OF THE GODDESS CREATRESS
COMMENTARY ON THE ORIGINS OF ART

Marija Gimbutas

University of California, Los Angeles

MANUAL LOVE PLAY—touching of vulvas, buttocks, and breasts—stimulated art creations some 30,000 years ago? That is the hypothesis posed by John Onians in the article "The Origins of Art" (published jointly with Desmond Collins) in *Art History, Journal of the Association of Art Historians*, I, 1 (1978), 1–25.

Considering the Aurignacian art of *c*. 32,000-26,000 B.C. Mr. Onians wonders why there are so many representations of vulvas, female figurines with large buttocks or breasts, and game animals: "There is no later culture, with one or two very isolated exceptions, which accords such prominence to the vulva. Nor is there a later culture which gives such prominence to representations of the entire female body in all its full and naked roundness" (p. 11). According to him, the Aurignacian art does not lend itself to ethnological comparisons. It does not invite comparison with totemism, shamanism, sympathetic magic, or initiation rites. If so, how are we to explain this early art? The conclusion is that the only help is the material itself, which exhibits the following: "The one activity to which the vulva is completely central is that of lovemaking" (p. 12). The Venus of Willendorf also suggests the association with love-making: "For those areas of her body which are shown in all their rounded perfection are precisely those which would be most important in the preliminary phases of love-making, that is, the belly, buttocks, thighs, breasts and shoulders, while the lower legs, lower arms, feet and hands are withered to nothing. There is no real parallel for this enormous imbalance of attention in any later art. Equally without parallel is the total neglect of the face. . . . This could once again relate to the restriction of interest during love-making, or more specifically the restriction to manual love play. This explains why the woman is so important in art" (p. 13). "If Aurignacian man ever day-dreamed, it is surely the sight of a nice edible reindeer or the touching of a nice rounded pair of buttocks which must have passed through his mind" (p. 15).

Illus. 23. The "Venus" of Lespugue, Haute-Garonne, Pyrenees, France, carved in mammoth ivory, and dated to c. 21,000 B.C. (Upper Périgordian). Her breasts and buttocks are shaped like double eggs, with the rest of the body tapering gradually. (Found in a damaged condition.) H: 14.7 cm.

Illus. 1. 1, Upper palaeolithic ivory waterbird and, 2, human female hybrid figurines, with prominent posterior, long neck, and an enormous human vulva engraved on the front. The figurines are symbolically decorated with chevrons, meanders, and parallel lines. Mezin on the R. Desna, Ukraine, c. 14,000-12,000 B.C. (no C-14 dates available; this date is based on the analogies with Kostenki site on the R. Don). Three views of each: a, front; b, back; c. profile. Scale 1:1.

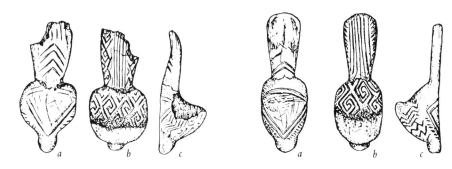

Illus. 2. Neolithic and copper age figurines with supernatural vulvas. 1, Marble figurine. H: 7 cm. Azmak tell, central Bulgaria. Karanovo I period, c. 5800 B.C. 2, Clay figurine from Bilcze Zlote, upper Dniester, western Ukraine. H: 12 cm. Cucuteni B phase, c. 3700-3500 B.C. (calibrated chronology).

This new hypothesis[1] on the origins of art is attractive and easily apprehended by readers (especially male) of the twentieth century A.D. But how are we to know that it was a human male who created art, and how sure are we that vulvas and venuses with large breasts and buttocks are portrayals of what a man experienced in touching or desiring to touch? Why not symbolic or philosophical concepts? Among other questions are the following: Is it true that the prominence of vulvas and the naked roundness of female body do not continue in the later cultures? Also, what of the anonymity of the face and the schematization of the body? Is it true that water and plant motifs (as the author asserts) never took the same place in early art because it was the responsibility of women?

In my opinion, early art was thoroughly symbolic, inspired by the urge to create another world, the mythic world. We do not know when man became the creator of myth, but certainly not as late as 30,000 years ago. The manifestation or belief in an afterlife and magical ceremonies is traced back to Neanderthal man some 50,000 years ago.[2] Ethnological evidence has shown that art is never dissociated from religious and social life. The same is true throughout prehistoric times and most of the historic era. Why then in the Aurignacian epoch did the meaning of art have to be divorced from society, its creeds, its values? Mme. Marthe Chollot-Varagnac, who recently published a corpus of thousands of incised upper palaeolithic bone and stone objects from the collection of the Musée des Antiquités Nationales, Saint Germain-en-Laye[3] came to the conclusion that all art, not only more or less naturalistic representations but also geometric motifs, is the outcome of mythical conceptualizations. "La conception magique" she says, was at the base of the psychic evolution of the hominids.

A number of signs and symbols and their associations with certain images of deities related to the concepts of cosmogony and cosmogeny are extremely long-lived: beginning in the upper palaeolithic period, they survived the economic changes in the onset of the agricultural era and continued further, some even to this day. The neolithic-copper age-bronze age symbolism of Europe and the Near East cannot therefore be disregarded as a source from which we can project backward. Its richness and extension into early historical times and to present-day peasant folklore in many cases provides a key to the symbolic meaning.

The portrayals of vulvas, breasts, and buttocks through the ages, from the Upper Palaeolithic and through the Neolithic, Copper

Age, Bronze Age, to modern times, some of which are illustrated in this essay, shed another light on the motivation of their creation than the one proposed by Mr. Onians.

The Aurignacian vulvas—semi-circles or bell-shaped with a dash or a dot at the opening—are abstract and schematic except for a few more naturalistic representations that make us believe that they are vulvas indeed. When we move into the later epochs, it becomes clear that the emphasized vulvas are not just "female signs" (the term used by Leroi Gourhan[4]), but are symbolic vulvas or wombs of the Goddess who is frequently portrayed as a human female and water bird hybrid.

The ivory figurines from Mezin in the Ukraine, dated to *c.* 14,000 B.C., are important for their symbolic associations. The vulva is the center of attention, engraved over the whole frontal part of the figurine (illus. 1). The long neck and protruding posteriors are clearly of a water bird. The meanders, chevrons, and parallel lines on the back and the sides belong to aquatic symbolism (the same associations systematically reappear over subsequent millennia). The large chevrons on the front of the neck are symbols of the Goddess.

Throughout the Neolithic, Chalcolithic, Copper Age, and Bronze Age of Europe supernatural vulvas appear as amulets (as clay triangles or round plaques with a "lens" incised), engraved on cult vessels or altars, and on several categories of figurines. The stereotypes of the figurines are: (1) The stiff "chrysalid" nudes with a large triangle instead of the abdomen, with arm stumps (for wings) or folded arms, and with cylindrical necks with no facial features or with masks (illus. 2,3,4). If legs are shown, they are schematized to cones. The almost lifeless bodies of the terracotta figurines of the Karanovo-Gumelnita and Cucuteni (east central Europe) of the fifth-fourth millennia B.C. and Cycladic marble figurines of the third millennium B.C. are engraved with groups of horizontal parallel lines suggesting that the body was wound symbolically with strings or bands. (2) The figurines with pregnant bellies, typical of the neolithic Sesklo culture of Greece. An enormous triangle is engraved below the protruding pregnant belly (illus. 5). The figurines of this "pregnant" aspect are portrayed in various degrees of schematization: some are "stand type" with a flat base (illus. 5, *2*); others are with prominent buttocks on which

VULVA

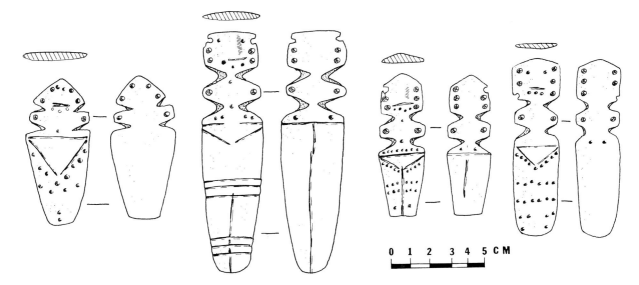

Illus. 3. Flat bone figurines with triangles over the abdominal area and masks with perforations for earrings. Ruse on the lower Danube, northern Bulgaria. Karanovo VI period, c. 4500-4200 B.C.

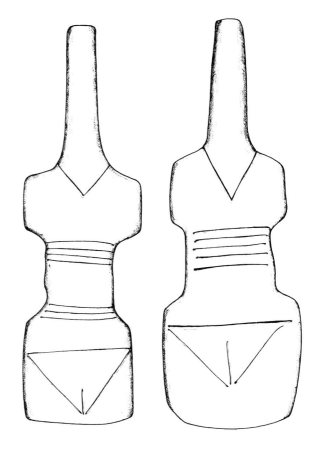

Illus. 4. Cycladic schematic abstract marble figurines with large vulvas and cylindrical necks, no arms, v-signs and groups of parallel horizontal lines around the body. Early Cycladic I. 1, From LOS (Norwich University of East Anglia Collection); 2, provenance unknown. H: approx. 19 cm.

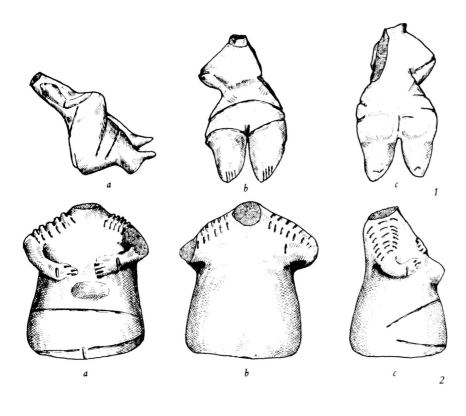

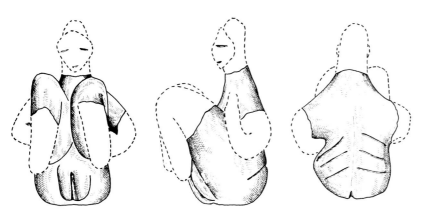

Illus. 5. "Pregnant" type figurines with supernatural vulvas from Achilleion IV, c. 6000 B.C., south of Farsala, Thessaly, northern Greece. 1,a, profile; b, front; c, back; 2,a, front; b, back; c, profile. Scale 1:1.

Illus. 6. Terracotta figurine in a birth-giving posture with an exposed vulva. Achilleion II, Thessaly, c. 6300-6200 B.C. H: approx. 6.5 cm.

they lean standing in a reclining position (illus. 5, *1*); still others are portrayed seated on a throne. If the neck is not broken, it is cylindrical and a mask is attached. In the mound of Achilleion, Thessaly, dated to 6500-5800 B.C. (author's excavation) such figurines were found placed on oven platforms and at grinding places. It can be surmised therefore that they were associated with seasonal rites and the idea of rebirth or resurrection. (3) The figurines

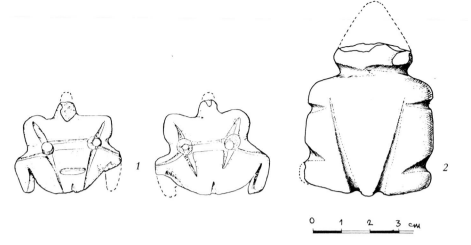

in a birth-giving posture, with upraised legs and exposed vulva (illus. 6).

The frog/toad-shaped amulets carved out of black or green stone, alabaster, or other material and molded in clay (illus. 7, 8), known from all prehistoric and historic periods of Europe, must have been related to the Goddess in the above-described aspects, particularly birth-giving and resurrection. There is a good deal of evidence, both folkloristic and historic (Egyptian, Greek, Roman, and later), that the Goddess herself is the toad and that she is also the vulva/uterus. Hence the belief in the "wandering womb" known from the Egyptian and classical sources, and as well as from the present-day folklore. Even Hippocrates and Plato described the uterus as an animal capable of moving around in every direction in the abdomen.[5] As a toad or vulva she is the symbol of resurrection. This symbolism is still alive in European folklore and it was even more so a century ago. I mention here several examples from nineteenth-century beliefs: The toad with a human vulva on the back was shown next to the portrayal of the Virgin on ex voto tablets of Catholic southern Germany (illus. 8, *2*). In western Lithuania, wooden tombstones were built in the image of a toad with a sprouting lily on the head.[6] The lily apparently symbolizes the new life. In northeastern Siberia, the Nikhs (Gilyaks) of Sakhalin and the lower Amur made pictures of a toad with buds at each extremity during the feast held in commemoration of the dead person. A ritual killing of a bear ("the glory of the forest", i.e., a vegetation spirit) was part of the celebration.[7]

The symbol of the vulva alternates with the seed/sprout/bud symbolism in pictorial art of east central European Copper Age

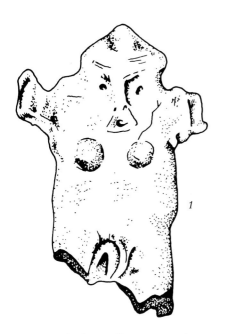

Illus 8. 1, A human female and toad hybrid with an exposed vulva from Maissau, a late Bronze Age cemetery in lower Austria, c. 1000 B.C. 2, A toad with a vulva on the back, which is painted next to the Virgin Mary, from a votive tablet of 1811, southern Germany. Scale 1:1.

(particularly well expressed in painting on Cucuteni B–Late Tripolye vases of the early fourth millennium B.C.) and of Minoan Bronze Age. The association of vulva and plant is as early as the upper palaeolithic art as was already demonstrated by Marshack in 1972. He rightly considered the vulva as a "non-sexual," that is, nonerotic, symbol, representing stories of processes that include birth and death, menstruation, and time-factored cycles relating to nature.[8]

The symbolism of the vulva traceable through the many milennia of prehistory and history suggests a different "activity" to which the vulva is central (that is, other than love-making as assumed by Onians), namely: birth-giving, rebirth, resurrection, plant regeneration.

The image of a bird-masked female with large hanging breasts emerged in the upper palaeolithic period: see the illustrated bird-beaked "Venuses" from the cave of Pech-Merle, Lot province of southern France of the Aurignacian culture (illus. 9). These finger-painted portrayals of human figures have artfully delineated female bodies with pendulous breasts, wings instead of arms, and the figure on the right has a bird head (mask). These paintings of human-bird hybrids were associated in the cave with serpentine meanders, parallel lines, series of dots, arcs, and hand prints. Bird-headed images with human breasts continue into the Neolithic and later periods.

THE BREASTS

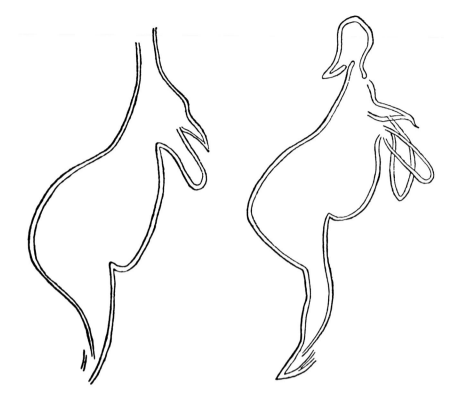

Illus. 9. Upper palaeolithic female nudes with pendulous breasts, wings for arms, and bird head masks (the figure on the right) from Pech-Merle (Cabrerets), Lot, southern France. H: approx. 70 cm. Painted with fingers. Chronology: probably Magdalenian.

The use of chevrons and parallel lines as symbols when applied to breasts of figurines can be traced to the upper palaeolithic period. One of the earliest examples is an East Gravettian (Pavlovian) mammoth ivory carving from Dolní Věstonice in Moravia (illus. 10, *1*). Only the breasts are naturalistically rendered on the rod-shaped abstraction of the human figure. The featureless head merges with the neck to form a single column; neither belly nor legs are indicated. Groups of parallel lines are incised at the upper end of the rod and below the notched breasts. A row of short lines are engraved from shoulder to shoulder across the back of the figurine. Beneath this are two groups of triple-line signs. Two short lines are incised beneath eight parallel lines in the center of the back.

The Dolní Věstonice site also yielded an even more abstract rendering of the female principle, signified solely by the breasts—an ivory pendant-bead of two breasts at the base of a conical neck (illus. 10, *2*). A double chevron incised beneath the schematized cylindrical neck is like the ornamentation appearing on the neck of beaked neolithic and chalcolithic figurines of east central and southeastern Europe. The concentric incisions to emphasize the nipples is a common characteristic of "nippled" vases of the Chalcolithic and Bronze Ages.

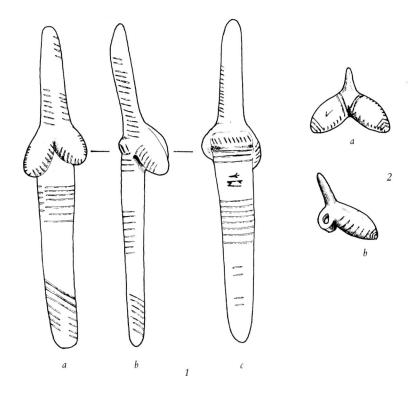

Illus. 10. Breast symbolism of the Upper Palaeolithic. 1, Mammoth tusk carving of a schematized human figure consisting of a pair of breasts, columnar neck and body incised with groups of parallel lines. 2. Pendant-bead in the form of two breasts attached to a conical neck. East Gravettian site of Dolní Věstonice, Moravia. 1,a, front; b, profile; c, back; 2,a, front; b, profile. Scale 1:1. c. 27,000-26,000 B.C. on the basis of radiocarbon dating.

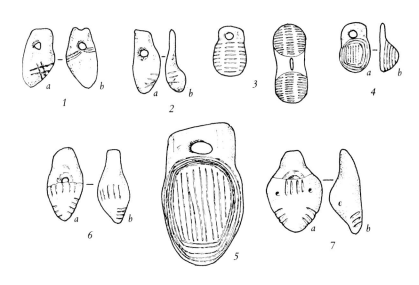

Illus. 11. Breast-shaped pendant-beads incised with parallel lines and Xs from upper palaeolithic sites. 1, La Ferrassie; 2, Saint-Germain-la-Rivière; 3,4, Barma Grande; 5, Arene Candide; 6,7, Grotta di Fadets. a, front; b, profile. Scale 1:1.

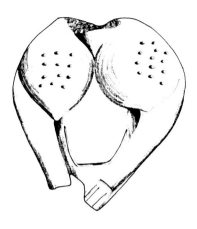

Illus. 12. Neolithic terracotta figurine with enormous breasts that are marked with incisions. Chaeroneia, central Greece. Sesklo culture, c. 6000-5800 B.C. H: approx. 7 cm.

Pendant-beads in the shape of a single breast have been recovered from sites of the Aurignacian (La Ferrassie, Grotte de Fossellone, Polesini, and Castanet), French Magdalenian (Saint-Germaine-la-Riviere, Pape di Brassempouy, and Saint-Michel-d'Arudy), Italian Gravettian, and Epigravettian (Grotta di Paglicci, Barma Grande, Arene Candide, and others) (illus. 11). Their presence in more than fifty upper palaeolithic sites documents the enormous spacial and temporal spread of this concept. Castiglioni and Calegari[9] have typologically and chronologically analyzed and classified these carvings of ivory, antler, bone, and canine teeth of deer or reindeer. The majority are incised with parallel lines in groups of three, four, or five; occasionally, a ∨ or ✕ appears beside the rows of parallel lines.

The upper palaeolithic tradition of marking the breasts with a group of parallel vertical lines or four lines continued in the neolithic and later periods evidently as a symbol for the concept related to milk, rain, nourishment, or of well-being in general. Parallel lines, ✕'s, notches, incisions were probably incised on breasts of terracotta figurines to express the concept of or invoke the Goddess for nourishment (illus. 12). Breast amulets carved out of greenstone are frequently found in Sesklo settlements (illus. 13).

The metaphor of the Goddess as the nourishing vessel is as early as pottery. Anthropomorphic vases recur throughout all phases of the Neolithic, Chalcolithic and Bronze Age. I am concerned here with vases with breasts and marked or associated with chevrons, zigzags, parallel lines, or streams—representations of vessels as the image of the Goddess.

Illus. 13. Breast amulets carved out of greenstone, probably worn as sacred breasts of the Goddess. Kyparisos tell, Thessaly, Sesklo culture, c. 6000 B.C.

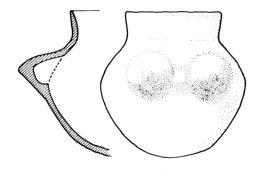

Illus. 14 Breast-decorated vase from the late neolithic Cortaillod culture, Switzerland. Saint-Aubin NE, Tivoli. Scale approx. 1:4.

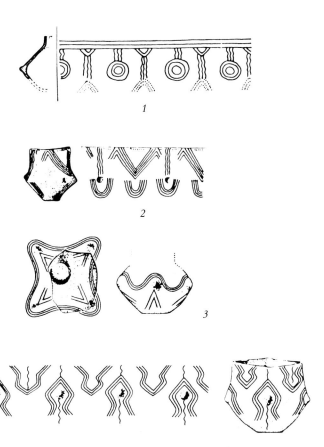

1

2

3

4

Illus. 15. Nipple-decorated motifs on Bükk vases, northeastern Hungary. Note the associations with wavy tri-lines (1,2), chevrons on M-signs (2,3), and snake heads (4). 1, Tiszadob-Ókenéz; 2, Tiszavasvari-Jozsefházá; 3, Tiszavasvari-Keresztfal; 4, Sárazsadány-Templomdom. Tisza-dob phase, c. end of the sixth millennium B.C. Scale approx. 1:6.

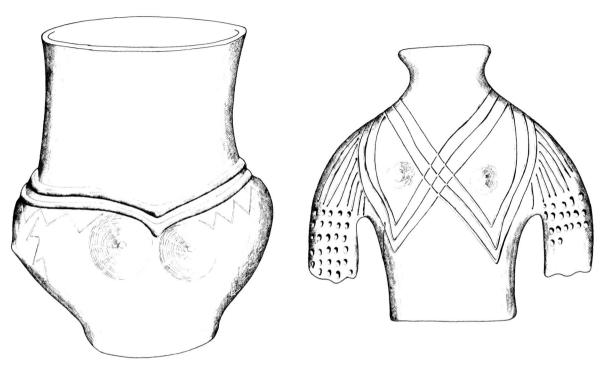

Illus. 16. Anthropomorphic urns with breasts from Fonyód, Baden culture, Hungary, c. 3000 B.C. H: (left) approx. 31.5 cm; (right) approx. 36 cm.

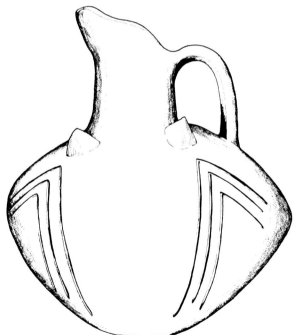

Illus. 17. Nippled lustrous-black jug with chevrons below. Troy I, c. 3000 B.C. H: approx. 23 cm.

Illus. 18. Nippled ewer from Thera (Santorini) exhibits a beaked face and necklaces, sixteenth century B.C. Thera exhibition, National Museum of Athens.

The breast-decorated or nippled vases start in the sixth millennium B.C., and for four thousand years the importance of the motif does not diminish. Occasionally breasts alone constitute the sole decoration of a vase, as seen in the illustrated example from the Cortaillod culture of Switzerland (illus. 14). Chevrons, grouped parallel lines, and zigzags of wavy parallel lines are usual accompaniments, indicative of streams of milk flowing from the breasts. The M and snake motifs are introduced on Bükk vase breasts (illus. 15). Breasts are shown in the midst of snake heads, and a wavy line emanates from them (illus. 15, *4*). Chevrons, zigzags, and parallel lines on vases with breasts continue throughout the succeeding

Illus. 19. Bands of zigzags and parallel lines are painted in white on a beaked anthropomorphic vase with human breasts as spouts. The cemetery of Mallia, eastern Crete, c. end of the third millennium B.C. H: 16.4 cm.

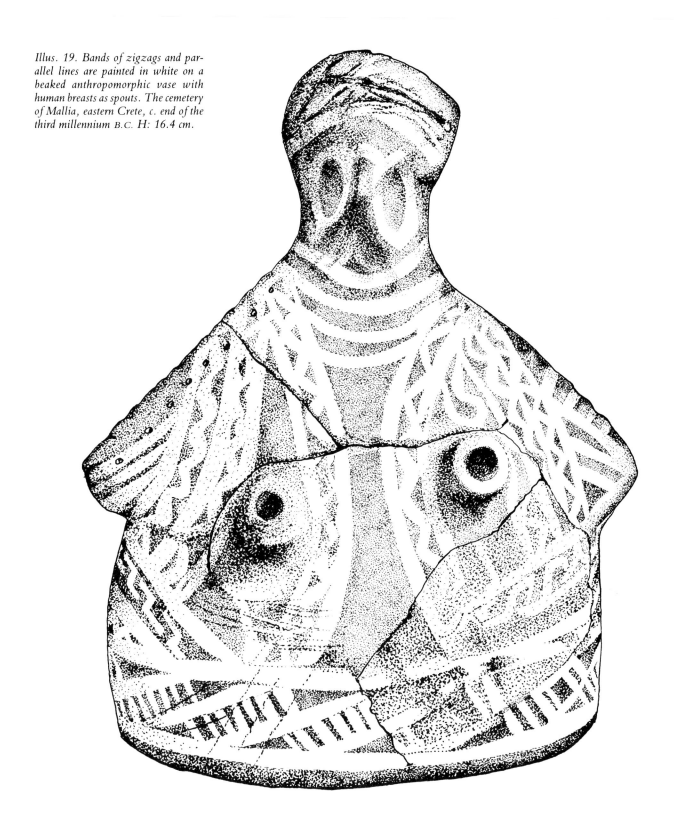

Bronze Age in east central Europe (Baden culture, illus. 16), western Anatolia (Troy, illus. 17), the Aegean islands, and Crete. At Thera hundreds of nippled ewers, dating from the sixteenth century B.C., have been excavated (illus. 18).

Anthropomorphic vases with perforated breasts as spouts, large-eyed beaked faces, and special headgear are characteristic of the Early Minoan period. Bands of zigzags, meanders, and parallel-lines dominate the rich decoration on one such specimen from the cemetery of Mallia (illus. 19).

In southeastern Italy, stone stelae ("statue-menhirs") with sculpted breasts and incised chevrons above and below (with their peaks between the breasts) have been discovered at Castelluccio dei Sauri in the area of Foggia, tentatively dated to the Copper Age, c. 3000 B.C. (illus. 20). From France, Spain, Portugal, and England statue-menhirs of the fourth-third millennia B.C. have breasts and a necklace as sole attributes of the Goddess. Occasionally her beak and eyes and vulva are indicated. The breasts and necklace as *pars pro toto* appear on slabs of gallery graves of Brittany (illus. 21). As the most important attributes of the Goddess they symbolize her presence in the grave.

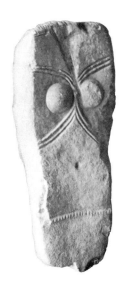

Illus. 20. Statue-menhir with breasts. H: approx. 1.5 m. Castelluccio dei Sauri, district of Foggia, southeastern Italy.

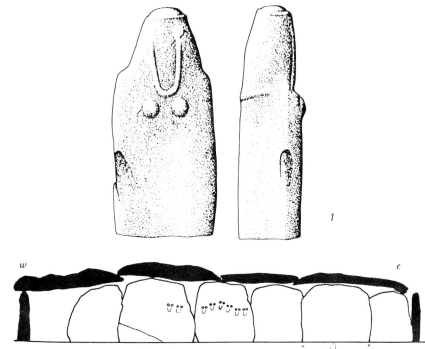

Illus. 21. 1, Statue-menhir of granite with breasts and necklace. H: 1.6 m. Câtel, Guernsey, Channel Islands, England (found in 1878 under a church). Probably belongs to the megalithic gallery grave of c. 3000-2500 B.C.

Illus. 21. 2, Slabs of a gallery grave bearing breast and necklace reliefs as symbols of the Goddess. Kerguntuïl, Tregastel, Brittany, c. 3000-2400 B.C.

Illus. 22. The Goddess in the form of amuletic breasts and schematized human body from the Iron Age in Denmark. She is marked with chevrons and parallel lines as in earlier prehistoric periods.

The breasts of the Goddess continued to be portrayed in the form of amuletic bronze ornaments even in the Iron Age of northwestern Europe (illus. 22).

The idea that the prominence of breasts in early art resulted from their importance in the preliminary phases of love-making is clearly far from the thoughts of the ancient artists. It is breasts of the Bird Goddess as the sacred source of milk/life and the symbolization of the concepts of nourishment and abundance which occupied the prehistoric artists.

THE BUTTOCKS

Illus. 23. Chapter frontispiece.

Symbolism linking the double egg, buttocks, and the magic of duality can be traced to the upper palaeolithic Gravettian "venuses" with buttocks sculpted without anatomical reality. A number of them have buttocks and breasts shaped like double eggs. One of the best examples of this symbolism comes from Lespugue in France (illus. 23). The female abstractions engraved on stone slabs from the Magdalenian epoch in Dordogne, southern France, are representations of buttocks with totally neglected other parts of the body. They are either struck through by an engraved line or by two lines, or contain a circle, that is, an egg, within the buttocks (illus. 24). A special series of upper palaeolithic mammoth ivory and coal figurines depict nothing else but female buttocks: the upper and lower parts of the body are reduced to cones. Such are the figurines from Petersfels, southern Germany, and Pekarna, Moravia (illus. 25).[10] Abstracted female forms whose primary fea-

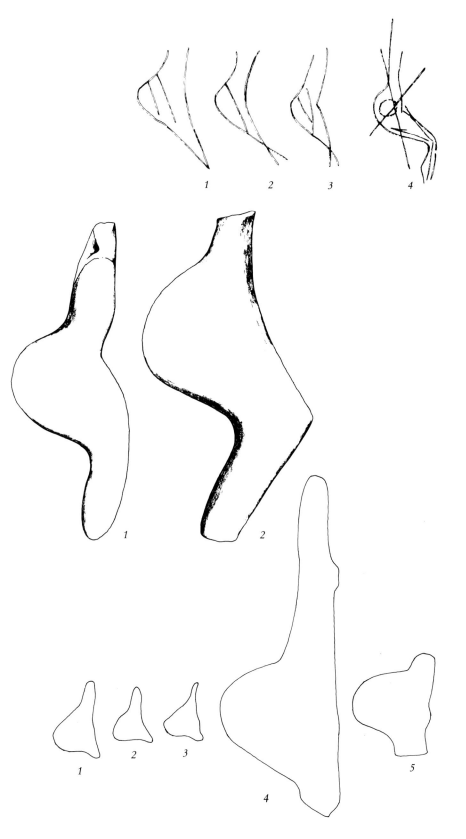

Illus. 24. Abstracted female forms whose primary features are the buttocks marked with one line, two lines, or a circle (an egg) and crossed lines. 1-3, Lalinde; 4, Fontalès, southern France (south of Les Eyzies). Engravings on stone slabs, Late Magdalenian.

Illus. 25. Upper palaeolithic (Magdalenian) schematic figurines featuring egg-shaped buttocks. 1, lignite pendant from Petersfels, south Germany. H: 4.3 cm. 2, Mammoth ivory figurine from Pekarna, Moravia, Czechoslovakia. H: approx. 9 cm.

Illus. 26. Profiles of schematic neolithic terracotta figurines with egg-shaped buttocks. 1-3, Early Pottery Neolithic, c. 6500 B.C., Sesklo, Thessaly, Greece; 4-5, Starčevo-Körös culture c. 5400-5300 B.C. from Röske-Lúdvàr (4) and Hódmezövásárhely, southeastern Hungary (5). Scale approx. 1:2.

 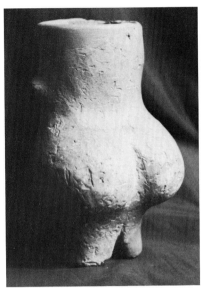

Illus. 27. Ornithomorphic vase with female buttocks from the Starčevo-Körös culture, southeastern Hungary, c. 5400-5300 B.C. Gorzsa at Hódmezövásárhely. Front and back views. H: 14.2 cm.

tures are the large egg-shaped buttocks continue in the European Neolithic, Chalcolithic, and Copper Age. Several examples are illustrated here from the Sesklo culture in Greece of the mid- seventh millennium B.C. and the Starčevo-Körös culture in southeastern Hungary of the mid-sixth millennium B.C. (illus. 26). The symbolic relationship between the upper palaeolithic and later figurines is obvious. There are also large anthropomorphic-ornithomorphic vases which have egg- or double-egg-shaped female buttocks (illus. 27). The images clearly combine the human female and waterbird features.

A distinct category of terracotta figurines from the end of the sixth, fifth, and fourth millennia B.C. in east central Europe (particularly of the Vinča, Lengyel, Cucuteni-Tripolye cultural groups) were portrayed with exaggerated egg-shaped buttocks (illus. 28-30). The buttocks were engraved or painted with snake spiral, concentric circle, and cross or whirl motifs. It is interesting to note that these figurines with egg-shaped buttocks either have no breasts or insignificant ones and pudenda hardly indicated. The buttocks were the center of interest; the other parts of the body are usually totaly schematized: the head is either an anonymous cylinder, or bird-beaked, arms are not shown or are stumps or wings.

The symbolic importance of buttocks is evident in pendants-amulets carved in the shape of buttocks of stone or bone (illus. 31), and in vases shaped as buttocks or double-eggs (illus. 32, 33).

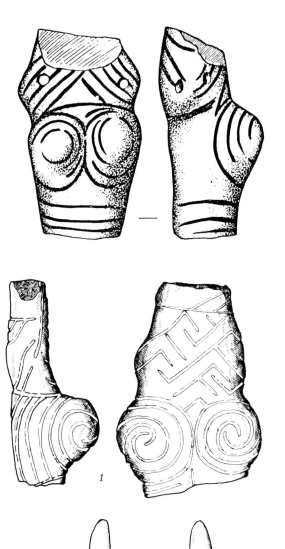

Illus. 28. Classical Cucuteni terra-cotta figurine with buttocks in the shape of a double egg. Vladimirovka, western Ukraine, c. 4500-4200 B.C. Scale 1:1.

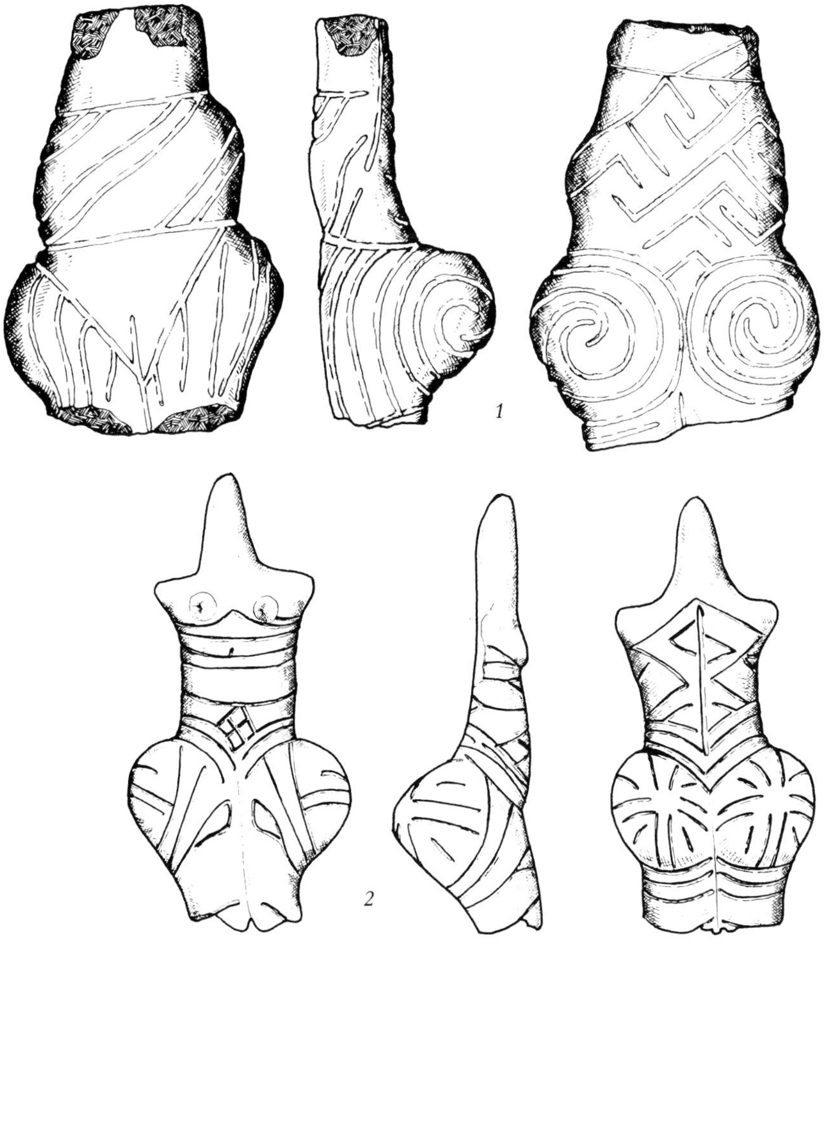

Illus. 29. Schematic terracotta female figurines with buttocks shaped in the form of double eggs and marked with a snake spiral and whirl design. 1. Kalojanovets, central Bulgaria. Karanovo IV, end sixth millennium B.C. 2, Novye Ruseshty, Moldavia, classical Cucuteni, c. 4500-4200 B.C. Scale 1:1.

Illus. 30. Cucuteni terracotta figurine featuring egg-shaped buttocks. The upper part of the body is schematized. Tirpeşti, Moldavia. Early Cucuteni period, c. 5000-4500 B.C.

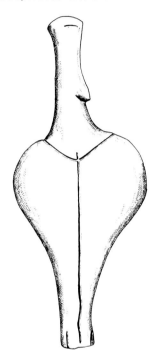

A painted double- or twin-egg motif on the interior of Cucutenian dishes and conical bowls is frequent. A snake stretches across the eggs (illus. 34). Two dots (symbol of duality?) occasionally flank the snake. A less abstract portrayal of twins in the embryonic state is rendered by two germs or seeds within a cosmic egg enveloped by a snake or a double embryo within the belly. The buttocks of Cucuteni figurines are marked by a double line within a double egg symbol which probably emphasizes duality (illus. 35). The double egg/buttocks symbolism cannot be dissociated from the symbolism of double seed or double fruit, known on Old European, particularly Cucutenian, painted vases (illus. 36 and 37) and which is still firmly preserved in the beliefs of European peasants of the twentieth century. Two is more than one. Two eggs or two seeds contain more germinating life power than one. It is believed that double seeds, double fruits, and double ears have magical power; they promote fertility and fertility is happiness.

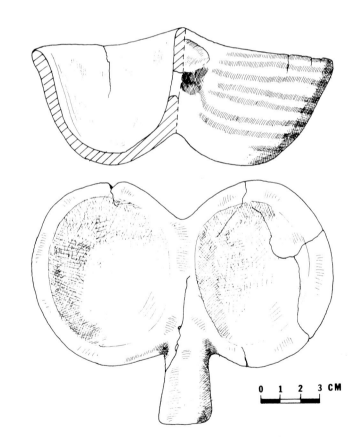

Illus. 31. Buttock-shaped amulet from Malta. Hal Saflieni Hypogeum, fourth millennium B.C.

Illus. 32. Buttock- or double egg-shaped vase. Pietrele near Bucharest. Karanovo VI (Gumelniţa) period, mid-fifth millennium B.C.

Illus. 33. A deep bowl with buttocks or splitting-egg symbol painted in white on red. Izvoare, Moldavia. Cucuteni culture, mid-fifth millennium B.C. 1, front (photograph); 2, back (drawing).

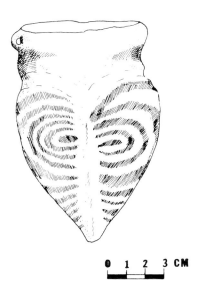

0 1 2 3 CM

Illus. 34. Cucuteni dish with double-egg/buttock motif with a snake winding across. Petreni, western Ukraine, c. 3700-3500 B.C. Diam: 51 cm.

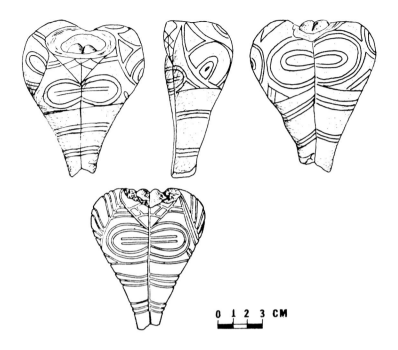

Illus. 35. Figurines with double-eggs or double-embryos within the bellies, and double-egg or duality symbols incised on the front and back. Novye Ruseshty, Moldavia. Cucuteni A culture, mid-fifth millennium B.C.

Illus. 36. Buttocks/double egg/double seed symbol painted in the central register of a vase. The upper register features a seed crossed by two lines and flanked by chevrons (Goddess's insignia). From Nedeia at Ghelaeşti, Moldavia, a Cucuteni site, c. 4000-3600 B.C.

Buttocks in prehistoric art were not buttocks of twentieth- century art. They were sacred parts of the body of the Goddess Creatress. This symbolism is inseparable from that of other symbols associated with the idea of beginning of life or germination, such as eggs, seeds, fruits. We are confronted with a philosophical thought about the beginning of life and the constant need of its promotion. The buttocks in upper palaeolithic, neolithic, and later portrayals were even farther away from the idea of the association with love-making than was the symbolism of the vulva and the breasts.

Illus. 37. Buttocks/double egg/double seed symbols decorate the neck and lower register of a vase. Note in the center a band of helixes flanked by seeds. Nedeia, Moldavia. Cucuteni culture, early fourth millennium B.C.

CONCLUSION

Our European prehistoric forefathers were more philosophical than we seem to think. They would certainly be stunned to hear the new hypothesis on the origin of their art (no philosophy, no questions of the beginning of life, birth and death, and resurrection). To us, naturally, the vulva, breasts, and buttocks are sex symbols—we cannot escape the ideals of the century we live in— to them they apparently were symbols of birth, life-giving, fertility, and regeneration. The rounded parts of the female body were the sacred and magic parts of the Goddess Creatress, the Giver-of-All.

NOTES

[1] Actually the hypothesis is not entirely new. Karel Absolon, who excavated at Dolní Věstonice in Moravia in 1937 and found the figurine illustrated in this article (illus. 10) wrote: "Sex and hunger were the two motives which influenced the entire mental life of the mammoth hunters and their productive art . . ." ("Modernist Moravian Art 30,000 Years Ago," *Illustrated London News* [March 25, 1939], p. 469). Ten years later, he called the upper palaeolithic figurine art "a dilluvial plastic pornography" ("The Dilluvial Anthropomorphic Statuettes and Drawings, Especially the So-called Venus Statuettes, Discovered in Moravia," *Artibus Asiae*, XII, 3 [1949], 208).

[2] A. C. Blanc, "Some Evidence for the Ideologies of Early Man," *Social Life of Early Man* (New York, 1961); Alexander Marshack, *The Roots of Civilization* (New York, 1972); P. I. Boriskovskii, "Problems of the Emergence of Human Society and the Archeological Discoveries of the Past Decade," *Soviet Anthropology and Archeology,* XIII, 3 (1974–1975), 25.

[3] Marthe Chollot-Varagnac, *Les Origines du Graphisme Symbolique. Essai d' analyse des écritures primitives en préhistoire* (Paris, 1980).

[4] A. Leroi Gourhan, *Treasures of Prehistoric Art* (New York, 1967).

[5] A. Gulder, *Die urnenfelderzeitliche "Frauenkröte" von Maissau,* Mitteilungen der Prähistorischen Kommission der Österreichischen Akademie der Wissenschaften, 10 (1962); Asta Ekenvall, *Batrachians as Symbols of Life, Death, and Woman,* (Göteborg, 1978).

[6] Marija Gimbutas, *Ancient Symbolism in Lithuanian Folk Art,* Memoirs of the American Folklore Society, 49 (Philadelphia, 1958), Figs. 51–58.

[7] L. Black, "The Nivkh (Gilyak) of Sakhalin and the lower Amur," *Arctic Anthropology* 10 (1973), 1 ff.

[8] Marshack, *Roots of Civilization,* p. 318.

[9] Ottavio Cornaggia Castiglioni and Giulio Calegari, "I Pendagli 'A Busto Ginemorfo' Del Paleolitico Superiore Centro-Occidentale Europeo, con un Inventario Ragionato Dei Reperti Italiani," *Museo Civico Di Storia Naturale Di Milano,* 66, 1–2 (1975), 25–52.

[10] A number of miniature of schematic "buttock-figurines" carved out of ivory or reindeer antler, dated by radiocarbon analyses to the eleventh-tenth millennia B.C., were recently discovered in Germany: Gönnersdorf at Andernach, north of Koblenz in the Rhine area, Nebra in Saxony-Anhalt, and Ölknitz in Thuringia. In addition to the figurines, in Gönnersdorf 500 plaques were engraved with similar "buttock-figurines." G. Bosinski and G. Fischer, *Die Menschendarstellungen von Gönnersdorf der Ausgrabung von 1968* (Wiesbaden: Steiner, 1974); R. Feustel, *Statuettes feminines paleolithiques de la Republique Deocratique Allemande* (Paris: Bull. de la Societe Prehistorique Française, 67, 1970); H. Delporte, L'Image de la femme (Paris: Picard, 1979).

SOURCES OF ILLUSTRATIONS

Illus. 1. Reproduced from Eugene A. Golomshtok, "The Old Stone Age in European Russia," Transactions of the American Philosophical Society, *Vol. XXIX, Part II (Philadelphia 1938), p. 352, Fig. 60.*

Illus. 2. Photo by Kónya, 1971.

Illus. 3. Marija Gimbutas, The Gods and Goddesses of Old Europe, c. 7000–3500 B.C. *(London: Thames and Hudson, 1974), Fig. 103, Plates 15, 144.*

Illus. 4. Jürgen Thimme, ed., Art and Culture of the Cyclades *(Karlsruhe, 1976), Plates 40, 41.*

Illus. 5, 6, and 7. 1. Author's excavation, 1973 and 1974.

Illus. 7, 2. Author's excavation, 1969.

Illus. 8. R. Kriss, Das Gebärmuttervotif *(Augsburg 1929); Alois Gulder, "Die urnenfelderzeitliche 'Frauenkröte' von Maissau in Niederösterreich und ihr geistesgeschichtlicher Hintergrund,"* Mitteilungen der Prähistorischen Kommission der Österreichischen Akademie der Wissenschaften. X: 1-157; Asta Ekenvall, *Batrachians as Symbols of Life, Death, and Women,* Kvinnohistoriskt arkiv. 14 *(Göteborg 1978).*

Illus. 9. Amédée Lémozi, La grotte temple de Pech-Merle *(Paris 1929).*

Illus. 10. Karel Absolon, "The Diluvial Anthropomorphic Statuettes and Drawings, especially the so-called Venus Statuettes, Discovered in Moravia," Artibus Asiae, *Vol. XII, 1949, pp. 201-220.*

Illus. 11. Ottavio Cornaggia Castiglioni and Giulio Calegari, "I Pendagli 'A Busto Ginemorfo' Del Paleolitico Superiore Centro-Occidentale Europeo, con un Inventario Ragionato Dei Reperti Italiani." Museo Civico Di Storia Naturale Di Milano, *66 (1-2), 1975, pp. 25-52.*

Illus. 12. Courtesy of Volos Archaeological Museum.

Illus. 13. Courtesy of D. Tlupas Collection, Larisa.

Illus. 14. A. Sauter and A. Gallay, "Les premières cultures d'origine mediterranéenne," Ur-und Frühgeschichtliche Archäologie der Schweiz, *II (1970).*

Illus. 15. Nándor Kalicz and János Makkay, Die Linienbandkeramik in der grossen ungarischen Tiefebene *(Budapest: Akad. Kiadó, 1977), Plate 171.*

Illus. 16. Nándor Kalicz, Die Péceler (Badener) Kultur und Anatolien *(Budapest: Akad. Kiadó, 1963), Plate VII.*

Illus. 17. Heinrich Schliemann, Ilios, the City and Country of the Trojans *(New York: Arno Press, 1976 edition), p. 227, No. 58.*

Illus. 18. Thera exhibition, National Museum, Athens.

Illus. 19. Arthur Evans, Palace of Minos, *Vol. 1 (London), p. 116, Fig. 84.*

Illus. 20. Courtesy of Archaeological Museum, Foggia. Author's photo, 1979.

Illus. 21. Jean Arnal, Les Statues-menhirs, hommes et dieux *(Paris: Editions des Hespérides, 1976), pp. 117, 123.*

Illus. 22. J. Glob, The Bog People: Iron Age Man Preserved *(Ithaca: Cornell University Press, 1969).*

Illus. 23. Alexander Marshack, Ice Age Art. *An exhibition catalog, California Academy of Sciences (1979).*

Illus. 24, 25. Alexander Marshack, The Roots of Civilization *(New York: McGraw-Hill Co., 1972).*

Illus. 26, 1-3. D. R. Theocharis, The Dawn of Thessalian Prehistory *(Volos: Volos Archaeological Museum, 1967);* 4, *Excavated by O. Trogmayer. Courtesy of Szeged Museum, Hungary;* 5, *N. Kalicz,* Dieux d'argile *(Budapest: Hereditas, Edition Corvina, 1970), Plate 16.*

Illus. 27. Courtesy of Hódmesövásárhely Museum, Hungary. Author's photo. Published in Idole, práhistorische Keramiken aus Ungarn *(Vienna: Naturhistorisches Museum, 1972).*

Illus. 28. Tatjana S. Passek, Periodizatsija tripol'skikh poselenii, *Materialy i Issledovanija Arkheologii SSR, No. 10 (Moscow and Leningrad: Academy of Sciences USSR), p. 94, Fig. 49.*

Illus. 29, 1. Mincho Dimitrov, Novi nakhodki ot neolitnata kultura Karanovo IV v Starozagorsko, Bulletin of Bulgarian Museums *I 1969 (Sofia 1971), p. 21.*

Illus. 29, 2 and 35. V. I. Markevich, "Mnogoslojnoe poselenie Novye Ruseshty I," Kratkie Soobshchenija Instituta, *No. 123: 56-68. Moscow.*

Illus. 30. Silvia Marinescu-Bîlcu, Cultura Precucuteni pe teritoriul Romaniei, *(Bucharest: Acad. R. S. Romania, 1974), Fig. 77.*

Illus. 31. J. D. Evans, The Prehistoric Antiquities of the Maltese Islands *(London: The Athlone Press, 1971).*

Illus. 32. D. Berciu in Materiale Cercetari Archaeol. *(Bucharest 2, 1956).*

Illus. 33. R. Vulpe, Izvoare. Sapaturile din 1936–1948 *(Bucharest 1941).*

Illus. 34. T. S. Passek, La Céramique tripolienne, *Izvestija Gos (Moscow: Akademii Istorii Materialnoj Kul'tury).*

Illus. 35. See credit from Illus. 29, 2.

Illus. 36. Vladimir Dumitrescu, Arta preistorică in Romania *(Bucharest: Editura Meridiana, 1974).*

Illus. 37. A. Niţu, St. Cucoş and D. Monah, Ghelăieşti (Piatra Neamţ) I. Săpaturile din 1969 in Aşezarea Cucuteniana "Nedeia," Memoria Antiquitatis III, p. 11.

Illus. 3-8, 10-12, 14, 16, 17, 19, 24-26, 29-33, 35, 36: Drawings by Linda Mount-Williams.

MINIATURE ART FROM TERQA, 1700 B.C.
NEW SOURCES FOR MID-SECOND MILLENNIUM ART IN MESOPOTAMIA

Marilyn Kelly–Buccellati
California State University, Los Angeles

Illus. 5. Haematite seal from the excavations at Terqa next to its modern rolling. The design shows the emphasis of the drill holes in the Khana style as in the garment fringe and in the hats of the deities. TQ5-T111

CYLINDER SEALS AS THE main source for miniature art in Mesopotamia have been a major contribution from this area to the history of Western art. The noted art historian in the field of ancient Near Eastern art, Henri Frankfort, was able to write as early as 1939: "The cylinder seals of Mesopotamia constitute her most original contribution to art" (Frankfort 1939, p. xiii). Mesopotamian sphragistics, as the study of cylinder seals and their impressions is called, has long been pursued by art historians because of the intrinsic beauty of Mesopotamian seals exhibited in their rich expression of iconographic and formal stylistic traits which in all periods paralleled those of monumental art. The importance of cylinder seals for the history of Mesopotamian art is heightened by the paucity of preserved monumental art for some periods. Thus a continuous history of Mesopotamian art can only be seen through its miniature art.

This essay deals with cylinder seals and their impressions excavated in the ancient city of Terqa, located in eastern Syria along the middle Euphrates River. The miniature art evidenced by these seals is one of the most important finds from the excavations at Terqa, on account of the contribution they make to our understanding of the Mesopotamian artistic tradition and, beyond that, of the historical development of an otherwise obscure period of the Near East. It is fitting that the first publication of this choice material should appear in a volume dedicated to Franklin D. Murphy, who has been an essential catalyst in making the excavations possible and has always shown an insider's interest in the work there.

The seals and sealings from Terqa are rolled for the most part on legal contracts and on the clay envelopes protecting them. Their historical importance lies in the fact that they are beginning to fill a gap both in space (i.e., the middle Euphrates River) and time (the period from 1750 to 1500 B.C.). Terqa is one of the few sites in Mesopotamia where we have material from this time period and, further, it is one that provides a link between the southern states in Sumer and Babylonia and the rich tradition of western Syria, highlighted in recent times by the major discoveries at Ebla.

Author's Note. The Joint Expedition to Terqa has been sponsored in part by the Samuel H. Kress Foundation and the Ahmanson Foundation, with whom Dr. Murphy is associated, as well as by the Ambassador International Cultural Foundation. The five seasons completed thus far (1976 to 1980) have been directed jointly by the writer and Giorgio Buccellati, with an international team from several American and European universities.

THE MID-SECOND MILLENNIUM SEAL STYLE

From about 1800 B.C. on, the typical Old Babylonian seals made in Mesopotamia have depicted on them the standard scenes of either a worshipper before an enthroned deity, or an individual giving homage to an enthroned king. While other motifs are found, Old Babylonian seal cutters and their customers preferred this theme. These scenes were diversified through the depiction of a variety of deities, subsidiary figures (such as different types of worshippers, the addition of interceding goddesses, animals associated with the deities, etc.), and smaller motifs placed in the field such as a star, crescent, bird, tortoise, mongoose, etc.

The style of carving of Old Babylonian seals varied also according to the skill and training of the seal cutter, the city the seal was produced in, as well as the time within the Old Babylonian period in which it was carved. In general we can see that the best seals, made of haematite, were carved with attention to the fine linear details of the figures and their costumes (illus. 1). The carving was started with a bow drill, and continued with various engraving tools.

In Old Babylonian seals the major figures take up the full height of the seal which determines the frame of the representation once the seal is rolled out. The relation between the size of the figures and the height of the seal stone was established as standard in the earliest cylinder seals carved in Mesopotamia, with deviations, previous to the Old Babylonian period, only in the best Akkadian seals (ca. 2300 B.C.) where more emphasis was given to the pro-

Illus. 1. A typical Old Babylonian Seal with its impression from Ibezeikh in southern Mesopotamia with a bearded god seated on the right and a worshipper in the center followed by an interceding goddess.

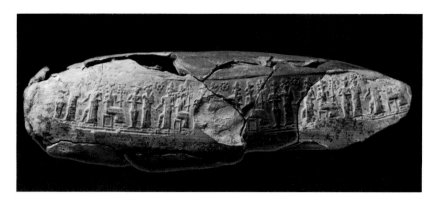

Illus. 2. Seal impression from Terqa rolled in a continuous band along one side of a clay envelope covering a cuneiform tablet. In this case the tablet was contained in two envelopes with the side of the outer one pictured here. The design, repeated several times in this rolling, includes a god holding a saw on the right faced by a worshipper, next is placed a naked goddess before a god seated on the left. TQ4-T68

portion of the figures in relation to the landscape depicted (Kantor 1965). This Akkadian practice, however, was sporadic and quickly fell out of use, so that in the following Ur III period we again find the main figures occupying the entire vertical space available. This compositional rule was so strong that it prevailed even when one of the figures is seated (illus. 2). In our example a bearded god on the left is seated on a plain stool with his feet resting on a low platform. The other three figures in the composition are all standing; their heads, however, are the same height as the seated figure. The artist was not trying to depict figures placed on different levels, as shown by the fact that the stool and footrest of the deity on the left, as well as the feet of the three standing figures, are all placed on the same continuous ground line. The only possible conclusion to be drawn is that the rule of composition whereby the main figures had to occupy the full height of the seal was so strong that it had to be followed even though the dictates of realism would have precluded such an arrangement. This is by no means the only place where the Old Babylonian artist, following tradition, ignored realism even though art in the Old Babylonian period was in many respects realistic.

Given this trend toward realism, the question then should be asked: to what extent do these seals reflect actual religious ceremonies? We know that statues of the deities were placed on altars in Mesopotamian temples. In the temple of Ninkarrak (the Mesopotamian goddess of Good Health) at Terqa we have excavated the sanctuary with the altar as well as a hoard of over six thousand beads which were probably used as part of the jewels of the goddess (illus. 3). It seems probable that this goddess, as well as all the other Mesopotamian deities, actually wore the clothes and jewels ascribed to them in the texts (Buccellati and Heimpel 1981).

Illus. 3. The jewels of Ninkarrak found in the sanctuary near the altar of her temple at Terqa. The hoard included more than 6000 beads in a wide variety of stones and shapes including several Egyptian scarabs.

Illus. 4. A portion of a seal rolling on the exterior of an envelope from Terqa. This fragment shows part of the figure of a worshipper holding the typical offering animal—a kid. TQ5-T82

Illus. 6. The side of a Khana period tablet from Terqa showing two seal impressions. The impression on the right includes a worshipper before a winged goddess standing on top of a lion. The impression on the left, reversed with respect to the other, depicts two deities next to two worshippers. TQ4-T1 and 4

As stated above, the themes on Old Babylonian seals were centered on scenes of an enthroned deity or a king being worshipped by a single adorer, who is sometimes introduced by an interceding goddess. The worshipper often carries a kid as an offering (illus. 4). From the texts we also know that offerings made to the deities included such animals. Also, the gesture of homage that a worshipper makes with his right hand (illus. 5 and 6), that is, fingers extended and close together with the hand before the mouth, is seen not only in cylinder seal designs but also elsewhere in monumental art, for instance on the famous stela with the Code of Hammurapi, where the king is shown in this posture in front of the god Shamash. That this gesture was actually used is difficult to determine but there is no doubt that its depiction was long lived since it can still be seen in Achaemenid art, for instance in the Treasury at Persepolis where a servant standing before Darius makes the very same gesture (Ghirshman 1964, fig. 255). Its frequent appearance in Mesopotamian art as well as its use later on by the Achaemenids certainly argues for a lively tradition in practice as well as in art.

Illus. 5. Chapter frontispiece.

The seals that were produced during the Khana period (1750-1500 B.C.) at Terqa are stylistically related to those made in Mesopotamia during the Old Babylonian period. There are, however, some significant differences between the two styles, as is borne out by the techniques used in carving, by their compositional arrangements, and also by their iconographies. These differences in the Khana artistic style mark the beginning of a distinctive new type of art, which then continued in Mesopotamia for most of the remainder of the second millennium.

THE KHANA STYLE FROM TERQA

It has been known for some time that late Old Babylonian seals show an increased use of the drill. However, the beginning of this type of carving has been obscure because there was not enough well-dated evidence bearing on this question. With the excavations at Terqa, the presumed capital of the Khana Kingdom, we are now amassing a large corpus of Khana seals and seal impressions. From this corpus it is clear that the increased use of the drill, which is typical of the Khana style, started in Terqa at least as early as the reign of Samsuiluna, the son of Hammurapi. Seals carved in the Khana style were used to seal documents dated to the reign of a king of Khana, Yadikh-Abu. Yadikh-Abu is mentioned in a year date of Samsuiluna, king of Babylon, which names the twenty-eighth year of his reign after his victory against a certain Yadikh-Abu (Rouault 1981). Since this name is not a common one for a king, and since other evidence from Terqa points to the fact that Yadikh-Abu reigned in this time period, we can date the use of the Khana style to sometime before 1721 B.C. In all probability this style had started sometime earlier in Terqa, as is suggested by the very large number of this type of seal impressions on the tablets dated to the reign of Yadikh-Abu. These sealings indicate that by then the style was already well developed at Terqa.

Most distinctive of the characteristics of the Khana style are the holes left by the use of the bow drill. On earlier Mesopotamian seals these holes were obliterated by the careful use of engraving tools to carve them away. In the Khana style seals, however, the holes were left as an obvious part of the stylistic effect the artist wanted to produce. This can clearly be seen in illustration 5 where the fringe runs vertically down the center of the garments worn both by the worshipper holding the kid offering, on the left, and by the second worshipper on the extreme right. In each case the vertical line of dots corresponding to the holes left by the carver on the cylinder seal is visible. How this fringe is depicted can be contrasted with the linear borders on the garments in illustration 1, an earlier Old Babylonian seal. Returning to the seal in illustration 5 we can see that the god wearing a slit skirt and holding a saw has his appearance accentuated by the use of a series of drillings for the depiction of his horned miter. These drill holes are repeated below his foot with a double row of three dots indicating a mountain or hillock associated with the sun god Shamash. This seal and an example of the type of saw he is carrying were found in the excavations of the Ninkarrak temple at Terqa (illus. 7). Here we

Illus. 7. A bronze saw from the Temple of Ninkarrak at Terqa. This saw, with well-preserved teeth, has an antler handle. TQ3-100

Illus. 8. The envelope of a Khana Tablet from Terqa with a single seal rolled the entire length. The sealing, best preserved on the right, includes two figures on either side of a seven-globed standard and a god on the left facing a worshipper. TQ4-T85

Illus. 9. Seal rolled criss-cross fashion on the envelope of a Khana period tablet. The same seal was used to make this rolling as was used to make the impression seen in illustration 2. TQ4-T173

can also point to the fact that the Khana seal cutter was technically able to use engraving tools to achieve the effects he wanted, as seen, for instance, in the straight parallel lines of the dress of the god Shamash in illustration 5.

In the area of composition, also, Khana style seals stand out as being related to, but different from, Old Babylonian seals. This is the case both in the overall composition of the seals as well as in the composition of individual figures or groups of figures. In the Khana style the principal deities are often placed on the left side of the composition facing subsidiary figures which are to the right of them (see illus. 8, also 2, 5, 6). This is contrary to the position of seated deities on Old Babylonian seals where they are placed on the right facing figures on the left (see illus. 1). This change in position is also reflected in the object they are often holding—a seven- or nine-globed staff (illus. 9; this is the same seal as illustration 2 but in this case rolled on the top of the exterior envelope). An identical staff appears in Old Babylonian glyptic but not as frequently as it does in the Khana style. Seven or nine globes can also be mounted on a full-length standard (illus. 10). It is not known what these objects were used for, but they were probably part of the ritual furniture in temple ceremonies.

Illus. 10. Two seal designs from a Khana period tablet excavated at Terqa. The upper design shows two figures flanking a seven-globed standard with a god holding a similar staff facing a worshipper. Below the seal design depicts a deity with his attendant and a nude hero with characteristic hair curls down either side of his face. TQ4-T144

Through the excavations at Terqa a corpus of miniature art is being amassed which is throwing considerable light on the artistic style of the second quarter of the second millennium in Mesopotamia. We are now beginning to see the major contributions that this particular tradition made to the developmental history of Mesopotamian art. This material is, thus, bridging the gap in Mesopotamia between the relatively well-known Old Babylonian period, especially during the reign of Hammurapi, and the Mitanni seals, popular around 1500 B.C. It is significant that the Mitanni style, as an inheritor of Old Babylonian characteristics, existed mainly in northern Mesopotamia, while the Old Babylonian style was centered in the south near Babylon. The transmission of ideas as well as artistic style must have been effected through the central Euphrates Kingdom of Khana; thus Khana was the geographical and chronological intermediary between these two cultures.

CONCLUSION

Bucellati, Giorgio, and Wolfgang Heimpel
  1981   "Two Views of Inanna," *Syro-Mesopotamian Studies* 4.

Frankfort, Henri.
  1939   *Cylinder Seals*. London: Gregg Press. Reprinted 1965.

Ghirshman, Roman
  1964   *The Arts of Ancient Iran*. New York: Golden Press.

Kantor, Helene J.
  1965   "Landscape in Akkadian Art," *Journal of Near Eastern Studies* XXV(3):145-152.

Rouault, Olivier
  1981   *Terqa Final Reports,* 1, *L'Archive de Puzurum*. Bibliotheca Mesopotamica. Malibu: Undena Publications.

BIBLIOGRAPHY

Dimensions of pieces illustrated: illus. 1, H: approx. 2 cm; illus. 2, H: 3.5 cm; illus. 4, H: 3 cm; illus. 5, H: 2.1 cm; illus. 6, H: 13.5 cm; illus. 7, L: 36.7 cm; illus. 8, H: 7.5 cm; illus. 9, H: 15 cm; illus. 10, H: 3.5 cm.

A MOCHE V BOTTLE
WITH COMPLEX FINELINE DRAWING

Christopher B. Donnan

University of California, Los Angeles

MORE THAN A thousand years before the beginning of the Inca Empire, a people we now call Moche flourished on the coastal plain of northern Peru. The Moche had no writing system, yet they produced a vivid artistic record of their activities and their environment. Indeed, the realism and subject matter of Moche art make it one of the most appealing of all Pre-Columbian art styles.

Since 1968, intensive study of Moche art and culture has been a primary focus of Andean archaeology at UCLA. Much of the success of this research has been due to Franklin Murphy. His fondness for ancient art and his personal interest and encouragement have been of key importance in the formation of an archive consisting of more than 110,000 photographs of Moche art from collections throughout the world. This archive serves as a continuing resource for teaching and research.

Current research in the Moche archive is focused on the end of the Moche style, and the development of the Chimu style that replaced it. The transition between these two styles, which occurred sometime between A.D. 600 and 800, has puzzled Andean scholars for many years, and only recently has sufficient evidence begun to accumulate so that the nature of the transition can be reconstructed.

This report deals with a Moche bottle decorated with an unusually complex fineline drawing. The drawing exhibits several features that have not previously been noted in the Moche style, and constitutes an important source of new information concerning the nature of the Moche-Chimu transition.

The bottle (illus. 1) is part of a private collection and has no provenience data. It measures 20.3 centimeters in height. There is no visible evidence of repair or restoration, although in the lower part of the chamber there are two small holes which appear to have been made in recent years. On the basis of its form and decoration, the bottle can be assigned to the final phase of the Moche style, Phase V, and is almost certainly from the last part of that phase.

Spiraling downward around the chamber of the bottle is a long procession of figures. This procession, which is reproduced in illustration 2, has been simplified by omitting the circles and dots that serve as background filler elements. Each figure is numbered to facilitate discussion.

Number 1 is positioned between the spouts of the bottle and is not part of the spiral that frames all the other figures. The figure is splayed and has a companion dog. The splayed posture is rare

Illus. 1. The Moche V bottle with complex fineline drawing. Photo by Robert Woolard.

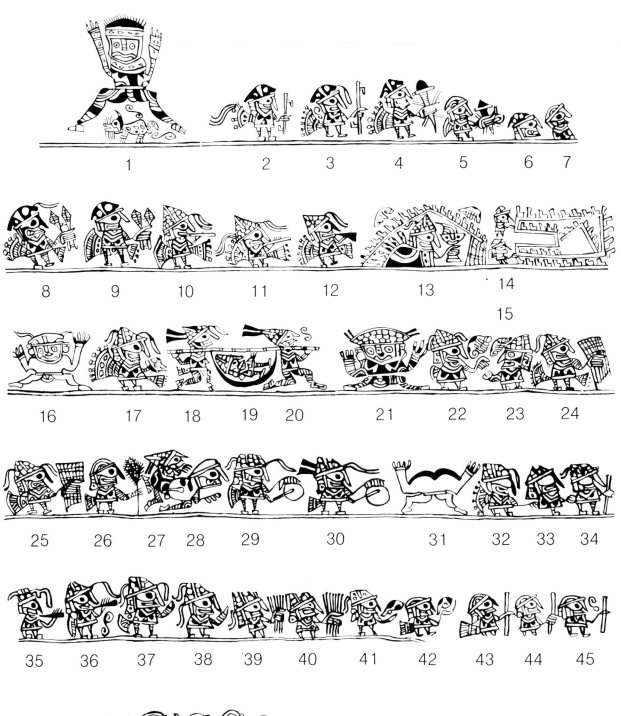

1   2   3   4   5   6   7

8   9   10   11   12   13   14

15

16   17   18   19   20   21   22   23   24

25   26   27   28   29   30   31   32   33   34

35   36   37   38   39   40   41   42   43   44   45

46   47   48   49   50   51   52   53   54   55   56   57

in Moche art, and when used generally indicates that the individual is dead. This figure does not have other typical Moche death features, however, and thus may well be alive.

Numbers 2 through 5 carry weapons. The first two have spear throwers, and the second two hold clubs and spears. Since numbers 5 through 7 are positioned below part of the spout on this bottle, they are reduced in size to fit the available space—number 5 is shorter than number 4, number 6 is represented only by a human head, and number 7 is shown as a head and torso without the legs. Thus, numbers 6 and 7 are almost certainly *not* meant to be simply a human head and a legless figure, but rather full figures shown in abbreviated form because of space restrictions.

Numbers 8 through 12 hold musical instruments. Numbers 8 and 9 hold rattles, numbers 10 and 11 play *quenas,* and number 12 plays a straight bugle.

Number 13 is a seated figure, with dragonfly wings, holding a goblet with a face on the chamber. He is under a gabled roof which has a step design along the upper edge. There are two conch shells above the roof. It is interesting to compare this individual with one depicted in another Moche V fineline drawing (illus. 3). Here a figure with dragonfly wings holds a goblet in one hand, but is seated in a tule boat rather than under a gabled roof. It is likely that the two are representations of the same individual. The fact that they are holding goblets suggests that they are in some way related to the Presentation Theme, a ceremony involving a ritual presentation of goblets (Donnan 1978: 158-173).

Numbers 14 and 15 are touching a large angular object. This object is almost certainly a plan view of a U-shaped architectural structure known as an *audencia.* An audencia consists of a large mound with walls extending forward on both sides. The mound and its two extended walls enclose three sides of a rectangular area in front of the mound. In the plan view representation of the mound, there is a side view of a gabled roof, suggesting that the mound served as the platform for a structure with a gabled roof.

Audencias have been found at Moche V sites, where they apparently served a highly religious-ceremonial function. Through time they became increasingly associated with socio-administrative activities, and reached their most developed form during the Chimu kingdom. They are particularly evident in the audencia-storage complexes at Chan Chan, the capital of the Chimu kingdom (Keatinge 1977).

Illus. 2. Fineline drawing from the chamber of the bottle shown in illustration 1. Drawing by Donna McClelland.

Number 16 is another individual shown in splayed posture similar to number 1, but he lacks the complex body paint and the companion dog. Number 17 appears to be holding a conch shell.

Numbers 18 and 20 carry number 19 in a sling or hammock suspended from a long pole. This arrangement is unlike the various Moche representations of a figure being carried in a litter (cf. Larco Hoyle 1939:11; Kutscher 1950:4; Kutscher 1954:80) since here the individual is lying down rather than seated upright. In many respects these three figures seem to be precursors of the "burial" processions rendered by Chimu craftsmen in both sheet metal and ceramic, where the deceased is carried in a pod-shaped container attached to a long horizontal pole. The pole is carried by two individuals who rest it on their shoulders (Lapiner 1976: fig. 612; Moseley and Mackey 1973: 334).

Number 21 is similar to numbers 1 and 16 in being shown in a splayed position. He has complex body paint like number 1, but he is wearing a headdress and, like number 16, lacks the companion dog.

Numbers 22 and 23 are facing each other. Number 22 has a conch shell above his outstretched hand. Number 23, whose feet are pointing forward, appears to be looking backward and reaching back so that his hand is almost touching that of number 22. In front of his face is another conch shell.

Illus. 3. Fineline drawing of an individual seated in a tule boat. This drawing is derived from a Moche V bottle in the Museo de America, Madrid. After Cordy-Collins 1972, fig. 16.

Numbers 24 through 26, 29, and 30 are musicians similar to numbers 8 through 12. Numbers 24 and 25 carry panpipes, number 26 carries a staff rattle, and numbers 29 and 30 carry drums.

Numbers 27 and 28 are very unusual and warrant particular attention. At first glance it appears that number 27, similar to numbers 29 and 30, is holding a drum and that a human head is mounted on the front of the drum. One can see, however, that number 27 has two legs and that number 28 has one leg and one arm. Clearly the artist was depicting two distinct human forms. If so, two interpretions can be suggested. One is that this is an erotic depiction with number 27 mounting number 28 from behind—the penis is shown analogous to the drumsticks held by numbers 29 and 30, and the testicles are indicated at the base of the penis. The other is that number 27 is actually playing a drum, but the drum is in the form of a human body with head, hands, and legs. The Inca are known to have made drums of human bodies, in which the stomach cavity served as the resonator (Cieza de Leon 1880, bk. 2, ch. 46; Anonymous Discurso 1906: 154; Poma 1936: 334). This custom has not yet been documented for earlier periods in Peru, but it may well have had antecedents long before the Inca period.

Returning to the procession of figures, number 31 is splayed and headless. Similar to number 16, he lacks complex body paint and the companion dog.

Numbers 32 through 34 are apparently blind. Numbers 32 and 33 appear to be following in the procession by holding onto the figure in front of them, while number 34 carries a long staff. It is curious that number 33 has only one leg.

Numbers 35 and 36 are playing straight bugles, numbers 37 and 38 do not appear to be holding anything in their outstretched hands, while numbers 39 and 40 each hold several short sticks. These sticks are commonly shown in Moche art, particularly in fineline drawings of Phase V (illus. 4); unfortunately, we do not understand their function.

Numbers 41 and 42 have *ulluchus* above their outstretched hands. The ulluchu is a highly symbolic motif, possibly derived from a plant form, which occurs in various ceremonial contexts (McClelland 1977).

Numbers 43 through 48 hold long staffs and tend to become progressively smaller and simpler as the design panel becomes narrower near the base of the bottle. This simplification and size reduction continues in numbers 49 through 57—the artist omits

Illus. 4. Fineline drawing of individuals holding bundles of sticks. This drawing is derived from a Moche V bottle in a private collection. Drawing by Donna McClelland.

the legs and arms on number 50, then omits all but the head on the subsequent figures, and finally ends with a series of small circles that probably are symbolic of additional figures. The abbreviated treatment of the figures, which was dictated by the diminished space, is analogous to the treatment of numbers 5 through 7, and should not be interpreted literally as a representation of human heads and figures without arms and legs.

Two particularly unusual aspects of this bottle warrant comment. First, although numerous Moche bottles have designs that spiral around the chamber, the procession almost invariably spirals upward toward the top instead of downward toward the base as is the case with the one under discussion.

Second, an unusual degree of variation is used in representing the eyes, hands, and legs of the various individuals. Four distinct eye forms are used: the circular eye with a small dot pupil, as seen on the splayed figures (numbers 1, 16, 21, and 31); the almond-shaped eye with a larger dot pupil on most other figures; the almond-shaped eye with a circle and a small dot pupil on number 23; and the almond-shaped eye without a pupil on the three blind individuals (numbers 32 through 34).

At least four distinct hand forms are used. The splayed figures (numbers 1, 16, 21, and 31) have one form. A second is exemplified by numbers 4 and 8, a third by numbers 29 and 38, and a fourth hand form can be seen in numbers 10 and 26. One may even argue that the hand on number 23 and those on numbers 18 and 20 may represent two additional forms.

Two distinct leg forms are used. One is the form used on the splayed figures (numbers 1, 16, 21, and 31) and the other is the form used on all other individuals except numbers 18, 20, 27, and 28. The latter exceptions have a leg form that is similar to the splayed figures: a bent knee and a tapered thigh and calf.

The distinctiveness of the eye, hand and leg forms used on this bottle is puzzling if we assume that the entire design was painted by a single artist. One may suggest that the different forms of eyes, hands, and legs used with the splayed figures came as a result of the artist depicting the figures front view rather than in profile. More likely, however, the artist was simply attempting to make the splayed figures distinct from all others in the scene. At this time it is impossible to say whether the variation in the other figures was deliberate. We should not, however, rule out the possibility that more than one artist was involved in painting the bottle, or that the artist who painted it was copying parts of the scene from bottles painted by others and in so doing simply copied the distinct manners of depicting eyes, hands, and legs.

Several aspects of the scene painted on this bottle are very rare, and may be unique in Moche art. If numbers 27 and 28 are engaged in erotic activity, the fact that it is depicted in fineline drawing is itself very unusual. Also unusual is the depiction of three blind individuals holding on to one another (numbers 32 through 34).

If we correctly interpret the object in front of numbers 14 and 15 as being an audencia, this drawing would be the first reported architectural plan view in all of Moche art. The implications are that the Moche conceptualized the audencia's architectural form as it would appear from above, and that its depiction carried a symbolic meaning. This view is particularly interesting in light of Keatinge's arguments that the U-shaped audencia had important religious-ceremonial functions in Moche V which were in the process of shifting to the socio-administrative functions that would characterize its use in the Chimu kingdom (Keatinge 1977).

Finally, the grouping of two figures carrying a third figure in a sling suspended from a horizontal pole (numbers 18 through 20) is very unusual—possibly unique in Moche art—and is almost certainly the precursor to the "burial" processions depicted by Chimu craftsmen. If all the Chimu examples of the "burial" procession are representations of a specific funeral, the fact that the same funeral is shown on this bottle indicates that it occurred during or before Moche V, and continued to be represented in the art of the people on the Peruvian north coast for centuries.

As we survey the entire scene depicted on this unique bottle, it is clear that we are witnessing an extremely important event, or series of events, loaded with ceremonial content. The scene incorporates various ideas and concepts that were particularly current during the last phase of the Moche style, and provides the antecedent for some aspects of iconography that were to be of particular importance during the Chimu kingdom.

REFERENCES

Anonymous
1906   "Discurso de la sucesión y gobierno de los Yngas, Un Juico de Límites entre el Perú y Bolivia." *Prueba Peruana* (Madrid) 8:149–165.

Cieza de León, Pedro de
1880   *Segunda parte de la crónica del Perú.* Biblioteca Hispano-Ultramarina, vol. 5. Madrid.

Cordy-Collins, Alana Kathleen
1972   "The Tule Boat Theme in Moche Art: A Problem in Ancient Peruvian Iconography." Master's thesis, Department of Archaeology, University of California, Los Angeles.

Donnan, Christopher B.
1978   *Moche Art of Peru: Pre-Columbian Symbolic Communication.* Los Angeles: Museum of Cultural History, University of California.

Keatinge, Richard
1977   "Religious Forms and Secular Functions: The Expansion of State Bureaucracies as Reflected in Prehistoric Architecture on the Peruvian North Coast." In *Annals of the New York Academy of Sciences* 293:229-245.

Kutscher, Gerdt
1950   *Chimu, eine altindianische Hochkultur.* Berlin: Gebr. Mann.
1954   *Nordperuanische Keramik.* Berlin: Casa Editora, Gebr. Mann.

Lapiner, Alan
1976   *Pre-Columbian Art of South America.* New York: Harry N. Abrams.

Larco Hoyle, Rafael
1939   *Los Mochicas.* Vol. 2. Lima.

McClelland, Donna
1977   "The Ulluchu: A Moche Symbolic Fruit." In Alana Cordy-Collins and Jean Stern, eds., *Pre-Columbian Art History.* Palo Alto: Peek Publications, 1977. Pp. 435-452.

Moseley, Michael E., and Carol J. Mackey
1973   "Chan Chan, Peru's Ancient City of Kings." *National Geographic,* 143(3):318-345.

Poma de Ayala, Felipe Guamán
1936   *Nueva cronica y buen gobierno.* Travaux et Memoires, vol. 23. Paris: Institut d'Ethnologie.

Author's Note: I wish to thank Donna McClelland for providing me with the superb line drawing of the scene painted on this bottle, and for her valuable comments about its interpretation.

THEORY AND PRACTICE IN THE STUDY OF ROCK ART

Clement W. Meighan
University of California, Los Angeles

"Antiquity willfully veils the truth so that the fool will go astray and only the wise may know." Phaedrus

THIS EPIGRAPH ALSO heads the monumental survey of North American rock art done by the late Klaus Wellmann (1979). It reminds us that rock art—the marks and pictures made by prehistoric man on the living rock—remains a part of the past in which the truth is veiled, an appropriate caution to those who would understand and interpret the enigmatic and anonymous artistic productions of the ancient past.

The first step at understanding any subject is the acquisition of a comprehensive body of reliable data since we need to define the phenomena before we can analyze them. The need to assemble and organize the scattered and often fragmentary information on rock art sites led to the establishment in 1977 of a formal Rock Art Archive at University of California, Los Angeles, set up by C. W. Clewlow and myself, and arising out of our own fieldwork with rock art sites and the frustrations of analyzing and publishing such data. Clewlow co-authored the major work on California rock art (Heizer and Clewlow 1973) and was particularly aware of the inadequacies of old notes, poor photographs, and spotty recording, much of which was done not by amateurs but by professional archaeologists.

The UCLA Rock Art Archive got immediate support and interest from many quarters, an indication that this kind of facility filled a real need. Personal encouragement came from Franklin D. Murphy, who assisted with an important initial grant through the Ahmanson Foundation. Other organizational grants were obtained from the Grancell Foundation and the Foundation for Rock Art and Archeology. The Institute of Archaeology at UCLA, under Director Giorgio Buccellati, incorporated the Rock Art Archive into the Institute as one of its regular research laboratories. Scholars concerned with rock art generously contributed manuscript material documenting their own fieldwork, so that we now have the original documentation on hundreds of rock art sites in many parts of the world. The donors include many of the leading investigators of rock art, all of whom saw the value of contributing basic site documentation to a central and organized repository, the first of its kind in the United States. Among the donors were R.F. Heizer, Campbell Grant, V. L. Pontoni, Franklin Fenenga, Paul Steed, Georgia Lee, and several members of the American Rock Art Research Association, many of whom are not Los Angeles residents, but are scattered from Oregon to Texas.

The Archive immediately became useful as a research resource and has provided the data for numerous studies, publications and

Illus. 1. Pleito Creek, a site of Chumash rock painting in southern California. Photo courtesy of Georgia Lee.

analyses, done by UCLA students as well as visitors from many other institutions. The Archive has also served to disseminate knowledge of rock art to the general public through exhibitions of rock art, most notably an exceptional photographic exhibit organized by C. W. Clewlow and JoAnne Van Tilburg. This exhibit has been shown in galleries, offices, and banks since November 1979 and continues to be exhibited in new locations on a regular basis. Public awareness was also served by a conference in November 1980, funded by the California Council on Humanities in Public Policy, which developed guidelines and policy statements for preservation of rock art sites.

While the Rock Art Archive has the advantage of an excellent data base for California and the Western United States, it deals with rock art worldwide and is not restricted to a specific region. Significant data are on file from Clewlow's fieldwork in Guatemala, with an impressive rock painting of Olmec style. There is also a major compilation of data from Mexico, Central America, and the Guianas of South America. Some of the data are contributed by scholars not at UCLA, such as the published bibliography of Matthias Strecker on Central America (1979). Other data are from field expeditions of the Rock Art Archive, including the work of Clewlow in Guatemala and my own recording of an important rock art site in Costa Rica.

From all this activity, much has been accomplished, but a need remains to develop new statements on methods and procedures in rock art studies, and it is to that end that the present discussion is directed. A review of approaches to the study of rock art must inevitably be partly repetitive and include some well-known material which has been recognized and published for many years. The active research and discussion of current scholars seem to be leading to a new formulation of rock art studies, with better procedures for both recording and interpretation. It is this new formulation that I examine here, following up on similar comments made previously (Meighan 1978).

I use the term "rock art" as the inclusive term for all varieties of art produced using natural rock surfaces. Some writers use the term "pictograph" for painted rock art (illus. 1) and "petroglyph" for rock art that is chipped or pecked into the rock surface (illus. 2); however, "petroglyph" has also been applied to both varieties of rock art. Further, there are other kinds of rock art to which neither term seems appropriate. Among them are the giant ground

Illus. 2. Petroglyphs chipped into rock surfaces. Upper: Abka, Sudan, *showing giraffes and a hippopotamus, animals not now found within hundreds of miles of the site location in the Sahara Desert. Giraffe is about 18 inches tall. Lower:* La Española, Costa Rica. *Bird and human figures in a complex symbolic arrangement. Decorated area about 4 × 6 feet.*

figures of both California and western South America that were produced as rock alignments in the desert, or by removing rocks from the surface to provide a light image on a darker rocky background. In England there are found images produced by stripping away the turf to allow the underlying bedrock (a white chalk) to show through. These are striking forms of rock art, but, because of size and method of execution, they are neither petroglyphs nor pictographs and must be set aside as a special category, sometimes called ground figures, although I prefer the term "geoglyph" for this kind of rock art.

Another common form of rock decoration in both Old World and New is the modification of rock surfaces by making numerous small pits, sometimes covering entire boulders. This is neither a "glyph" nor a "graph," and, to be literally correct, it is probably not "art" either. There is a consensus that "rock art" seems a useful term to encompass all the varieties of technique by which early man modified the natural stones in his environment.

Rock art may vary a great deal in sophistication. Most studies of rock art locations deal with primitive and prehistoric examples, many of which are both simple in art forms and rude in execution. However, very elaborate and sophisticated artistic representations also occur as rock art. The Olmec example of a costumed priest, recorded by Clewlow, is a case in point. One must also consider elaborate religious paintings in Asia, inscribed mantras in Nepal and Tibet, and similar productions as forms of rock art. Such art is primarily in the province of the art historian and linguist, and it has its own developed methods of description and interpretation, somewhat different from those used by students of prehistoric rock art.

Some rock art approaches sculpture, either by modifications of the surface involving relief carving, or more commonly by decorating a naturally shaped rock that bears some resemblance to a living creature—for example, putting eyes and a mouth on a "lizard-shaped" rock to make a three-dimensional form. For some sites, it is difficult to decide whether the work is rock art or sculpture, as in the site of Lavapatas in Colombia, where a stone riverbed has been shaped and covered with grooves and channels as well as small sculptured figures (illus. 3). Any arbitrary definition here can be argued; in general, nothing that is statuary is a part of rock art as it has been defined.

Also excluded from rock art are portable pieces. Although some rock art can be moved, and on occasion is moved with winches and bulldozers, none of it was intended to be moved from the place where it was produced. Hence, I consider decorated artifacts as something separate from rock art, even though rock art motifs may occur on inscribed stones, as in California and some sites of the French Paleolithic where "sketches" of the large animals appearing in the rock art were also inscribed on small cobbles, apparently as practice pieces. While there is clearly a relationship between such portable artifacts and the associated rock art, they are not themselves rock art in my definition.

An important aspect of rock art, often as a result of the natural setting, is its contribution to a sense of monumentality and per-

Illus. 3. Lavapatas, Colombia. Two views of a rock art site which includes sculptured figures in a stream bed.

manence, even when the art itself is rather limited in scope and scale. Small and simple figures placed in a cave, on a house-sized boulder, or on a spectacular cliff are enhanced and made more impressive by their surroundings, and it is clear in most rock art locations that the effect was desired (if not intentionally planned). Spectacular rock art sites tend to be in spectacular places.

RATIONALE FOR THE STUDY OF ROCK ART

Since so much of the study of rock art has been left to nonarchaeologists, one may ask whether it might not be preferable to treat this as a kind of art history and turn it over to other specialists. It is noteworthy that the only continent-wide surveys of rock art in North America (Grant 1967, and Wellmann 1979) were not done by professional anthropologists but by an artist and a physician, respectively. Further, the majority of members of important research organizations such as the American Rock Art Research Association are not archaeologists. This is probably a good thing, in view of the diversity and complexity of rock art sites and the fact that scholarly study of such sites requires a variety of talents. In spite of the impressive contributions made by scholars outside of archaeology, the professional "digging" archaeologist should play a more active part in defining and analyzing rock art. Whatever else it may be, rock art is a part of the archaeological record, and where it occurs it has to be fitted into the archaeology of a given region. For archaeologists to ignore the rock art associated with their sites is to leave out an important part of their data—in some cases, it could be argued, the most important part of their data.

Judging from published reports, many archaeologists take the position (by omission) that rock art may be interesting but is not archaeology. Unfortunately, many art historians appear to take the view that rock art is interesting but not art. This has left the whole area of study to a few dedicated individuals of quite varied backgrounds. It seems fair to suggest that archaeologists take up the challenge and make some efforts to contribute to rock art studies, because such studies are part of their own data, and because archaeologists are equipped with the background and training needed to make useful contributions.

The obligation of archaeologists to contribute more substantially to the study of rock art has some element of urgency. Aside from their technical knowledge, most archaeologists can also bring to bear anthropological knowledge, and this is essential. It provides a much needed corrective for many extreme interpretations put forward by persons who know nothing of the cultural level or way of life of the people who produced the rock art, and who believe that similarities in simple art motifs are all that is needed to demonstrate historical connections between hunter-gatherer nomads of the desert with advanced civilizations. Hence the "relationships" postulated between the central desert of Nevada and the Aztec empire, between ancient Egypt and New World rock art, and many similar fringe discussions which ignore not only chronology but also the cultural level of the people who produced the rock art.

A second element of urgency which should inspire archaeologists to devote more time to rock art studies is the ongoing destruction of rock art sites in all parts of the world. Rock art sites are among the most vulnerable of archaeological remains. Being mostly exposed, they are subject to deterioration from wind and weather. More important, being visible, the sites are subject to the destruction of various acts of human vandalism. One day of activity by one or two vandals can destroy the art of generations of ancient craftsmen. All archaeologists are painfully aware of the damage that can be done to archaeological remains through vandalism, but not all have recognized that the threat is more severe for rock art sites, and that vandals can devastate such sites far more rapidly than they can damage middens or buried remains.

The tragic destruction of a major panel at the Courthouse Wash site in Arches National Park, Utah, is an example of what can happen to a rock art site when vandals set out deliberately to scrub ancient paintings from the rocks. A recent discussion (Noxon and Noxon 1980) defines three types of vandalism at rock art sites: "ignorant vandalism" (graffiti and other marks left by visitor), "malicious vandalism" (deliberate defacement or removal of rock art), and "professional vandalism" (removal of rock art for sale or personal use). All three forms of vandalism are common and occur in varying degrees of severity. Since rock art sites cannot be guarded continually, the only protection against loss of the record is through a major effort to acquire a total and accurate record of existing rock art, a task to which archaeologists should contribute. To leave a rock art site alone on the assumption that it can be studied "next year" is to run a strong risk that the data may disappear or be severely diminished by the time someone gets around to doing the thorough recording.

To the kinds of vandalism mentioned above may be added a new form which seems to have started in recent years: "political vandalism." Where rock art can be attributed to specific tribal groups, as it can in numerous locations in the Southwest (Michaelis n.d.; Schaafsma 1980), it is clear evidence of the occupation and use of certain territory by that group in the past. Tribal hostility or competing land claims motivate one group to destroy the evidence left by another group, and the evidence grows that such destruction by Indians has taken place in some locations. Another kind of potential "political vandalism" is destruction by Indian fanatics to prevent any non-Indian from seeing the rock art; this has been threatened orally by some individuals, but so far as I know it has not actually happened yet. This is an ironic reversal of the fanaticism of some early Christian missionaries who did their own vandalism as an effort to stamp out paganism and all symbols of it. There is no way to control people who vandalize believing that they are acting under divine guidance—a mental aberration that also causes destruction in well-guarded art museums.

In any event, the threat to rock art sites is real and growing as the population increases and the number of visitors to rock art sites goes up. From old photographs and drawings in the UCLA Rock Art Archive, it is clear that many sites have remained remarkably intact during the last century or so, but there is no guarantee that any of these sites will remain equally undamaged in the future. The dimensions of the threat to rock art sites are little appreciated. From discussions with many groups and visitors to such sites, it is evident that the public perception of rock art sites is that they are few in number, very well known and studied, and reasonably well protected. None of these beliefs is correct. California, alone, has thousands of rock art sites (Heizer and Clewlow 1973). Few of them have been studied in detail, and many that are well known to local residents have never been visited or recorded by an archaeologist. Finally, the protection ranges from minimal to nonexistent, and is in fact impossible for small sites in remote areas.

DESCRIPTION OF ROCK ART

Development of an orderly and more or less standard way of *describing* rock art sites is a goal that has by no means been attained, and the development of descriptive methods has been tackled by many authors. For Baja California, one set of approaches is defined in Meighan's and Pontoni's work (1978). In addition, the general manuals on recording rock art are devoted primarily to field methods rather than to classification and descriptions. Yet some progress has been made in an area where few standards or formal procedures had been established. Since archaeologists are accustomed to doing detailed research on individual sites, they should be qualified to study individual rock art sites, then build from particular sites to a general study in the same way they work with excavation sites. Archaeologists are well trained to record excavations, stratigraphy, and the like. They also have established methods for describing collections of data through such tools as typology. Finally, archaeologists are equipped with many ways of determining chronology and sequence. Unfortunately, our scholarly armament is not directly transferable to rock art sites—the dating methods will not work, there is no stratigraphy, and even typological description is little developed. It is no wonder that many archaeologists find themselves more comfortable doing what they can do well—excavate sites and analyze collections of artifacts. Just the same, it is precisely because the study of rock art is less developed and understood that it is a challenge; it provides an opportunity for new kinds of archaeological investigation, and for an important contribution to our understanding of past peoples.

It would appear to be not particularly difficult to do descriptive recording and classification of what is present at a rock art site, but like many apparently routine chores it is more difficult than it may seem. First of all there is the difficulty of observation. Rock art is often in inaccessible places and not easily visible. This problem is compounded by weathering of the rock surfaces, lichen growths, fading of colors, and sometimes partial destruction of the art by natural or human causes. In addition, light plays a very important role, for figures that can be clearly seen in the morning may be invisible under the afternoon sun. It is common for rock art observers to comment, "Every time I go back to that site I see something I didn't see before." The "seeing" alone may call for repeated visits under different lighting conditions.

There is also the individual element in "seeing"; two observers may record the same rock art very differently. This can be readily observed by comparing the drawings made by several individuals against the photographs of the same rock art. Clearly, some people are more reliable recorders than others, partly because of varying experience and partly because of difficulty in recording faint details. If a recorder draws only the lines that are vividly clear to his eyes, he may complete a set of meaningless lines—a "connect the dots" picture rather than the picture the aboriginal artist actually drew. On the other hand, attempts to fill in faint details may lead to imaginary drawings which are fanciful reconstructions. To overcome these recording problems, it is desirable to have records made by different observers at different times.

An additional check on the recorder's drawings is in the photographic record, so that it is essential to have photographic documentation as well as written records. Photographs can rarely substitute entirely for drawings, however, because of the faintness of some rock art, superimpositions, and similar problems where the human eye is able to record details the camera does not see. On the other hand, photographs are essential to give a feel for what the site and its setting look like, to serve as a check on the drawings, and to capture aesthetic qualities not always present in record sketches. Some rock art actually looks more impressive in photographs than it does in reality; this, because the clarity of the images can be enhanced photographically through use of lighting, adjustments of exposure time, and filters or special films.

The dilemma of recording rock art also includes the problem of sampling. Since so much of rock art analysis is based on content of the art, it is essential to have complete documentation of the site so that we know what is truly present in the art. Unlike excavation methodology where a total sample of the data is rarely attainable, the study of rock art is much easier because of the surface visibility of the art, making it possible (if often laborious and time consuming) to record 100 percent of the data. In the matter of sampling, the archaeologist studying rock art has a tremendous advantage over the excavator, since the rock art scholar can record and deal with a total sample of his site data. In some cases, such as the site of Los Pozos (Baja California) recorded by Pontoni and her crew, this total sample may be a very large recording task involving several thousand individual elements. However, most rock art sites do not contain anything approaching this number of elements, the average for California sites being less than a couple of hundred individual drawings. There are a few exceptions in California, notably the Inyokern petroglyphs recorded by Grant, Baird, and Pringle (1968) with many thousands of elements present. However, that is by far the largest rock art site record published for California, and it may well represent the upper limit of petroglyph density for the state.

In any event, it is not appropriate in rock art studies to analyze partial data—recording only part of the rock art present at a site will inevitably add sampling error to the many difficulties of interpreting the site. These difficulties are major when the recorded art includes only the most striking and elaborate elements of a site—the common way in which rock art has been recorded in brief visits when a few snapshots were taken. In such cases, the record may be very misleading about the nature and content of the art present at the site. This seems self-evident and not worth such lengthy discussion, but it is worth emphasizing since the majority of older site documentation does not include *all* of the rock art present, and there is no way of knowing what fraction of the site was recorded nor how that fraction was selected. One therefore begins by obtaining a 100 percent sample of the rock art present at the site, a chore that can be truly tedious when there are hundreds of repetitions, but a necessary beginning to put us on firm ground when we describe what is present at the site. This also allows for statistical comparison of the frequency of various elements present in the art.

Having figured out how to get a reliable record of all the art in a given location, one can move to the second aspect of recording: classification. This is essential to allow for comparative studies as well as to reduce the volume of data to an orderly system so that the content of the art can be readily understood. Archaeologists should be reasonably good at this because their universal concern for typology in classifying artifacts gives them a good basis for understanding the practical and theoretical problems of classifying a large number of variable items into an orderly scheme. However, typology of rock art is no easier than typology of artifacts, and the same problems are present. With rock art, the "splitter" will reduce the art to its smallest visible components: dots, straight lines, and curved lines. Such a literal classification of minutiae generally does violence to what the artist had in mind and is more apt to obscure than clarify interpretation. The "lumper," on the other hand, may well miss subtle and significant differences in his rock art classification so that he groups together things of quite different meaning (for example, by assuming that simple representations of frogs, lizards, and humans are all depictions of the same thing).

The result of typology in an assemblage of rock art is a motif index—a tally of those elements present in the rock art. Just as with artifact typology, there cannot be a universal motif index. What is significant at one site is not necessarily significant at another, and the classification has to come out of the realities of the data rather than being an intellectual scheme divorced from the nature of what is being classified. In rock art, for example, the classification (motif

Illus. 4. Assemblage of individual painted elements, Gardner Cave, Central Baja California. Human figures are life size.

index) of a site containing nothing but simple geometric figures cannot be done in the same way as with a site dominated by representational pictures (such as the hundreds of engravings of fish at Fish Hill in Baja California). For purposes of comparing one site with another, it would be advantageous to have a standard terminology and method of classification, but that is no more feasible or desirable with rock art than it is with artifact collections. Hence, we share a common approach and terminology on a gross scale, but the application to a specific collection may well vary, based on the decriber's judgment of what is meaningful in his particular collection of data.

Beyond classification and counting of individual elements or motifs lies the important problem of recognizing assemblages of things that belong together—"compositions" of elements all painted at the same time and intended to be a "scene." Much rock art in California appears to be in the form of individual pictures done one by one, but there are many examples of sets of things all arranged into an overall picture. We would clearly miss the meaning of such scenes if we confined our recording to a mere counting of component parts without recognizing the overall image the artist was striving to produce (illus. 4).

Good examples of "scenes" are the four froglike creatures arranged around a circle (Seaver n.d.), and the four horsemen in a row (Reinhardt n.d.) (illus. 5). All evidence of preservation, color, and style indicates that these compositions were done by single artists at a specific point in time. In the upper example, we might well enter four "frogs" and a circle as separate elements in our motif index, but on a different level we have to see the assemblage of these elements as the intended picture and hence the clue to meaning. Similarly, in the lower example, the artist who painted the horsemen was not painting individual men on horses, but a procession of men on horses—something quite different.

Just as there are problems in deciding what the motifs of a given site may be and how to arrange these motifs in a classificatory scheme, there are obvious problems in making decisions about which things belong together. These decisions are usually based on preservation, uniformity of color and style, and physical arrangement of the various elements indicating a grouping of some kind. Some scenes are easily recognizable and would be agreed upon by all observers; others are much more tenuous and may not be defineable (situations where there are many superpositions, the preservation of the art is poor, or where the artist's concept of spatial organization may have been quite different from that of a modern observer). Mistakes in grouping together several elements are, of course, possible, but the observer is obliged to attempt such groupings. Generally this aspect of the study is more reliable when it is done directly in the field while looking at the rock art—reliability goes down when such judgments are based on photographs or drawings.

One problem not addressed in detail in this paper is the matter of recognizing and defining style areas, primarily because the first step in analysis is to concentrate on the study of the individual sites rather than on the area. It is characteristic of archaeological field work to begin with individual sites and build up to a more general picture of regional characteristics. Archaeologists have been justly

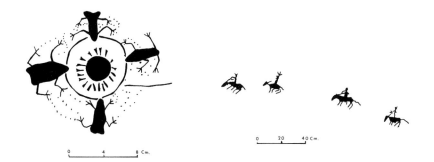

Illus. 5. Two rock scenes composed of multiple elements. Left: Scene from a Santa Barbara County site (SBa-519; drawing after Seaver, n.d.). Right: The "Four horsemen" from a Los Angeles County site (LAn-717; drawing after Reinhardt, n.d.).

criticized for a tendency to get so immersed in this way of proceeding from individual sites that they never do get to more general statements. However, what is present in a single site is a test of whether the style areas so far defined in the literature are correct in their boundaries and their characteristics. Each careful site description makes a contribution by raising questions about style areas and how to make them conform to observed evidence of the sites.

CHRONOLOGY

One of the first things an archaeologist learns is that not everything in his site was made on the same day. Similarly, not all the art in a rock art site is necessarily of the same age. With rock art, as with other archaeological remains, a significant amount of the study time must go to determining when the rock art was made, over how long a time the site was used, and whether or not there is a sequence of styles and motifs representing use of the site by new artists or new cultures. A report on a rock art site which does not mention chronology (of which there are many) implies that all the art there present represents the same group of people and a short period of time, but these assumptions, that may sometimes be true, have to be documented and not be taken for granted.

Chronology questions pertaining to rock art are slowly being answered by a number of investigators, although difficult problems remain since most conventional dating methods are not applicable to rock art. New and more refined dating methods are needed. The first step is to recognize that chronology is important and must be investigated. One important contribution of Wellman's 1979 volume, a massive study of North American rock art, is the explicit mention of chronology for his sites and style areas. Some regional studies have also dealt with chronological problems: for Baja California, a chronology of styles is suggested by Meighan (1978:7–10); this is not entirely convincing but represents a first attempt to develop chronological data. Similarly, Grant, Baird, and Pringle (1968) discuss chronology of Coso rock art, mainly in terms of content of the art and superpositions. Smith and Turner (1975:24–26) list a number of dating methods applicable to sites in the California desert and elsewhere; unfortunately, many of these methods are experimental and unproven, and few if any have been systematically put to use in the specific search for chronology of rock art.

A serious source of uncertainty in developing absolute dates for rock art sites is that nearly all ages proposed for rock art depend heavily upon associational dates; that is, the date of something else is presumed to apply to the associated rock art and thus the art itself is not dated directly. Although there have been a few experimental attempts to provide direct radiocarbon dates to pigments, and hence to date the painting directly, all of these are inconclusive. Hence the published dating of rock art rests largely upon:

1. *Dating of associated artifact materials, particularly in rock art sites with habitation refuse.* Objects dated by radiocarbon or obsidian dating are used to provide an age for the site, on the assumption that the paintings date from the same age as the people who lived at the site. This is plausible, but it must be remembered that the date is not derived from the paintings. Also, this type of dating does not tell much about the span of time during which rock art was produced—a site with a long time span might contain rock art all done during a very short period within the history of the site. It is also possible that the rock art was done before the site became a habitation area, or more likely, *after* such use. Dating the occupation of a rock art site is not useless, but there must be suitable reservations about a chronology derived in this way.

2. *Stylistic resemblances to something that is dated elsewhere, such as decoration on dated pottery types.* Such dating carries conviction only when the styles are reasonably complex and distinctive; matching up circles and spirals in rock art sites with similar elements on dated artifacts is not sufficient because of the universal distribution of such simple design elements.

3. *Time markers portrayed in rock art.* Late period sites are sometimes marked by elements that can only pertain to a known historical period: Christian crosses, men on horses, even ships and trains. Early sites are sometimes marked by portrayal of objects known to have gone out of use at a particular time, such as spear-throwers. Portrayal of animals now extinct can also serve to identify the age of some rock art.

Of course, a few fortunate people in the Old World can work with rock art sites bearing an inscription and a date, but this does not apply to any prehistoric rock art, and is never found in the New World (with the exception of recent graffiti).

Perhaps in the future dating methods will be developed which can reliably be applied to things related to the process of making

Illus. 6. Superimposition: bird painting on top of deer which in turn overlies two smaller deer, the legs of which can be seen projecting. Such superimpositions establish the sequence of the paintings and styles. The large deer is life size. Central Baja California.

rock art: the paints or pigments, patination and weathering of rock, and the like. All known methods of this kind, however, are much affected by chemistry, which is in turn affected by temperature, exposure to rain and wind, and so on. Hence it seems unlikely that accurate methods of this kind can be applied to many sites in different environmental zones, or even to all the rock art of a single site. Dating methods of general applicability remain to be discovered, although some insight on the age of rock art may be obtained in local areas.

Aside from the question of age in years, important chronology data lie in the sequence of artistic production within the site. This is most commonly tackled by recording superpositions (illus. 6), although standard archaeological methods of seriation (cf. King 1978) are appropriate and deserve much wider use than they have had.

INTERPRETATION

The problems of *interpreting, understanding,* and *explaining* rock art cannot even be approached in any meaningful way until there is adequate description and a body of controlled information for analysis. Site data are as essential for rock art studies as they are for all areas of archaeological investigation. The detailed record on individual sites provides the building blocks from which to make regional and general statements; these detailed records are what provide the test of speculations and also raise significant questions to be addressed. For most regions, the data base is still very inadequate and the conclusions about rock art are based on overview studies which often do not sustain general statements, or are shown to be in error when a careful compilation of site data becomes available.

Since much less than 1 percent of California rock art sites has been described by the standards previously discussed, it is clear that our present efforts at interpretation must be tentative. Yet all site reports should make an effort to go beyond mere description to offer some ideas of what the rock art may mean.

Not only must the description of rock art sites differ from that of an excavated site, but its interpretation also must be developed by quite different approaches than those we use with excavation data. This is necessary since we are dealing with data that are more humanistic than scientific. We are trying to decipher what something *meant* to people of the past, rather than how something was used, how it improved environmental adaptation, or how it related to most of the common areas of inquiry in the analysis of excavated sites. Hence our best evidence for understanding rock art remains ethnographic analogy, and our best references are accounts of ethnography and folklore. We can add to this the need for varying kinds of content analysis among which is the assumption that what is present in the art is a fair reflection of what people had on their minds. And based on recent studies we can discuss basic psychological processes conditioned by the biology of the brain—a line of interpretation that is not provable and will certainly not appeal to some of the hard scientists in archaeology. It may be that in the future a scientific, hypothesis-based approach will prove a better way to do rock art studies, but now our present lines of evidence would be considered "anecdotal" and passé by the new archaeologists. The most enthusiastic of rock art scholars would agree that conclusions about the meaning of rock art are not provable in the scientific sense. The interpretation of rock art, however, need not be considered antiscientific; it is a response to the nature of the data. The goal is to present a line of reasoning which will be a plausible explanation of the observed phenomena—the same scholarly goal toward which site excavators work, even though attainment of the goal with rock art sites is more tentative and exploratory than much field archaeology of today. Scientific *proof* of meaning is likely to remain beyond us with the exception of those very few sites where we have direct testimony from the people who produced the rock art, as with the puberty-related rock paintings of San Diego County. But for the most part, Indians of the historic period have denied authorship of the rock art in their territory; the people who made the images are long gone and not available to tell us what they had in mind, and we have to do the best we can with the existing record (both artistic and written).

The abundance of unfounded speculation about rock art and the inability of "proving" the meanings of rock art sites have discouraged all but a few archaeologists from making interpretive efforts in rock art studies. Indeed, most archaeological reports do not acknowledge that rock art exists, even though it may be a physical part of the site. Particularly in recent years, archaeologists have tended to shy away from untestable hypotheses, and to concentrate on questions more amenable to mustering scientific evidence. Yet, even though the prehistoric artists cannot tell us what was in their minds, they are *showing* us what was in their minds through the art they produced. Conversely, analysis of the content of a rock art site ought to tell us what the artists did *not* have in mind, and this is also valuable. For example, interpretations of hunting magic are certainly more plausible when the art is dominated by pictures of game animals than when such representations are entirely absent. And far-out interpretations, such as Runic writing in Modoc County (Crotty, n.d.), fall immediately when one looks closely at what is in fact present in the art. It is our endeavor to provide plausible and reasonable explanations of the rock art we see before us, and a plausible and reasonable explanation is certainly of value even though it is not provable.

An important premise is that interpretations of rock art must consider multiple possible meanings. It is simplistic to assume that all rock art sites are assignable to some single function such as hunting magic, astronomical significance, or drug-induced visions, to mention three of the most popular interpretations in the current literature. Many other interpretations are possible, and for each site the art must be examined against many possibilities to see if the evidence favors one or another interpretation.

Of the wide range of meanings that may plausibly be attributed to known rock art sites, the following are among the possibilities that must be considered:

Boundary markers or representations of group symbols having territorial significance.

Clan or personal symbols representing the "I was here" message.

Supplication, exemplified by the so-called rain rocks or baby rocks consisting of boulders with many drilled pits—marks made by individuals to accompany a prayer or request for some benefit.

Hunting magic; ritual intended to increase the supply of game.

Astronomical significance; comets, solstice-related symbols.

Initiation rituals including puberty ceremonies.

Representations of mental experiences such as visions, guardian spirits, mythical beings, phosphenes. These may or may not be drug induced.

Important historical events (e.g., coming of the Europeans).

Witchcraft; magical control over enemies, dangerous animals.

Mortuary marks in commemoration of the dead.

"Doodling" or more or less random marks done to while away time and lacking any particular significance.

Aesthetics—the enhancement of special places with striking and colorful images.

The situation is further complicated by the fact that a single site might have been meaningful in more than one way, for example, a site incorporating rock art in puberty rituals could also be a sacred place where astronomical meanings were also present. Furthermore, it is not impossible that the same people could have produced rock art sites of different styles and meanings—one site for hunting magic, another for initiation of shamans.

Among the more interesting of recent interpretations has been the effort of several scholars to seek what might be called universals of mental experience and to relate some art to imagery which is biological in origin, hence likely to occur among all humans. There are two strands to this line of interpretation. One deals with drug-induced visions and the fact that certain drugs tend to cause standard kinds of visions or hallucinations; the other, which consists of a much simpler kind of mental image that can be spontaneously and easily generated by anyone, has been shown to be universal in human populations, and does not require the effect of drugs. The latter, more simple images are referred to as phosphenes, and the relationship of phosphenes to rock art is well discussed by Wilbert (n.d.).

The idea of phosphenes as a stimulus to Chumash rock art in California has also been put forward by Blackburn (1977). He, however, links this notion to that of hallucinations produced by drugs (such as *Datura* and peyote), whereas the two kinds of imagery should be kept separate. As mentioned, phosphenes require no drugs or chemical stimuli, and when such stimuli *are* used the visual hallucinations generally go far beyond the simple geometric figures of phosphenes; indeed, the use of drugs is intended specifically to acquire rich and elaborate visions with enhanced colors and sounds, imaginary creatures, and the like, taking the user to another world very different from the ordinary everyday world. Wellmann (1978) presents a good summary of the relationship that may exist between rock art and hallucinogenic drugs.

Blackburn's suggestion that phosphenes may be a stimulus for Chumash rock art does not seem plausible in terms of the content of Chumash rock art, which has some simple geometric elements but is, on the whole, far more elaborate and colorful in its content. Further, what simple elements exist are often parts of complex arrangements so that they do not stand alone as representatives of the art style. On the other hand, since Chumash rock art also includes many imaginary and fantasy creatures of strange anatomy and proportions, the suggestions that *Datura*-induced visions may be the stimulus for some of the art is not unreasonable, even though it cannot be proved with present evidence.

Examination of these issues is not unimportant and may prove to be a key to the understanding of much rock art. It is certainly reasonable, and supported by abundant ethnographic data, to suppose that "mental experiences" were carefully sought, examined, and remembered by the Indian artists, and furthermore that mental images of all sorts, whether received in dreams, through drugs, or through physical hardships, were considered *significant* learning experiences not to be idly dismissed. Hence, even a low-level experience like phosphenes, which people in contemporary cultures do not notice—or ignore as being of no importance—might be expected to be both noticed and considered important by hunters and gatherers who watched for and interpreted the limited sensory experiences that came to them. It is hard for contemporary man to appreciate this, for our lives are full of sensory enrichment (some would call it overload) in ever-present music, colored lights and television, art, and the tremendous diversity of sights and sounds that surround us. It is difficult for us to conceive of the much narrower range of sensory experience available to a California Indian in aboriginal times. If we bear this in mind, however, it is easy to appreciate why phosphenes could have been far more noticeable and important to a California Indian than they are to us. This makes the discussion in the Wilbert article fairly plausible, since the rock art in his study is composed almost exclusively of phosphene-like images.

The move toward such interpretations suggests a possible typology of the kinds of stimuli that may have given rise to the various styles of rock art we see. It is remarkable how much variety in content occurs in rock art sites, and it is also remarkable how an individual site or region will specialize or pursue a given kind of rock art while minimizing or omitting other possibilities. When the artist sets out to make his drawing, he can draw anything that comes into his mind, limited only by his drawing skill. The fact that rock art sites exploit only a very narrow range of the universe of things that the artist can think of indicates that this is never "free form" art but is controlled by historical, cultural, and probably biological limiting factors.

One possible set of historical factors may be suggested by a consideration of rock art as perhaps originating from three kinds of mental states:

1. Sensory deprivation of which phosphene-related art is the best example. Phosphenes are best triggered and most prominent when the normal biology is under stress (deprived of light, causing the "prisoner's cinema," or through fasting, mutilation, and fatigue). Individuals under stress could well see phosphenes as important and meaningful images, and either at the time or from later recollection put such images into rock art and the associated beliefs. Since some rock art is known to be associated with puberty rituals, and since participants in such ceremonies are often under physical stress (fasting, endurance tests, sometimes physical punishment), it is plausible to suggest a relationship with phosphenes and the origin of such elements in rock art.

2. "Real world" observations, in which peoples were stimulated to portray important things in their world, either for magical reasons (realistic images of game animals, for example), or because the things and events were so striking as to be considered extraordinary. In this category of rock art would lie most of the efforts at naturalistic representation, ranging from pictures of comets through

scenes of warfare or ceremony, to exciting events of the early historic period, such as missionaries or soldiers on horseback, and even the rock art which portrays trains, steamships, and the like. Also in this class of rock art are calendrical symbols and art associated with observation of astronomical bodies (see Hudson, Lee, and Hedges 1979). An aboriginal example of such a historical record of an exciting event may be seen in the single portrayal of two men shooting at each other with bows and arrows (Grant, Baird, and Pringle 1968:80). How is this picture, the only one of its kind in a site with several thousand petroglyphs, to be understood? It clearly cannot be hunting magic, the common interpretation for the site as a whole. Perhaps it is merely a record of an actual conflict, so striking that one artist felt compelled to commemorate the event with a drawing.

3. Sensory enrichment. In this class of rock art are images derived from "other world" experiences, particularly visions, whether drug induced or not. Such art characteristically shows considerable elaboration of designs and colors as well as "unreal" and imaginary creatures. It also includes standardized images of gods, spirits and religious beings. See, for example, the linkage between rock art and the Katchina cult (Schaafsma and Schaafsma 1974).

This scheme does not address the "meaning" of rock art, but it may be useful as pointing to the origins and emphases that gave rise to the variety of rock art styles. This seems a more meaningful frame of reference than a mere division of rock art into "crude" and "sophisticated" categories. Of course, once a particular kind of rock art came into existence, it would become traditionalized and conceptualized as the proper way to produce rock art, which explains the long persistence of particular styles in particular areas.

Such a notion of cultural origins may also lead to some supporting observations for the various interpretations that have been proposed. For example, one would expect rock art derived from sensory enrichment to have some relationship to the other world and hence to shamanic practices. One might also expect such art to be esoteric and in the hands of religious practitioners, rather than art done by ordinary people.

Left out of this discussion is rock art that is not art at all but merely activity confined to the making of a mark. The best example in California is the so called cupule style, which results in boulders covered with shallow pits. These are places where people went to make a supplication for some desired effect (such as having a child), and made a mark on the rock as part of the ritual. A comparable concept is seen in some African wooden images full of nails, each nail being driven by a supplicant as part of his own personal prayer. Physically, cupule sites belong in the general category of rock art sites, but they represent the simplest variety of such sites and are probably not related to sensory experiences as defined above.

There is also a continuum of what might be called the intensity of meaning, with some rock art sites being secular, rock art produced by anyone (e.g. the "supplication" rock art of the cupule style), whereas other sites were no doubt sacred and secret, visited only by certain classes of initiated people, the rock art produced only by religious practitioners. The more elaborate rock art appears often to have been intended partly to enhance the ambiance of a *place,* and to be embellishment of a particular location which was important for other reasons. In other words, the art did not come first—the meaning of the place gave stimulus to the art. At least some rock art is probably similar in intent to the artistic productions lavished on medieval cathedrals.

Finally, it should be mentioned that rock art, like other art, had personal meaning as well as group meaning, and some of the more knowledgeable people saw much more in it than others. Just as some people can recognize the saint by its halo, but do not know which saint is portrayed, others initiated in the religious knowledge not only know which saint is portrayed but recognize many other symbolic elements in the art and may be able to provide long and detailed "explanations" of the picture. Our interpretations, made from a different cultural background and at a different time from the rock art, are unlikely ever to reach the sophistication of those ancient people who were initiated in the knowledge of their culture. But we may well be able to make plausible "general" interpretations that would come close to the meaning of the art as it was viewed by the ordinary person in the society that produced the art.

The big difficulty in interpretation, of course, is symbolism in that a given rock art element may have stood for some standard meaning known to the artist but not to us. Pictures are easier to interpret than symbols, although the pictures themselves may be symbolic of something, for example, a human figure that represents not a person but a spirit or deity. However, even allowing for symbolism in realistic pictures, it is certainly easier to develop plausible interpretations from complex and pictorial rock art than it is to develop interpretations of simple geometric figures like phosphenes. In the future we may develop ways of getting at the meanings of the simpler kinds of rock art, but for the present our interpretations are clearly of varying degrees of plausibility which tend to go up as the content of the rock art becomes more complex and more pictorial, and down when the rock art consists of only simple geometric elements.

Archaeologists who take up the challenge of rock art interpretation find themselves drawn closer to a set of scholars who are important to rock art studies and yet peripheral to standard archaeological research. This includes folklorists, students of symbolism and aesthetics, and ethnographers concerned with mental processes and intellectual patterns of tribal peoples. It is a new direction for archaeological research to take, since the work of such scholars is rarely used or cited in archaeological writing. It remains to be seen how archaeologists can combine new approaches with the strengths of their developed methodologies to gain a new understanding of rock art sites.

BIBLIOGRAPHY

Blackburn, Thomas
  1977 "Biophysical Aspects of Chumash Rock Art," *Journal of California Anthropology* 4(1):88–93.

Crotty, Helen H.
  n.d. "Petroglyph Point Revisited; A Site in Modoc County, California." MS in UCLA Rock Art Archive [1980].

Grant, Campbell
  1967 *Rock Art of the American Indian.* New York: Thomas Y. Crowell.

Grant, Campbell, James W. Baird, and J. Kenneth Pringle
  1968 *Rock Drawings of the Coso Range, Inyo County, California.* Pub. No. 4. China Lake, Calif.: Maturango Museum.

Heizer, Robert F., and C. William Clewlow, Jr.
  1973 *Prehistoric Rock Art of California.* 2 vols. Ramona, Calif.: Ballena Press.

Hudson, Travis, Georgia Lee, and Ken Hedges
  1979 "Solstice Observers and Observatories in Native California," *Journal of California and Great Basin Anthropology* 1:39-63.

King, Thomas J., Jr.
  1978 "A Petroglyph Assemblage from Cerrito de Cascabeles." In Meighan and Pontoni, eds., 2:124-177.

Meighan, Clement W.
  1978   "Analysis of Rock Art in Baja California." In Meighan and Pontoni,
          eds., 2:1-19.

Meighan, Clement W., and V. L. Pontoni, eds.
  1978   *Seven Rock Art Sites in Baja California.* Socorro, N.M.: Ballena Press.

Noxon, John, and Deborah Marcus Noxon
  1980   *American Rock Writing Research Newsletter* 2(7).

Reinhardt, Gregory A.
  n.d.   "Pictographs with a Historic Component: LAn-717, a Los Angeles
          County Rock Art Site." MS in UCLA Rock Art Archive [1980].

Schaafsma, Polly
  1980   "Kachinas in Rock Art," *Pacific Discovery* 33(3):20-27.

Schaafsma, Polly, and Curtis F. Schaafsma
  1974   "Evidence for Origins of the Pueblo Katchina Cult as Suggested by
          Southwestern Rock Art," *American Antiquity* 39:535-45.

Seaver, Joan T.
  n.d.   "Indian Caves: An Analysis of Rock Art from SBa-519, Santa Barbara
          County, California." MS in UCLA Rock Art Archive [1980].

Smith, Gerald A., and Wilson G. Turner
  1975   *Indian Rock Art of Southern California.* Redlands, Calif.: San Bernar-
          dino County Museum Association.

Strecker, Matthias
  1979   *Rock Art of East Mexico and Central America: An Annotated Bibliog-
          raphy.* Los Angeles: UCLA Institute of Archaeology.

Wellmann, Klaus F.
  1978   "North American Indian Rock Art and Hallucinogenic Drugs," *Jour-
          nal of the American Medical Association* 239(15):1524-1527.
  1979   *A Survey of North American Indian Rock Art.* Graz, Austria: Akade-
          mische Druck u. Verlagsanstalt.

Wilbert, Werner
  n.d.   "Two Rock Art Sites in Calaveras County, California." MS in UCLA
          Rock Art Archive [1980].

OBSERVATIONS
ON THE SOCIAL FUNCTION OF ART

Walter Goldschmidt

University of California, Los Angeles

Illus. 1. Sebei children with homemade wheel toy.

ART IS UNIVERSAL. This generalization is unassailable. No peoples known to ethnography or history have failed to engage in transforming substances, altering surfaces, manipulating sounds, stringing together words or engaging in motion in ways that are not, in the ordinary sense of the word, utilitarian, but which are intended to evoke some kind of emotional response either in the performer, or his public, or both. But in some places and among some people these activities are ever-present; every surface and shape comes under the artist's manipulation, the sounds of music are everywhere and the aesthetic impulse—whatever that may be—is given full rein. Bali comes to mind as one such place; the Bakuba; New Guinea; the Northwest Coast tribes—students of the arts could go on and on. The same can be said for epochs and areas in history: the Golden Age of Greece, sixteenth-century Venice, nineteenth-century France, and so on. By contrast other places are drab—not by nature but in cultural expression: most of East Africa in contrast with West Africa, the Basin-Plateau Indians in contrast with the Northwest Coast. There is no more important question in anthropology than: Why this difference?

From time to time, Franklin Murphy and I discussed the relative prevalence of artistic expression in cultures, raising the issue as to why some peoples displayed a rich aesthetic and others a constricted or impoverished one. I was motivated to this discourse by the fact that the people with whom I spent much of my research life, the Sebei of Uganda, fell at the extreme of the latter category. We agreed that the subject was worthy of detailed examination, but never found the time to undertake such a study or even to set forth the manner in which one might be conducted. Here I offer some thoughts that might inspire those more competent than myself to pursue the matter in greater scholarly detail.

The problem must first be set in its proper theoretical context. For if art is universal, it must be because it is more than merely ornamental; it must play some significant role in human affairs. My examination of the peculiarly unsatisfactory quality of Sebei aesthetic expression has led me to the conviction that art is indeed a crucial element in human social life and furthermore that in recognizing the social role of art we gain a better perspective on the human condition.

Some small progress toward such understanding can perhaps be made by engaging in an inquiry that students of art are rarely tempted to make: to examine an instance in which artistic expression is minimal; to try to understand, so to speak, the negative case. The aesthetic environment of the Sebei is a remarkably drab one, as will be readily apparent in my brief inventory of their aesthetic expression.[1] I have also illustrated this characteristic, by contrasting Sebei aesthetics with that of the Hupa, to be discussed below (illustrations 3-10). I know of no object that the Sebei fabricate simply for the sake of its appearance, feel, or other aesthetic stimulus. There is very little surface decoration or concern with form in the manufacture of utilitarian objects. I once saw a Sebei woman decorate a leather cover for a milk gourd with beadwork, but it was a crude product and an exceptional instance. The spears lack the elegance of those found among the neighboring Pokot; and although the leather shields have a graceful shape, they do not have the surface decorations found on the otherwise less satisfying shields of the Maasai. The architecture is purely utilitarian; the surfaces of the mud and wattle houses are never decorated as elsewhere in Africa. I once—and only once—saw chalked graffiti on a house surface, a crude infantile product undoubtedly made by a schoolchild. Only very occasionally is a house finished with elegance, carefully mudded with an even color, and surrounded by grass and flowers. The single exception that comes to mind is the household of a very unusual Sebei man who was in other respects a nonconformist. Occasionally cattle owners will transform the lyre-shaped horns of their animals (particularly the "Bull of the herd," which represents a kind of alter ego). But this is less frequent than among other East African cattle-keeping people I know, and they never painted their cattle as the closely related Pokot do.

I should mention that the Sebei live in an unusually gratifying physical environment. Mount Elgon, which is their home, rises above a plain that offers vistas of exceptional beauty. The plain itself varies, depending upon the aspect and the season—sometimes shimmering as the impounded water two thousand feet below reflects the moving sun, sometimes in subtle pastels of beige and light olive, while the exciting and shifting mass of Mount Debasien, rising up from the plains to the north, gives dramatic form to this vast earthen sea. Scenes on the mountain, with its red earth, green canopy, and frequent spectacular waterfalls are reminiscent of Chinese paintings. The Sebei are not unmindful of these views; they are frequently to be seen sitting on rock outcroppings overlooking the vista below, apparently enjoying the beauty. That this view has affected them is indicated by the relatively high frequency of "vista responses" in the ink-blot test administered to them. They are thus not lacking in "aesthetic sense."

Sebei rituals, especially the puberty initiation rites involving circumcision, are accompanied by song and dance. Music is largely vocal; the chief instrumentation currently employs the leather-covered single-head drum and the seven-string mandolin, both recent borrowings from their Bantu neighbors. They more frequently beat sticks against a log when they sing and dance at beer parties. The Kudu horn trumpet was apparently used only during wartime. What other instrumentation they once had has entirely disappeared. Nor is music an important part of daily life. I have elsewhere in Africa seen men walking down the path or sitting quietly while playing music, but never among the Sebei. Their frequent beer parties sometimes end in song and dance but more often in quarrels. The eminent ethnomusicologist Klaus Wachsman recorded Sebei songs in a "music festival" I arranged in 1954. There was a wide range—lullabies, children's songs, songs for rituals, war songs. Wachsman was disparaging of the quality of Sebei music; significantly, he said that it was a mixture of Nilotic and Bantu elements. When the big Uganda Uhuru celebrations were being planned in 1962, the Sebei feared an onslaught of raids from the neighboring Kenyan Pokot, so the men gathered together in a bivouac for several nights. There was military practice and speech-making and feasting and a kind of prayer and talk—very much talk. But there was neither singing nor dancing!

If there is one art form that might be said to be highly developed among East African pastoralists, it is body decoration. Apparently, the Sebei once engaged in elaborate mudded and painted hairdos like those found among the nearby Karamojong and Pokot, but the earliest photographs of the Sebei, made at the very first contact in 1890, show no evidence of this. As one of the old chiefs told me: "The Sebei are easy to be converted to new fashions." Girls decorate their abdomens with rows of cicatrices that are said to be sexually exciting to their lovers, but these are just in rows, not arranged in the elaborate designs of other Nilotic people. Only occasionally do Sebei men or women display style or elegance, whether in native or Western costume. Nothing comparable to the tall aristocratic bearing of the Baganda or Ghanaian women with their stylish gowns and proud headscarfs can be found among the Sebei, although some Sebei women, as would be expected, show more style than others.

Illus. 2. Sebei child playing with his "cattle" of pebbles.

The oral literature, again, gives evidence that aesthetic expression is sparse. Adults could not recount cosmological or cosmogenic tales; there were no heroic accounts of past deeds, whether mythical or historical. Children know a body of folk tales told to them by their grandparents, but ordinary adults have "forgotten" them. Only children could be induced to tell us these tales. Once, when the Sebei lived in brush-enclosed encampments, the people gathered in a special area in the evening and told stories, but when settlement was dispersed over the land, this custom was lost and storytelling became less important and less social. Certainly their importance and probably their quality rapidly declined. Beer libations are accompanied by prayers, but these are not couched in poetic terms. Instead they are merely mundane directives to the ancestral spirits.

Finally, in this review mention should be made of the sparsity of play. Although play is not normally considered as a part of the aesthetic realm, I think it is relevant. Sebei children are quite inventive in their play activities. They fabricate wheel toys, make wheelbarrows with plantain log wheels (illus. 1) to push one another around in, and have elaborate fantasy play in which they enact adult roles—circumcising, bargaining for wives, exchanging cattle, and the like (illus. 2). School influence has introduced jackstones, soccer, and other children's recreations. I do not recall ever seeing an adult engaged in play. The widespread African game played with pebbles in a series of pits (which has so many different names it effectively has none—called *bao* in East Africa), is not found in Sebeiland. (I once saw two men playing it there, but I do not believe they were Sebei.) Nor does one see card games played at the beer parlors. In the olden days, newly circumcised youths engaged in games and contests during their period of seclusion, but these customs are no longer followed. There is no Sebei equivalent to softball or boules or other such adult pastimes.

Students of art naturally seek out places where the artistic impulse is given rich expression. This leaves people like the Sebei outside their normal discourse, and for this reason it seems worthwhile to examine the context of their behavior. Although such an account does not give much aesthetic satisfaction, it does raise issues central to any discourse on art. How do I account for their low level of artistic expression? First, let us eliminate any notion that the answer lies in a lack of capacity to appreciate aesthetic products. There is evidence of greater past involvement and enough current aesthetic responsiveness to eliminate any doubt in this matter. We must look for social causes.

Neither economic stage nor ecological condition can offer a solution. The aesthetic expression of the Australian aborigines, whose material conditions were as poor as any known to ethnography, had a rich drama, mythology, and graphic art—far greater than those of the Bushmen or the Paiute, whose environment and mode of life are comparable and whose technical apparatus was somewhat more advanced. East Africa is the home of nomadic pastoralists and some might suggest that the nomadic life is antithetical at least to the plastic arts. But the great tradition of rug making is a pastoralist's contribution to the world of aesthetics, as perhaps also is silver smithing. Amount of leisure time? The information already presented suggests the inapplicability of this measure. There is no reason to believe that the Balinese have more leisure than the less aesthetically oriented peasants in, say, Thailand. Finally, we cannot say that it is because the culture has less artistic spirit; that sort of nonexplanation received its ultimate parody from Molière when the doctor explained the sleep-producing property of opium by its "dormative principle."

Before turning to an explanation, it is essential to examine the theoretical orientation within which it is cast.[2] Human endeavor requires collaborative effort in unique degree, and collaboration in turn requires systems of mutuality. To achieve this commonality, humanity everywhere has constructed a way of understanding the world. This pattern of understanding is a symbolic system that we usually call culture, and as we know, it is culture that varies from people to people and from time to time. The infant is therefore born not only into a world of physical reality, but also into this symbolic world. This symbolic world is transmitted to the infant in ever greater detail by those who are already there—his parents and other relatives and the whole of the social order in which he is to participate. Thus the individual's understandings are shaped by the culture. It does not merely involve the way of doing things, but the manner of relating to people, motivations, and feelings.

By and large, these cultural perceptions of the world, of the society, and yes, even of the self, are transmitted through language, which organizes for each individual how the world is and how it works. But language is the communication of the intellect; it is a handmaiden to the cognitive process. It is, as we all know from bitter experience, a poor medium for the communication of sentiment. Yet each individual is not merely an engine of practical purpose, he is also a bundle of passions—love and hate, fear and lust—and a complex of moods and lesser emotions—despair and elation, anxiety and pride. These emotions and sentiments, though ego-centered, are essential ingredients to social interaction; they are both responsive to and directed at the people in the social surroundings. They are thus to be seen as significant elements in that process of collaborative action that is necessary for all major human endeavors.

Essential to the social system is a means of communicating, ameliorating, and orchestrating sentiment, and I believe it to be the central function of ritual. *Ritual is to sentiment as language is to cognition.* And it leads us to the function of aesthetic expression, for ritual *is* aesthetic expression. It always involves, in varying degrees, music, drama, dance, body decoration, and symbolic forms such as masks, altars, and other representations, all designed to establish and coordinate the feelings of the people involved.

If collaboration is the central issue, the kinds of collaboration that are necessary in a society differ in accordance with the major forms of economic activity—in current anthropological parlance, ecological conditions. It is no accident that social forms tend toward a certain similarity among peoples who share the same productive processes, even though they are not historically connected. And if this is so, if ritual, and the arts that are in the service of ritual, relate directly to the mode of production, it follows that any abrupt and serious shift in the economy will throw these institutions out of joint. As they become increasingly irrelevant to emerging conditions, they will wither and die, although if the change is gradual enough, they may themselves be transformed and replaced.

In the century or so before European contact, the Sebei had made a great change in their ancient Nilotic traditional economy; they turned from pastoralism to intensive hoe farming. In part this was because their mountain environment was suited to such pursuits and in part because they acquired new cultivated plants, maize and plantains, which were highly productive. With this rational change went many alterations in their social system, of which I enumerate but a few. They moved out of the brush-enclosed manyattas and spread over the land; their warfare shifted from raiding and counterraiding of the cattle kraals of their neighbors to defensive action; the age-sets which unified young men into warrior groups and older ones into authority figures lost their function, since defensive warfare must involve all able-bodied men; social position no longer rested on acts of derring-do, and indeed, there was no clear basis for personal status advancement. In short, changes that were in themselves ecologically appropriate and economically sound had the secondary effect of undermining traditional directions for social action and individual incentive. These secondary changes were in progress when another historical event overtook the Sebei—the invasion of their territory by Western culture. This change, here as everywhere, inhibited the endogenous development of institutions. It came before the Sebei had managed to forge a new culture based upon the newly acquired technology—indeed, even today their economy varies regionally between intensive farming and predominantly pastoral activities. Thus we find among the Sebei a lack of cultural integrity. I believe this to be the key to understanding the limited artistic expression among the Sebei.

In my work in East Africa, which involved the comparative study of four tribes, I had the collaboration of Professor Robert Edgerton, who sampled each population and administered an extensive interview and tests to about 120 persons in each tribe. The list included the Rorschach, a picture-test of our devising, and other provocative stimuli, as well as specific questions and some open-ended interviews. The inner life as revealed by responses to Rorschach tests reflects a lack of cultural commitment and a lack of internal consistency in their beliefs and attitudes. Edgerton makes the following summary characterization:

> The Sebei as a people remain shadowy. That the reality of Sebei responses should prove to be so illusory may in part result from the extreme variability of their responses; of all the [four] tribes [in this study], their responses are most varied. More striking is their lack of positive expression in their beliefs, attitudes, and values. It is very much as though they had no commitment to them, no favorable sentiment about their world. [3]

Edgerton found the Sebei expressing diffuse anxiety, fear of death and the malignant power of women, and profound hostility and jealousy. In my summary of Sebei religion I wrote:

> Sebei ritual as a whole dwells on dangers, disasters, the immanent evil in the universe. These negative forces are not particularized; the emphasis is not on the evil of witches or the individual representations, nor on particular situations out of which danger arises, nor is it related to breaches of tabu or the commission of sins, though such may also bring disaster and are in the ambience with which the Sebei dwell. Most ritual symbols and symbolic acts are ameliorative in character: the spitting, libation, anointing and cleansing are designed to remove unspecified but strongly felt contaminating elements that adhere to persons, things, and situations. Sebei ritual life is not concerned with good and evil, right or wrong, but with retaliation and amelioration. [4]

These comments apply not merely to the religious life that survived three-quarters of a century of European overrule, but that which existed at the time of first contact; that is, the condition of ritual behavior that existed after the transformation from pastoralism to farming. The responses express, I suggest, a low degree of collaborative sentiment and appear to serve largely the amelioration and projection of negative emotions.

These qualities are revealed also in the evidence at hand for the inner psychic life of the Sebei. Edgerton had a Rorschach specialist make a review of their responses for a nonstatistical subjective evaluation of the Rorschach protocols.[5] She read them "blind," that is, with minimal information about the people themselves. "There is no type, no one person" among the Sebei, the analyst said of these responses, but a great range and variation. The one consistent response pattern was a tendency to use vague responses—clouds and rocks. These are generally treated as expressing a lack of creative imagination.[6] She felt they were being used as a kind of protective façade, enabling the respondents to distance themselves from the issues, either to avoid facing deeper psychic problems or to avoid revealing themselves too much. It was less true among respondents who remained more closely associated with the older herding pattern of life than it was among those who devoted themselves to farming, but even these pastoralists maintained a guarded position.

Fantasy life was not totally absent, but rich expressions of fantasy were clearly not characteristic of Sebei responses, and the analyst specifically noted that there was little reference to religious or supernatural concepts. An exception to this picture of vagueness and inconsistency tells us something of importance. The analyst, without knowledge of the cultural context, remarked on certain responses that she considered bizarre. They were references to lightning: "the children of lightning," "lightning pulled by animals." But lightning is one of the few still recognized, feared, and personified forces of nature, placated, when it strikes, by a special ritual. It evokes responses so filled with imagery that in her ignorance the analyst saw them as pathological, when they are in fact expressions of feelings that have been reinforced by a surviving fragmentary segment of an earlier system of belief. These responses show how belief has served to give meaning to the percepts, to give dramatic form to the environment, and to transform the capacity for fantasy into aesthetic expression.

A brief contrast can perhaps demonstrate how ritual and arts serve the social order, and I indulge myself by discussing another people whose culture I studied.[7] Among the Hupa Indians of northwestern California, the aesthetic expressions are associated with their religious life and the manner in which the individual should conduct himself. The Hupa and their neighbors, the Yurok, to whom the great anthropologist Alfred Kroeber devoted much of his attention, have a rich mythology, an elaborate set of ritual paraphernalia, and religious rites in which the material representations of dance, music, and, yes, even games are associated. Hupa society is unique for a people whose economy depended upon the products of nature in that clans and lineages were absent, in that the possession of property, including access to the basic resources, was held by individuals, and in that social status was measured by the acquisition of wealth in the form of this highly valued religious paraphernalia. The acquisition of such wealth was, as is usual, fundamentally through inheritance, but an individual was expected to be industrious and increase his property, he was expected to further his own interests assiduously, and he did so in no small degree through taking aggressive legal action in a highly litigious society. There was also an unusually strong imperative to proper conduct, which was expressed in the sense of sinfulness with respect to sloth, gluttony, and sexuality. Indeed, reflected here is the protestant ethic in an extreme form. These are elements in a social system designed to create a high degree of tension, both between individuals and internally within individuals.

Hupa rituals, particularly the World Renewal or White Deerskin Dance, in which the wealth is given public display, are designed to allay these tensions and thus to reestablish harmony. At the same time, this ritual reinforced the social order in an unusual way; leadership in the rite is the responsibility and prerogative of individual wealthy men who are assisted by their network of friends and associates. Thus these rites express not merely individual status—express it in elegantly decorated wealth objects that are themselves sacred—but also demonstrate and publicize social alliances that are so important in this litigious community. And to this function, as already indicated, all the arts of the Hupa are brought to bear. In view of the unusually individualistic character of these northwest California societies, where harmony must be attained through cooptation of independent and aggressive individuals, it is interesting that their music is also unusual (indeed, unique) among American Indians in that it involves syncopated part singing, according to Professor Charlotte Heth (personal communication).

The poverty of Sebei aesthetic expression can be seen in the

Illus. 3. Gourd containers belonging to a Sebei cattle keeper.

Illus. 4. Utilitarian baskets and other objects used by the Hupa in preparing acorn soup.

contrast to that of the Hupa in the illustrations. Illustration 3 shows all the gourds used for storing milk and water and other uses that were the property of a single Sebei household. Though they are naturally elegant in shape, they are totally without decoration. Illustration 4 is a display of equally mundane Hupa paraphernalia—the artifacts associated with the gathering and preparation of acorns—the large collecting basket, the cooking vessel and eating bowls at the left, decorated winnowing baskets, the basketry hopper and pestles, and the carved stirring paddle used while boiling the acorn meal with hot stones. These handmade utilitarian items carry traditional decoration, but are by no means the finest expression of Hupa basket weaving. Illustration 5 is a Sebei hand-wrought iron necklace worn as decoration, contrasted with the elegantly crafted net-making shuttles of the Hupa (illustration 6).

The two women, each in ceremonial dress, further exemplify the contrast. The Sebei girl (illustration 7) is preparing for her initiation; the beads on her head and around her neck are purchased from the market; only the crude cowry girdle and the unusually

Illus. 5. A Sebei iron necklace.

elaborate cicatrices are Sebei products. The Hupa girl (illustration 8) is modeling the ceremonial costume of elaborately beaded and carefully designed skirts and basketry hat; only her elegant blouse is not of native manufacture. The contrast is reflected also in the ritual performance. Illustration 9 shows Sebei youth dancing as part of their circumcision rite; illustration 10 is a scene from the Hupa White Deerskin dance.

Culture is a structure of collaboration, and collaboration is based upon communication; only through a consensus can a community engage in the collaboration necessary to achieve a higher level of

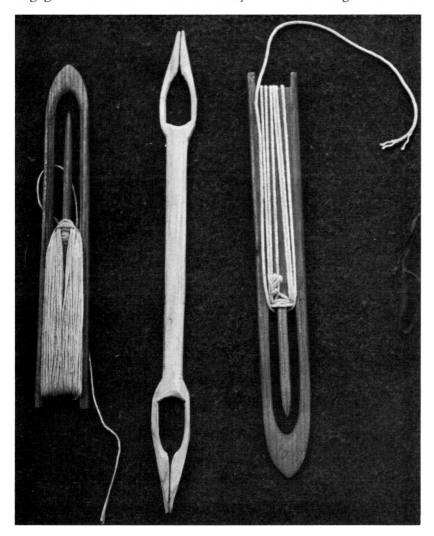

Illus. 6. Hupa net-making shuttles.

Illus. 7. Sebei girl dressed for her initiation rite.

Illus. 8. Hupa girl modeling dress worn on ceremonial occasions.

Illus. 9. Sebei initiates dancing.

Illus. 10. Scene from the Hupa White Deerskin Dance.

productivity. Language is the communication of the intellect; through it individuals come to share an understanding of the world around them, that enables them to manipulate it to their own ends. The arts (and rituals, which are traditionally an orchestration of the arts) are the communication of sentiment; they enable the individuals that make up a society to share feeling, and thus to subordinate their sense of individuality to a larger social whole.

Intellectually oriented, pragmatic Western society has given far more attention to the communication of cognitive understanding than to the transmission and sharing of sentiment, although the latter is too insistent to permit its total neglect. Our word-oriented culture, especially as it operates in the academic world, translates feelings into words in order to deal with them as a part of the cognitive system. But emotions are emotions, regardless of the words used to express them, and they suffer in the translation.

It is in the light of these considerations that we must look back at the poverty of aesthetic expression among the Sebei. We see that the transformation of Sebei society diminished the sense of commitment and purpose, and led to the kind of flaccid emotional tone that rendered the world hostile and fearful. The psychological stance of the Sebei was negative, just as their military position had become defensive. It was not a social milieu in which the arts were likely to flourish, and without aesthetic expression the people in turn remained uninspired.

I am not saying either that the situation caused the impoverished aesthetics or that the absence of art caused the emotional poverty. What I am saying is that aesthetic expression, being an element in communication, is part of the feedback mechanism in that essential circularity between personal action and social expectation. I am also saying that aesthetic expression, particularly traditionalized, community-wide aesthetic expression, is an essential ingredient in a viable social order. With respect to the Sebei, loss of purpose (which I take to be one with their deficit in aesthetic expression) was having dire consequences at the time of the European takeover. Although they enjoyed a rich and healthy environment on their mountain bastion, the Sebei were being decimated in one quarter by the raids of their more inspired pastoral neighbors to the north, and were being pushed out of their territory by the aggressive agricultural Bantu to the west. Had not these processes been halted by colonialism, one of two things would have occurred: either the Sebei would have been eliminated as a separate and independent people (killed off or absorbed by others), or they would have undergone some revitalistic religious movement which would have inspired them to new purpose. And you may be sure that such inspiration would have had as a necessary component a revitalized aesthetic expression.

In the light of these considerations, let us examine certain historic phenomena as revealed by archaeology. Consider a recurrent matter in the archaeological development of any civilization: the standard event of a "florescent" period, as it is usually called. What is this florescent epoch in the normal growth of civilizations? It is a period of expansion, of growth, of greatness. It is also a period of high artistic creativity. Is this recurrent association fortuitous? Is the art merely a by-product of the political growth? Or is the aesthetic expression a more integral part of the process, an essential link in a causative cycle, a crucial ingredient of the sociocultural mix that makes for greatness? The plight of the Sebei suggests that the latter is the case.

We may take the inquiry further back, to the very beginnings of human culture as it is known to ethnography and history. I have become intrigued with a peculiar aspect of the curve of human development from its beginnings on the African savannas some three million years ago. For about 98 percent of the history of the bipedal primates that ultimately became us, the development was miniscule and the hominids as a whole remained unimportant. Although culture, in its pragmatic sense, was the essential element in the formation of this hominid ecological niche, these practical accomplishments did not originally transform our ancestry into the earth's dominant species. The archaeological record over these eons has revealed no evidence of either ritual or aesthetic expression. Only well into the Mousterian, not over fifty thousand years ago, do we get evidence of ritual expression in the form of intentional burial with interred objects; and not until the Upper Paleolithic, some thirty thousand years ago, do we get clear evidence of any aesthetic expression. Thereafter, cultural development moved at an entirely different pace; man conquered the whole terrestrial environment, spread across the face of the globe, and rapidly advanced his power and his numbers. How crucial to this development was the emergence of the arts? Was aesthetic expression merely a source of pleasure and satisfaction for the artist and his public or was it necessary for the unleashing of the true human potential?

Scholars, with their propensity for dealing with the verbal and the cognitive, have suggested that it was the acquisition of language that was the critical element in this takeoff. Perhaps it was not language, but the orchestration of sentiment through aesthetic expression in religious ritual.

Let us return from these speculations to the bleak Sebei aesthetic landscape and come to terms with it in relation to other elements in their culture. We find it associated with a lack of cultural commitment, a general poverty of religious expression, and a psychological outlook at once fearful and hostile. As seen, at the time of colonization, the social order was in such disarray that the Sebei had not been able to mount the military force to withstand an attack on their flank, so that both their population and their territory were dwindling before Europeans arrived in eastern Uganda. The ultimate cause of this precolonial social disorder was the fundamental reordering of an economy that had rendered obsolete older Sebei institutions and for which they had not found new ones functionally relevant to the emerging order when a massive external force stopped the process of endogenous growth. It is in the context of these historic events that we come to understand the artistic poverty of these people and thereby learn to appreciate the crucial function of the arts in the maintenance of the social order.

NOTES

[1] My work among the Sebei, in which I was assisted by my wife, Gale Goldschmidt, involved fieldwork in 1954, 1961-1962, and briefly in 1972. For details of Sebei culture see my *The Culture and Behavior of the Sebei* (Berkeley and Los Angeles: University of California Press, 1976), which includes a full bibliography. Initial work among the Sebei was supported by a Fulbright Research Scholarship and by grants from the Wenner-Gren Foundation, the National Science Foundation, and the National Institute of Mental Health. I want also to express gratitude to Professor Jacques Maquet for his insightful comments on this paper. Gale Goldschmidt, whose photographs are used to illustrate this article, thus also gives homage to Franklin Murphy.

[2] This brief statement is drawn from a work now in progress, tentatively titled *Dynamic Anthropology*. Some preliminary ideas were expressed in a series of lectures, "Three Times Two, Three Dualities in the Structure of Human Behavior" (MS).

[3] The *Individual in Cultural Adaptation* (Berkeley and Los Angeles: University of California Press, 1971), p. 122.

[4] *Culture and Behavior of the Sebei,* p. 337.

[5] These data are from research files kindly supplied by Professor Edgerton.

[6] These are the so-called vista responses, and may reflect the impact of the physical rather than the social environment in the Sebei perceptions.

[7]My wife and I did research among the Hupa in 1937, with support from the University of California, Berkeley. The Hupa and Yurok share an almost identical culture, and my analysis draws on data from both societies. For further details see my "Ethics and the Structure of Society," *American Anthropologist* 53:506–527, which has an extensive bibliography, and *The Hupa White Deerskin Dance,* with Harold Drivers, University of California Publications in American Archeology and Ethnology, 35(1940):103–131.

PLURIFRONTAL FIGURINES IN LEGA ART IN ZAIRE

Daniel P. Biebuyck

University of Delaware

Illus. 1. Lega (Zaire), wood, blackened, white faces, h. 23.7 cm, Musée royal de l'Afrique centrale, Tervuren, collected in the field by Daniel Biebuyck. The bicephalous figurine, called Sakimatwematwe, Mr. Many-Heads, was part of a collectively owned basket of initiation objects. It was used at the highest levels of the closed bwami *association.*

As Chancellor of the University of California, Los Angeles, Dr. Franklin Murphy was instrumental in the acquisition of two outstanding collections of ethno-art and material culture. I became intimately associated with those collections when I was a professor and Curator of African Art at UCLA. The important set of art-works and other material objects from Zaire, Rwanda, and Burundi assembled by Jean-Pierre Hallet was obtained for the university as a direct result of the impulse, the efforts, and the far-reaching vision of Dr. Murphy. Soon after, the great Sir Henry Wellcome Collection was transferred to the Museum and Labo-ratories of Ethnic Arts and Technology at UCLA.

I cannot forget the circumstances under which the Hallet collec-tion was acquired. The UCLA African Studies Center invited me to act as a consultant just after it had become available for sale. Arriving in Los Angeles on a Friday evening, I discussed the work schedule with Hilda Kuper and Ralph Altman; on Saturday Altman and I searched furiously through the partly crated collection in Bakersfield to assess its artistic and ethnographic significance. On Sunday morning, Altman and I, in the company of many distin-guished members of the UCLA faculty, were received by Dr. Mur-phy at his home to get an immediate report on the status of the objects. That day impressed on me forever the depth of humanistic understanding and genuine excitement that the Chancellor showed for a field that was far removed from his own scholarly speciali-zations. Somewhat conflicting statements had been made previ-ously about the aesthetic and ethnographic significance of the Hal-let collection. I tried to put it into the right perspective: the many objects were of mixed quality (old and new pieces, some outstand-ing, some inconspicuous) but were drawn from several ethnic groups. The objects illustrated diverse facets of central and east African cultures and were of irreplaceable ethnographic and edu-cational value. They exemplified different aesthetic modes, styles, and techniques; they were derived from many ethnographic con-texts (e.g., daily lives of hunters, cultivators, and pastoralists; par-aphernalia of rank and status; cults connected with ancestors, shades, and nature spirits; initiations; sociopolitical control). As the discussion proceeded, we all became excited about the pros-pects, and I felt that Dr. Murphy had perceived at once the unique value of the collection as a research and educational tool. When the objects were later acquired for the university, Dr. Murphy showed relentless interest in seeing that the collection was properly cared

Illus. 2. Lega (Zaire), wood, black-ened, white faces, h. 22.4 cm, Musée royal de l'Afrique centrale, Tervuren, collected in the field by Daniel Bie-buyck. The plurifrontal figurine, individually owned, was identified as Kimbayu "the man whose heart is dead" in the context of the kinsamba rite of the highest bwami grade.

for, cataloged, validated, and publicized (see R. Altman, *Balega and Other Tribal Arts from the Congo* [Los Angeles: University of California Dickson Art Center, 1963).

Private discussion with Dr. Murphy revealed his very real and deep affective response to the aesthetics of the objects. He also realized that the full appreciation and understanding of them were impossible without the knowledge of usages, functions, meanings, and contexts associated with the objects. It is in this perspective that I wish to analyze a single feature of form and content in Lega art.

The Hallet collection contains a large number of sculptures in ivory, bone, and wood from the Lega, a population located in the forest regions of eastern Zaire. Among the anthropomorphic fig-urines, some have two or more faces (Altman, 1963, figs. 12 and 19). A similar morphological feature occurs in many Lega artworks contained in public and private collections in Canada, Europe, and the United States. Multifaced (plurifrontal) and multiheaded (polycephalous) figurines are one of the recurring iconographic motifs of Lega art. Others include one-eyed and one-armed pieces, statuettes with one or two raised arms, figurines with zigzag shapes or flat perforated bodies, sculptures carved in peg or pole forms, and figures with swollen abdomens. These typical morphological models are in sharp contrast with the vast number of carvings that simply represent a normal or truncated but always stylized human body or a bust or head.

These and many other types (e.g., masks, spoons, zoomorphic figurines) of sculptures are of intrinsic importance to the closed *bwami* association, which dominates the artistic, intellectual, ritual, and sociopolitical life of the Lega (for further information, see D. Biebuyck, *Lega Culture: Art, Initiation, and Moral Philosophy among a Central African People* [Berkeley and Los Angeles: University of California Press, 1973]). Depending on generic and functional cat-egories (as perceived by the Lega), the sculptures are owned, used, and interpreted by bwami members of the two highest grades (each divided into several levels). Thus, the carvings are not merely emblems of rank, status, and prestige, but they are also symbols that express, in association with sung aphorisms and danced drama, the principles of the moral code in the initiation context.

The plurifrontal and polycephalous motifs are sculpturally ren-dered in many ways on the anthropomorphic figurines. In its sim-plest form, the figurine has a single head with two opposing faces, one in the front and one in the rear. The more complex forms have two jointed but flattened heads or two separate heads on a single body. In rare pieces the complete figurine is doubled: two personages stand back to back, completely joined or linked just at the buttocks or the heads. Faces are also carved on parts other than the head: at the height of the shoulders or the hips and in the back; in some instances the entire sculpture both frontally and dorsally consists of a superposition of faces (illus. 1-5). In many cases, then, these are not the classic Januslike bifacial or bicephalic sculptures, but rather carvings that have various combinations (never juxtaposition, but opposition and superposition) of three to eight faces. Some rare carvings consist merely of two heads joined at the neck. The majority of this category of artworks has either two or four faces in opposition (i.e., looking frontward and backward, downward and upward). In other words, plurifrontality has been worked out by the artists according to some preferred manner. Although operating clearly within the restraints set by the patrons' demand for plurifrontal pieces, the artists have much freedom and leeway to manifest creative originality, effect, and surprise. Local traditions cultivated by successive generations of artists within their lineage groups have set some limitations to the range of creativity. It would be impossible, however, to link specific formal patterns with distinctive territorially based social and ritual units in Legaland. Segments of lineage groups have traveled and so have traditions; the bwami members who sponsor the carvings regularly participate in initiations held in ritual communities other than their own; artists who are frequently members of the association have traveled and learned elsewhere; the objects themselves have traveled partly because of inheritance patterns.

It is noteworthy that plurifrontal sculptures rarely exhibit immediately visible sexual distinctions (genitalia or breasts). Cultural features such as different types of hairdos or tattoos, which might indicate sexual distinctions, are also absent. There may be complete uniformity of the two sides of the sculpture and of the faces. Sometimes one face is slightly longer and narrower than the opposing one. (There is a tendency to identify the longer one as the female face, but strict emphasis is not placed on this.) In rare instances an incised motif of a different pattern distinguishes one side of the sculpture from the other (illus. 4-5).

Given the recurrence of the plurifrontal motif and its multiple sculptural variations, the questions arise about their precise func-

Illus. 3. Lega (Zaire), ivory, yellowish patination, h. 13.1 cm, Musée royal de l'Afrique centrale, Tervuren, collected in the field by Daniel Biebuyck. The figurine with two sets of opposing faces was individually owned by a member of the highest grade and identified as Mr. Many-Heads.

tions and meanings as well as whether or not functional and cognitive distinctions are linked with the formal variations. The latter question is easy to answer: there are no functional or cognitive differences between the various morphological subtypes. In other words, identical functions and meanings are associated with the objects regardless of the number of faces and their placement. This important point obviously has emerged from research in the field context. Creative imagination, relative freedom of expression, and extraordinary sense for stylization and schematization characteristic of Lega artists are not the only factors at work. Part of the value of initiations rests on their secrecy; part of the secrecy can be maintained by creating an atmosphere of deliberate confusion for the noninitiates. The symbolic messages contained in gestures, poses, attitudes, somatic features, and designs expressed in Lega artworks are so surprising, sometimes so deliberately antithetical and so strictly circumscribed by the philosophical code that out-of-context speculations about them are meaningless. Even if the exact meanings of plurifrontal pieces found in areas adjoining and related to the Lega were known, the validity of the generalizations could not be guaranteed, because Lega interpretation of forms and of their connotations is not part of the general culture but rather of the specialized initiatory knowledge.

It is an essential feature of Lega initiatory thought (surely not limited to the Lega) that an object by itself "does not speak," that the Lega "have made it speak." By this they mean that form has no intrinsic meaning for them, that its meanings are created (according to secret patterns) by their makers and users. It should therefore not be surprising that a great many, if not all, objects (natural or manufactured) convey several meanings (immediately connected or unconnected, complementary or antithetical) in single or different contexts; that regional and local preferences may be manifested in the interpretation. (Although organization, structure, and ideology of bwami are basically similar throughout Legaland, autonomous ritual and sociopolitical entities cultivate originality to various extents.) Singular and connected meanings inversely may be expressed and enhanced by the use of diverse objects. Since an object has distinctive components and properties (which can be perceived as complementary or antithetical to one another), the focus can be either on the totality or on one or more select features (not always the most obvious ones). Among the plurifrontal figurines, for example, some have only one eye or one arm; others have a flat perforated body; others wear a skullcap of cowries. Sculptures occur singly (which is rare) or in a configuration (static or dynamic) of similar or different objects (sculptures and nonsculptures). When part of a configuration, the objects may be used sequentially or simultaneously as contrastive or complementary sets. During Lega initiations, I observed plurifrontal sculptures (of any type) manipulated in these various ways, and hence the striking diversity of meanings associated with them.

The basic identification given for any subtype of multifrontal sculpture is Sakimatwematwe (Biebuyck 1973: 220–221), Mr. (Father; Possessor of) Many-(Big)-Heads (lit., Father-[Big]-Heads-Heads). This name sometimes is replaced by Sameisomabili, Mr. (Father) Two-Eyes (Faces). The latter term, although more specific than the first, is used as a synonym for the less precise Mr. Many-Heads. The verbal exegesis is as usual contained in an aphorism: "Mr. Many-Heads has seen an elephant on the other side (bank) of the large river." When the object is used with this basic meaning, the action is always very simple: the object is viewed singly, and it stands on the ground or is held in the hands of a dancer who may occasionally point to the multiple faces. The overt reference of the aphorism is to a person whose many eyes (faces) enable him to see things that are hidden from others. The metaphor relates to the high initiate (owner and exegete of these figurines): he has the extraordinary power of sight and insight because hidden things have been revealed to him through initiation. The figurine is meant to evoke the status of the high initiate: having witnessed superior things, he is wiser than others; seeing well and in many directions, he has a deep and balanced view of everything, a sense of fairness and justice as an ideal mediator between antithetical forces. The high initiate's multifacetedness expresses his own completeness as a central figure in the sociopolitical, legal, and moral systems. This basic theme is even better underscored in some ritual contexts where the multifaced sculpture is placed in the center of a circle of other sculptures. In such cases the figure is referred to as *kimini*, the great dancer. In Lega initiation, the great dancer is generally a person of high rank in the association; he not only has exceptional talent in choreographic performance and often acts as soloist but also is a skillful leader and organizer of everything connected with a successful dance (right objects, right manipulation, words, movements, music, atmosphere). The concepts "great dancer" and "preceptor" are closely intermingled in this case.

Illus. 4. Lega (Zaire), ivory, reddish patination, cowries glued to the head with resin, h. 15.3 cm, Musée royal de l'Afrique centrale, Tervuren, collected in the field by Daniel Biebuyck. The figurine was individually owned by a member of the highest grade. The side illustrated here is identified as the male initiate Kabukenge, Little-Beautiful-(Good)-One.

The idea of completeness leads to two more possible associations of the plurifrontal sculpture. First, it symbolizes the vital link between the highest initiate (*kindi*) and his initiated wife (*kanyamwa*). Neither is complete nor even imaginable without the other. This idea was strongly emphasized in the exegesis of the sculpture reproduced in illustrations 4-5. It depicts Kabukenge, Little-Beautiful-(Good)-One, and his wife Kagunza, Woman-with-Fallen-Breasts; the much admired fertile woman; the mother of sons who will continue their father's tradition who together have four eyes. Another sculpture represented the vital link between the candidate-initiate and his initiated tutor. Without a tutor the candidate (however important his position or advanced his age) is like a *kyegelela*, a drowning person (something drifting with the river). No person is a complete member of the highest grade level unless at least one wife is coinitiated and unless he has tutored others to reach high initiatory experience.

The preceding Lega interpretations for any of the multifaced figurines are by far the most frequently stated ones. It would be incorrect, however, to think that any statue of this type necessarily or solely expresses these restricted meanings. The term "Mr. Many-Heads" definitely refers to a particular morphological category (any object with more than one face or head). In principle the morphological category corresponds with a broad semantic and functional one: it glorifies the unique status of the high initiate as a complete man (a poised, intelligent, fair mediator and guardian) inseparably linked with the initiated kanyamwa wife, the junior candidate whom he has sponsored, and the senior initiate who has proctored him.

Other selective morphological features may occur in a statue conjointly with its multifrontality. Two examples may illustrate this point. Some double-faced figurines have only one arm. The theme of Kubokokumozi, (Mr.) One-Arm, is an important and relatively frequent one in Lega art and fits together well with that of plurifrontality. Literally, the high initiate, symbol of balanced action, has forgotten himself and engaged in a violent brawl in which he lost an arm. He has thus diminished himself morally and lost much of his effective power and appeal. Figuratively, the sculpture exhibiting the incompatible feature (one arm) very directly states what the great initiate is not: he is not a violent or meddlesome person; rather the high initiate is physically and morally intact (*busoga*, beautiful and good).

In another example, some multifaced figurines are adorned with the relatively infrequent dot or circle-dot motif. This motif is equated with "signs of (youthful) beauty" (i.e., tattoos). The general aphorism associated with this feature is as follows: "The one who had the signs of beauty engraved on the cheeks (face) no longer is in the place (in the status) where he used to be." This statement certainly refers to the transience of people and things, but unlike the first example it notes that the results of moral decay are not necessarily visible. The idea is often found in several proverbs expressing the notion that persons are not always just what they appear to be (e.g., a beautiful body but an implacable heart).

It was pointed out earlier that sculptures do occur in a dance context in certain sequential or simultaneous combinations of similar or different types of objects. In very rare instances, a two-headed sculpture was used to depict the character of Mukobania, the Sharer-of-Things who, however, causes strife and disaster in the group and turns into a Divider. The sculpture occurred jointly with a single-faced carving representing Kakulu, Little-Old-One, who fell victim to the dissensions caused by Mukobania. Mukobania, a high initiate, had invited others for a beer party (a bad thing to do); Kakulu, one of the participants, fell victim of an ensuing fight. Instead of being a Sharer-of-Things, Mukobania became a source of divisiveness. In another dance context, a similar four-faced wooden sculpture represented Kimbayu, "the man whose heart is dead"; he is inattentive to advice ("Who will teach him?" the proverb asks), brings discord, and is finally rejected by the group. The character was contrasted with another sculpture (without facial features) representing a lonely and destitute but good and receptive person, who finds refuge among his maternal uncles.

In these latter cases the plurifrontal figurine condenses the negative pole of symbolism. The figurine still basically represents the "physical" completeness of the initiate (in the sense that multiple faces are a symbolic expression of completeness, the high initiate still wears the outer signs of his status), but he is no longer a moral person. This is one method the Lega use in their initiation system on the one hand to signify *ex contrariis* the behaviors which an initiate should and should not adopt, and on the other hand to emphasize that sheer acquisition of a high grade is not a guarantee of continued moral excellence. The latter is a praxis; it must be constantly cultivated and exemplified.

Illus. 5. Reverse of illustration 4, this side is identified as Kagunza, Woman-with-Fallen-Breasts. Together the two faces emphasize the inseparable linkage of the high kindi *initiate and his initiated* kanyamwa *wife.*

Complementary oneness and opposition are expressed in other ways by the combination of many objects. First, there are natural (e.g., *lubumba*, mussel shell), manufactured (e.g., a mat and its seam, an ax and its shaft), and carved (e.g., the *kisumbi* stool, the multifaced figurines) objects that intrinsically (by their very forms) convey this message. Second, there are objects that in daily life are inseparably used together (e.g., needle and thread, needle and sheath of a monkey *tibia*). Third, there are objects that are conceptually linked (e.g., the sculptures representing Kakulu, Little-Old-Man, and Waiyinda, Pregnant-Adulteress; Kasangulu, Penis, and Nyabilimbio, Mrs. Thighs). Similar complementary oppositions are obviously perceived in the physical world (overtly, e.g., penis and vulva, forest and village; covertly, e.g., giant snail shell and hornbill beak).

In Western art studies, archetypal forms have quite precisely been isolated and characterized according to their subject matter. Similar studies of African art must yet be undertaken and developed. Their success will depend on the availability of carefully made, descriptive, and analytical studies of particular groups and on well-delineated small-scale comparative studies. The range of meanings contained in particular sculptural forms and design features recurring in distinctive ethno-arts cannot be inferred simply from analogies. The analogies and similarities first must be documented and proven. The janiform motif—more than the plurifrontal one—is widely but unevenly distributed in Africa and is found in masks, anthropomorphic and zoomorphic figurines, pole sculptures, staffs, scepters, and other objects (E. Von Sydow, "The Image of Janus in African Sculpture," *Africa*, 1932; A. L. Scheinberg, *Two . . . Aspects of the Doubled Image in African Art* [New York, 1975]). In areas of eastern Zaire among peoples geographically, historically, or culturally close to the Lega, the bifacial motif is frequently found, for example, on Bembe ʻ*alunga* bell masks, Boyo and Hemba *kabeja* heads and poles, and Lengola and Metoko *bukota* figurines. The motif does occur more or less frequently elsewhere in Zaire on masks (e.g., some Kongo or Ket), on figurines (e.g., some Luba, Kanyok, Songye, Luluwa, Yaka, etc.), and on other carvings as well (e.g. Luba stools, Mbala neckrests, Bembe scepters). In most cases, however, comparisons and conclusions are excluded for lack of basic research not only on what the objects as such represent but also on exactly what the janiform may mean. This is *a fortiori* true for broader comparative studies on similar works found among peoples in West and West Central Africa.

In some cultures the plurifrontal sculpture may be linked with the worship of particular nature spirits or with mythical ideas about twins and twinship; in others it may symbolize the successful passage of initiates from lower to higher statuses. Elsewhere it represents the guardian or the leader seeing in all directions; one who cannot easily be fooled, a master of balanced behavior that affects his role as mediator and judge. The degree to which the plurifrontal pieces are linked with bisexuality is problematic. Among the Lega, the simplest bifacial figurines are not identified as male or as female, and in fact sexual indications on the sculptures may be entirely lacking. The broader ideas and practices of the bwami association do indicate that perfection and plenitude of a status position are often conceived as a merging of male and female attributes. It was pointed out already that no man finishes the highest level of initiations without one of his wives being coinitiated to the corresponding female grade, and no woman who is not a wife of a high initiate can aspire to reach the highest female grade. This necessary complementarity is symbolically expressed in many ways during and after the initiations. In the spheres of dress and adornment, for example, high male initiates often wear hats that imitate the plaited hair of their wives. High female initiates, who normally have beaded diadems, are allowed to wear their husbands' hats in certain rites; they permanently carry hanging from their belts small sculptures (called "phalli that did not witness the circumcision rites") as outer signs of their quasi-male status. In the Lega initiation context, ideas about sexuality itself are not communicated by means of the plurifrontal sculptures but by the use of other objects, such as phallic-shaped bark beaters, giant snail shells, hornbill beaks, and miniature feather hats.

Author's Note. I did fieldwork among the Lega as a research fellow of "L'Institut pour la recherche scientifique en Afrique centrale" (Brussels and Lwiro). In recent years, analytical and comparative research on the arts of Zaire, including the Lega, was made possible through research grants from the National Endowment for the Humanities, the Samuel Kress Foundation, the Rockefeller Foundation, and the John Simon Guggenheim Memorial Foundation.

THE WARAO LORDS OF RAIN

Johannes Wilbert

University of California, Los Angeles

Instituto Venezolano de Investigaziones Científicas

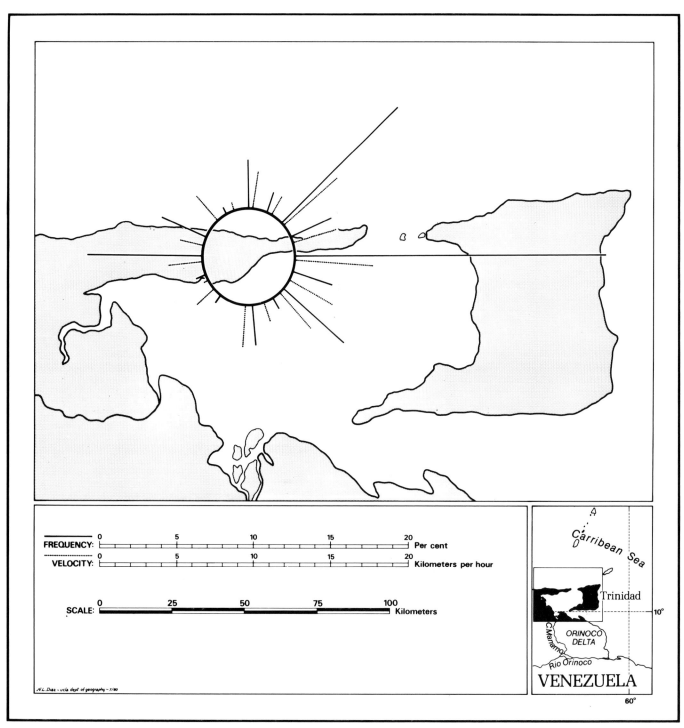

Illus. 2. Wind rose, Güiria, Gulf of Paria.

ONE OF THE BIGGEST surprises of my career as an ethnographer was to find the Warao—a South American Indian tribe I have been studying since 1954—in possession of an elaborate system of weather shamanism. I had often heard the tribal rainmaker sing his magic chants or had seen him blow against upcoming storms, but I had assumed that to be the extent of Warao weather magic. It was not until the rainy season of 1975 that I learned otherwise.

The Warao Indians inhabit the extensive swamplands of the Orinoco Delta on the east coast of Venezuela. Not only is their world, *hobahi,* "surrounded by water," but it is also crisscrossed by a dense network of drainage rivers, saturated by tides and ground-water, and flooded annually by the Orinoco River. Furthermore, Warao land is situated between 8° and 10° north latitude, subjected, that is, to the winter solstice humidity of the northeast trades as well as to the Amazonic monsoon-like rains following the spring equinox. From May to October rains are heavy to torrential; even during the so-called dry season there are rarely any rain-free days. With so much water from above and below, why would the Warao bother with shamanic rainmakers? One would suppose that rain-makers and rain gods are ordinarily found among peoples of arid regions, or among agriculturalists for whom a reliable pattern of precipitation is a condition of survival. In those regions food and drink depend on rain and on the manipulation of the supernatural masters of this precious commodity. But in the case of the Orinoco Delta, these conditions do not exist; there is a superabundance of water and the Warao, traditionally a nonagricultural people, do not need rain to fertilize fields. Consequently, the explanation for the presence of weather shamanism among these Indians has to be other than a conventional one.

The Warao are a tribe of roughly 16,000 individuals. With the exception of a common language, however, there is little cohesion among the members. Far more important for the individual's daily needs is the local group, averaging 50 persons, consisting of 13 women, 12 men, and 25 children. A remarkable achievement for a society at this level of cultural development is the availability of an array of professional careers from which each adult of a local group may choose a challenging and meaningful pursuit. There are such posts as shamanic craftsman, ritual musician, priest-, dark-, and light-shaman, for the men; positions for women include shamanic artisan, herbalist, priest-, and white-shaman. Thus rain-maker is but one career opportunity offered to individuals. What distinguishes the career person from others is that he or she acquires, in the process of enculturative learning, not only technical and mental skills, socioeconomic stability, and recognition, but also the benefit of supernatural patronage. Career people among the Warao live and labor sub specie aeternitatis, motivated by the usual mundane interests of personal advancement while keeping an eye on eternity. Warao rainmakers today do not enjoy the same power as other shamans or shamanic artisans, a result, I believe, of an acculturative process during which the tribal life-style has been changed and weather shamanism deemphasized.

The Warao refer to their weather shaman as *naharima,* "father of rain," and there is usually one in every local group. Rainmakers are generally elderly persons, and although most of them are men, I have also been acquainted with a "mother of rain" *(naharani).*

To become a rainmaker, a person seeks out an accomplished practitioner to whom he can apprentice himself. Nowadays, women do not undergo formal training but learn from their husbands by observation. Young people are not eligible, ostensibly because they are apt to abuse their power in youthful irresponsibility. In addition to being the proper age, the novice must have sufficient money or goods to compensate the teacher for his efforts; the apprenticeship period lasts three to four days.

I have known rain shamans who had engaged as many as six teachers successively for fear that none might be in full command of the wisdom of his office; and I know of yet another case where the aspiring novice traveled to the very end of Waraoland to find a competent master teacher.

An important difference between rainmakers or approaches of becoming one lies in the fact that one may acquire the art of rain-making by "listening," as the Warao would say, or by "dreaming." Some rainmakers, thus, learned their trade through informal education only, while others also underwent a shamanic initiation which brought them face to face with the Lords of Rain. Although I cannot prove this, it is likely that in the past all rainmakers were trance initiated and that today's "secular" practitioners are symptomatic of a deculturative process.

For the study period, master and apprentice retire to an isolated place to practice the chants and transmit and learn the skills of the profession. At the end of instruction, the confident student applies his newly acquired power by calling or repelling a thunderstorm.

To call a storm, the rainmaker addresses the rain gods by means of traditional incantations. Done properly, a chant is expected to bring prompt results. To ward off a storm, the rainmaker rubs the palms of his hands together and, while holding them close to his lips, blows forcefully between them. After a few seconds, he flings his arms skyward and waves his hands toward the approaching storm, shouting:

> *Rainbow, Rainbow*
> *That is enough*
> *Listen to me*
> *It is enough*
> *Hear my words*
> *Let the rain go by*

In the case of a trance-initiated weather shaman, the period of skill training is followed by an initiation ritual. During his apprenticeship, the novice has refrained from eating and drinking, while smoking tobacco heavily in the form of three-foot cigars. *Nicotiana rustica,* a high-nicotine species of tobacco, is preferred for this purpose and, like other Warao shamans, rainmakers rely on its potency for hallucinatory experiences.

In his emaciated state the novice soon falls into a trance, to meet Kanamuno, the black giant. This demon of colossal proportions approaches the novice with wide open mouth, lifts him up, and swallows him. Without being crushed or hurt the initiate experiences his passing through the giant's body as a long journey, which ends with his ejection, as an old man, from the buttocks of the devourer. In his new form and in the land of the Lords of Rain, the novice meets the deities, is recognized by them, and is endowed with the power of saying their names.

There are rainmakers who have visited the rain gods without experiencing the ordeal of transformation; but those who have, claim to possess the power of a patron god in their breast—the trademark of true Warao professionalism.

Kanamuno, the black transformer giant, has a female companion, Tarita, which leads me to surmise that, in the past at least, rainmaker initiations for women also took place. In any case, not only is isolation during initiation sought for greater concentration, but also to avoid any unexpected noise that may awaken the novice during his narcotic sleep (while still inside the devourer), cause him to become disoriented, fall ill, and die.

The Warao recognize eight Lords of Rain (illus. 1). Their generic designation is *kabo arotutuma,* and they reside on eight world mountains at the cardinal and intercardinal points around the horizonal edge of the universe. According to their geocentric world view, the Warao picture the earth as a disk surrounded by the sea. The world mountains along the circular outer edge of the sea support the cosmic vault.

The rain gods live in mansions on top of these sky-bearing mountains. The doors of their houses face the center of the universe. During the rainy season, when the doors are wide open, the rain gods sit on benches in the doorways, looking toward the world. The doors are closed the rest of the year.

Both the mansion and the personal appearance of a rain god have an air of opulence about them which the Warao tend to associate with wealthy Venezuelans. Indeed, the Indians do not envision the rain gods as Warao at all, but as Criollos[1] *(hotarao)* with the peculiar difference that the lords have large flaring heads. During the rainy

Illus. 1. The Lords of Rain.

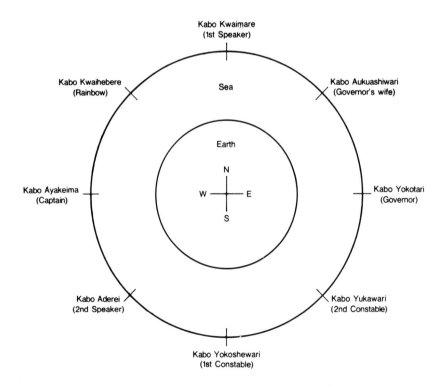

season the gods wear black and during the dry season they don white tunics. They wear sandals and spectacles, and smoke tobacco pipes. In their hands the rain gods carry large walking staffs that produce lightning. Their voices roll like thunder through the cloud-draped skies, while rain exudes from their bodies.

Of the eight Lords of Rain seven are male and one is female. Among themselves they form a stratified elite that parallels the political hierarchy of the subtribe. Table 1 lists the rain deities according to seniority and world location.

I found that the order in which the rain gods are ranked and placed along the horizon is deliberate rather than random inasmuch as the power vested in each lord corresponds, with inconsequential deviations, to the relative frequency and velocity of winds along the Delta littoral and the Gulf of Paria (illus. 2). Much more meteorological data, specifically for the Orinoco Delta, are needed to substantiate this claim. But I do not expect the Delta wind rose to differ markedly from the one presented here for the northern Gulf (table 2).

Illus. 2. Chapter frontispiece.

The political titles of the lords in tables 1 and 2 represent the English translations of their Waraoan equivalents, most of which, in turn, come from Spanish. The Warao refer to the governor as *kobenahoro,* the governor's wife as *kobenahoro atida,* the captain as *kabitana,* the constable as *fisicali* (from "fiscal"), and to the speaker as *dibatu.* The titles are used as terms of reference rather than address. The rain shaman calls the lords by singing, using their personal names. The chant included below was sung by a Warao, whose patron rain god is Kabo Kwaihebere of the northwesterly world mountain. Saying the name of his patron rain god is taboo. In addressing him the Indian uses the title Hubanashiko, "Rainbow," because during his initiation, he had adopted this rain god's name and is "embarrassed" now to use it publicly.

Translating the appellations of the Lords of Rain is fraught with difficulties because they rarely represent words or word combinations employed in common parlance. In fact, one of my informants, who had spent one year among the Pemon Indians of southern Venezuela, suggested even Cariban provenience in certain instances.

Nonetheless, the etymology of the personal names of the rain lords suggests meaningful connotations which, not surprisingly, appear to be associated with weather phenomena (table 3). It makes sense, for instance, that "Thunderers" would be associated with the easterly trade winds that carry much humidity around the winter solstice and with intertropical southern and southeasterly winds that bring the spring equinoctial storms with resplendent lightning. In contrast, the westerly night wind is dry and balmy, and the Rainbow (Lord of Prominent Summit) and the Lord of High Projection probably derive their names from the rainbow whose "feet" or ends are believed to be located on their respective mountains. It is also in association with these two lords that the issue of the flaring heads of rain deities is brought up most often, and I assume that the arc of the rainbow is the model for this somatological peculiarity of these two Lords of Rain.

As explained above, communication with the rain gods is possible only during the rainy season. Once they have retired into their houses, the rain gods no longer attend to the shaman's wishes; neither do they react to his protective spells, nor to his incantations to provoke a storm.

Incantations may be directed by a rainmaker to any one of the eight lords. Included below are the Warao text and my translation into English of a chant, recorded in August 1975 with the assistance of Jaime Zapata, senior rain shaman of the Winikina subtribe. This chant is addressed to Yokotari, the supreme Lord of Rain residing in the east.

TABLE 1
Warao Lords of Rain, Their Ranks, and Locations

	Name	Rank	Location
1.	Kabo Yokotari	Governor	East
2.	Kabo Aukuashiwari	Governor's wife	Northeast
3.	Kabo Ayakeima	Captain	West
4.	Kabo Yokoshewari	First constable	South
5.	Kabo Yukawari	Second constable	Southeast
6.	Kabo Kwaimare	First speaker	North
7.	Kabo Aderei	Second speaker	Southwest
8.	Kabo Kwaihebere	Rainbow	Northwest

TABLE 2

Relationship of Rain Lord Ranking and Wind Conditions

Rank	Wind			
	Location	Frequency (percent)	Direction	Average velocity (kph)
Governor	E	20	Easterly	5
Governor's wife	NE	11	Northeasterly	5
Captain	W	7	Westerly	3
Constable 2d	SE	5	Southeasterly	3
Constable 1st	S	3	Southerly	3
Speaker 1st	N	3	Northerly	3
Rainbow	NW	3	Northwesterly	2
Speaker 2d	SW	1	Southwesterly	1

Source: *Atlas de Venezuela,* 1979:195. Meteorological data corresponding to Güiria, Sucre.

TABLE 3

Names of Rain Lords, Titles, and Etymologies

Name	Location	Title	Etymology
Yokotari	E	Lord of Daybreak Thunder	*Hoko,* "dawn"; *tari,* "thunder"
Aukuashiwari	NE	Lord of Prominent Summit	*Aukuashi,* "summit"; *wari,* "long," "prominent"
Ayakeima	W	Lord of Nightwind	*Ahaka,* "wind"; *ima,* "night"
Yokoshewari	S	Lord of Manifest Radiance	*Hoko,* "dawn," "radiance"; *wari,* "long," "manifest"
Yukawari	SE	Lord Son of Prominence	*Uka,* son; *wari,* "prominent"
Kwaimare	N	Lord of Felicitous Heights	*Kwai,* "above"; *mare,* "felicitous"
Aderei	SW	Lord of Thunder	*Derei,* "thunder"
Kwaihebere	NW	Lord of High Projection	*Kwaihebere,* "to project upward"

WEATHER SHAMAN'S CHANT TO YOKOTARI

I

Ihi kabo arotu ihi	*You are the lord of heaven*
ihi weyo a buaranoko	*you rule where the sun comes*
arotu	*aflame*
ihi tata arotu	*you are the lord of yonder*
otuida arotu	*lord of remoteness*
hi [wai] karamuna	*I shall pronounce and*
nanoarate ine.	*repeat your name.*
Hi karamuna	*I shall raise it*
hi wai ka- karamuna	*your name I shall raise*
hi wai ka- karamuna	*your name I shall raise*
nanoarate	*and repeat*
hi wai karamuna	*your name I shall raise*
nanoarate ine.	*and repeat again.*
Otuida arotu	*Lord of remoteness*
ma nobo diawara	*my grandfather god*
ma nobo diawara	*my grandfather god*
hi karamuna	*I call upon you*
manobo diawara ihi	*my grandfather god*
kabo arotu ihi	*you are the lord of heaven*
kabo arotu	*lord of heaven*
otuida arotu:	*lord of remoteness:*
Y O K O T A R I .	Y O K O T A R I .

II

Karamunai	*You trembled*
hi karamunai	*you trembled*
hi karamunai	*you trembled*
hi karamunai	*you trembled*
nanoarate ine	*I shall repeat your name*
hi kanamane	*so you will rise*
hi kanamane	*you will rise*
hi kanamane.	*you will rise.*

Hi natorobo aida   Your mighty staff
orebekware   preceding
orebekware   ahead of you
kabo sisi a witu   right on the road of heaven
orebekane   ahead of you
hi urunaka tane   will not weigh you down
hi urunaka tane   will not weigh you down
neriwakate   so you be content
neriwakate ine   and I be content
hi urunaka tane   it will not weigh you down
neriwakane.   being comfortable.

Neriwakane   Being agreeable
hi anatoro aida   your mighty staff
memo sabane   pass me by
memo sabane   pass me by
hiyakakune   to the cuajo tree
doko mare   with its wind-blown leaves
nisinatahine   there you plant it and
hi abate ine.   I shall leave you.

III

Hi nasaribuna tane   With your voice like
domu turu tuyuna   the tigana bird's
tuyuna ware   the snake-necked tigana
taisi a yekoita   with its cry
ahi hatekore   its piercing cry
mu yaritanu   become enraged
mu yaritanu   become enraged
hi tehori   your body
mu yaritanu   become infuriated
mu yaritanu.   become infuriated.

Ori kanamanu	Arise
hi kanamane	to your full height
hi kobukane	stand up
hi kobukane	stand up
kabo sisia	on the road of heaven
hi kobukanewitu ine	stand straight [I say]
hi kobukane	stand up
hi kobukane	stand up
hi kobukane	stand up
kabo sisia.	on the road of heaven.

IV

Kabasimo hi tehori	Your body like a fiery wasp
hi te abane	brace your body
mu yari tanu	become enraged
ma nobo diawara ma nobo	my grandfather god my grandfather
ma nobo diawara	my grandfather god
ma nobo kabo arotu	my grandfather lord of heaven
kabo arotu diawara.	lord of heaven.

Kabo meho kasaba yana	Now then at the bosom of heaven
kasaba yana toate ine	there then shall I place
ma weraribuyawitu	my tongue's own words
ma nasaribuyawitu	my very words
kabo arotu	lord of heaven
isa ine nanoarane.	wherewith I repeat your name.

Ne mu yaritanu	Eh! Become infuriated!
mu yaritanu.	Become infuriated!

Miana	Blindly
diana.	that is all.

WEATHER SHAMAN'S
CHANT TO YOKOTARI

Rendering Warao religious chant in a form intelligible to the outsider is handicapped by a series of complicating factors; the accelerated speed of performance being one of them. The above example, for instance, took only one minute and fifty seconds to record. The general volume of the rendering is low and articulation often difficult to understand. Under normal circumstances, chants of this kind are often performed quite audibly in the quietude of predawn hours, but they are just as frequently whispered by the rainmaker, intelligible only to the immediate bystander.[2]

A second complicating factor is the use of uncommon language in ritual chanting; the use of the word *diawara,* for instance, in everyday language is discouraged by religious practitioners and rarely heard. A word like *weyo* is employed only by shamans, whereas the common man would say *"hokohi"* to designate the sun. But rather than dwell on the formal detail of Warao chants, let me comment, instead, on some aspects of content in order to facilitate the understanding of the text.

The first part of the chant (I) is an evocation, proclaiming the exalted station of the lord in question, his place of origin, and his personal name.

To have the power of the *kabo* shamanism means to be able to envision or to "scan" the body of a rain god while addressing him in song. The rainmaker's familiarity with the god's corporal features derives from the experience of his initiatory journey when he was transformed to become his elder, his classificatory father.

More importantly, kabo power entails the capability of pronouncing the rain lord's name. This is the true power of knowledge, knowledge of the essence of the deity as it is bound up in his secret name. The power of grasping and of naming the rain gods turns the weather shaman into the formidable person that he is, the *naha arima,* "Father," "Master of the Lord of Rain."

When the weather shaman utters his name the rain god must listen. Thus, the second part of the chant (II) shows the deity stirring and arising from his stool. He is encouraged to walk toward the zenith and to use his walking staff, step by step, until he can thrust it into a cuajo tree *(Virola sebifera* Aug.*).* Hit by the staff of lightning, the tree will fall and, so it is believed, produce a rainbow; evidence of the rain shaman's success at raising the god.

Encouraged, the rainmaker changes his suggestions to the deity to commands in part three of the chant (III). So that his body will exude capious rainfall, the shaman admonishes him to become irritated by the penetrating, high-pitched double whistle of the sun bittern *(Eurypyga helias)*, whose spread wings, incidentally, display a "sunburst" effect that turns the bird into a fitting symbol of a rain lord who resides "where the sun comes aflame." Furthermore, the god is provoked by the image of the fiercely aggressive and noxious wasp, *(tomonoho simo, Stenopolybia fulvofasciata,* DeGeer*)*.

All this the weather shaman accomplishes by directing his words to the heart of the cloud heaven where, as expressed in part four of the chant (IV), they echo and reecho to maintain the rain god in a state of rage.

Strangely enough, the Warao incantations to the Lords of Rain do not resemble humble supplications to obtain a gift of fertilizing rain from benevolent deities. Instead, Warao rain lords are provoked to unleash a deluge of rattling thunderstorms and to drench the world with cataclysmic downpours. This brings us back, then, to the question of the significance of Warao weather shamanism.

When asked directly, the Warao do not understand the question; the rain lords have no *anamonina,* they say, no transformational genesis. They are not of a previous form and are without beginning. Consequently, rain shamans have also existed since the beginning of mankind and need no further explanation.

Observing the role of the rain shaman over time, however, does offer some clues that help explain the phenomenon. Why does he make it rain? As punishment, is the stereotypic answer, punishment for the greed of his fellowmen.

As elderly persons, rainmakers belong to the nonproductive sector of society, and herein seems to lie the real reason why the young and energetic are excluded from the profession. Elderly weather shamans beg for food, goods, and favors, and will not be sent away empty-handed or humiliated. Thus, they ask for a share of the hunting bag, of the catch of fish, or of other staples. They ask that something be brought back for them from trading expeditions. They ask for shelter in provisional camps and, generally speaking, for consideration. If the requests are rejected, the offenders will pay by being scared and doused by thunderstorms. Even in response to annoyance suffered because of an insect sting or accidental injury, the weather shaman will retire to his hammock and sing or whisper for rain. Rainmakers thus receive much attention and are treated with great respect.

At first this explanation of Warao weather shamanism will impress the Western reader as exceedingly facile and the seeming opportunism of the septem as disappointing and degrading. When viewed from the perspective of the senior tribesman and woman, however, rain shamanism becomes a most effective institution. Care for the aged is accepted by the Warao as a social obligation of the entire group. Even at the food-foraging level this sharing of responsibility makes the system of old-age care work.

The severity of punishment meted out by the rainmaker is also easily underestimated by the outside observer. Can scaring the people by thunder and lightning or pouring water over them really lessen their selfishness and induce them to share resources?

To be considered first in this respect is the truly awesome spectacle of a tropical thunderstorm, especially when one has to endure it with the simple means of a primitive technology. The discomfort and sheer misery of having to sit out one storm after another in a boat on the river, under a branch, or in a palm-thatched house without walls are indescribable, particularly when one is faced with the prospect of weeks and months of such circumstances.

Then there is the cooling effect brought about by the wind that precedes the rain. The small fires of wet firewood do little to alleviate the cold, and weather diseases begin to take their toll. Bronchitis, common colds, and coughs all take a turn for the worse, as do rheumatic diseases and asthma, especially if cooling temperatures combine with strong northerly winds. Discomfort and illness of these kinds are no harmless bogeys in a swamp, but serious forms of punishment allegedly brought about through the intervention of the weather shaman.

One further aspect needs consideration in this connection. Before the recent introduction of agriculture, the Warao exploited the sago of the moriche palm *(Mauritia flexuosa)* as their staple food. The availability of this starch within the trunks of moriche palms fluctuates according to the pattern of precipitation throughout the year. But it is precisely during the period of heavy rains, between May and the beginning of August, that the sago starch becomes very scarce and seriously strains the food economy of the local group and tribe. Inclement weather, disease, and hunger conspire effectively against the general welfare of the Indians and make the weak among them vulnerable to death. Seen in this context, the rainmaker assumes a most important position in the group; he is the one who can divert a storm from his people's territory. But he can also conjure up the fear-inspiring specter of a rainy season in its grimmest form. These are, I believe, the essential reasons why the Warao bother with weather shamanism: it provides for their elderly, it engenders congenial social behavior, and it offers the hope of survival in an environment essentially hostile to man.

In closing, I must admit that, to date, I have not come across any other South American Indian tribe with a similarly developed system of weather shamanism. Of course, outside of the subcontinent one's attention is readily drawn to the *tlaloc* Lords of Rain in the pantheon of the Aztec.

The ethnohistorical question as to the provenience of weather shamanism among the Warao is initially posed by these Indians themselves who consider the rain gods foreigners like the Criollos. Compatible with this belief are the titles of the Lords of Rain which, with the exception of *dibatu* (speaker) and *hubanashiko* (rainbow), represent administrative and military ranks of Spanish derivation. As such they parallel the titles and rank order of modern political leaders of band and subtribes among whom the Warao, through the instigation of Criollos and missionaries, distinguish between a *kobenahoro* (governor) of a subtribe; and a *kabitana* (captain), a *fisicali* (constable), a *dibatu aida,* and a *dibatu sanuka* (first and second speaker) of a local band. Following the same etymological reasoning one could even derive the generic name *kabo* of the rain gods itself from Spanish *cabo* (corporal), although this is a low rank and would have required a reinterpretation of significance.

I do not believe, however, that explaining the origin and hierarchical order of the Warao Lords of Rain is quite so simple. While there can be no doubt that linguistically the elite terminology is largely Spanish derived, I suggest that the ranks the terms denote are not. Instead, the titles seem to substitute a set of more traditional ones which used to designate an autochthonous elite of "strong men" *(aidamo),* patriarchs *(araobo),* local headmen *(arahi),* and speakers *(dibatu)* on the one hand from the commoners and workers *(nebu)* on the other. Membership in these social strata is not by birth or for the lifetime of the individual. Rather, as in a cargo system, there exists an upward mobility within the ranks from worker to strong man through which every ambitious and socially successful male individual can aspire to ascend. This set of titles and their corresponding ranks are probably older among the Warao than post-Conquest, and, but for their "modern" colonial titles, the Warao Lords of Rain have nothing in common with

Spanish tradition. The white skin color imputed to them is a characteristic of all Supernaturals of the highest order in the Warao pantheon. Also, their attire, while apparently Criollo, does include several aboriginal elements such as the sandals, the staff, the pipe, and the goggles which point toward the advanced cultures of South America and Meso-America. Since Meso-American parallels to features of Warao culture have been uncovered in other contexts, the possibility of a relationship of the Warao Lords of Rain with those of Meso-America ought not to be dismissed without thorough examination.

NOTES

[1]Criollo: a Venezuelan whose ancestors have interbred for several generations among whites, Indians, and blacks.

[2]I transcribed the text of the "Weather Shaman's Chant to Yokotari" from a cassette recording. Translation was aided by field notes and by commentaries made by two Indians: Antonio Lorenzano and Cesáreo Soto. Dr. Dale Olsen kindly provided the musical transcription from a copy of the field recording. Transcription entailed slowing the music down from 7½ ips to 3¾ ips. Several text corrections made by Dr. Olsen in the process of musical transcription are gratefully acknowledged. I should also like to thank Dr. Floyd Lounsbury and Dr. G. Reichel-Dolmatoff for their helpful comments on the paper.

WANG CHIEN (1598-1677)
AND CHAO MENG-FU (1254-1322)
SOME NOTES ON A WANG CHIEN HANDSCROLL

Chu-tsing Li

University of Kansas

Illus. 1. Wang Chien, Landscape in the Manner of Chao Meng-fu, *dated 1662. Spencer Museum of Art, Lawrence, Kansas. (Section 1.)*

Illus. 1. Wang chien, Landscape in the Manner of Chao Meng-fu, *dated 1662. Spencer Museum of Art, Lawrence, Kansas. (Section 2.)*

Illus. 1. Wang Chien, Landscape in the Manner of Chao Meng-fu, *dated 1662. Spencer Museum of Art, Lawrence, Kansas. (Section 3.)*

AMONG THE WORKS of Chinese art in the Helen Foresman Spencer Museum of Art at the University of Kansas in Lawrence is a long handscroll by the seventeenth-century painter Wang Chien (illus. 1), which was acquired by the museum in 1967 (no. 67.1). This scroll, painted in ink and colors on silk and measuring $12 \times 144\frac{1}{6}$ ", is distinguished not only as a unique piece of creation among the works of Wang Chien himself, but also as an outstanding work of art historical interest in the development of Chinese painting. Whereas many details of the basic documentation of this painting have been published by this writer in the *Catalogue of the Oriental Collection* (pp. 115-117) of the Spencer Museum,[1] this paper is an attempt to point out its historical importance, especially in the context of the interest of Wang Chien in the Yüan Dynasty painter Chao Meng-fu, who lived about three hundred and fifty years before him.

Landscape in the Manner of Chao Meng-fu unfolds a long, continuous panoramic view of rivers, mountains, clouds, trees, houses, and other details in the unique Chinese handscroll format, which is often compared with a musical composition or symphony. A set of basic motifs appears again and again in various combinations that form patterns analogous to symphonic movements and dramatic sequences. In the opening scene, beginning with the two boats in the foreground, one can see three ranges of low-lying hills that lead our eyes to the horizon marked by a screen of high mountains painted in washes. From this view of deep spatial recession, one comes next to a group of high mountains ringed with white clouds around their waists. These mountain formations take on interesting and even arbitrary shapes, topped with a marvelous combination of color dots in blue, green, and yellow. From the valley below this group flows a stream through the pine forests down to the foreground. Moving further toward the left, one comes to another open scene, in which the village by the water, as the starting point, leads our eyes gradually, through three low-lying groups of hills, far back into the horizon, which is again screened by a background range of mountains done in wash. Then, as one passes through another village by the water, suddenly a mountain group rises from the foreground, again with strange formations ringed by clouds around the waist. A path on the mountainside leads us down to the foreground, while a stream guides us up into the valley. From this high group one next encounters a section which combines low hills in the foreground and high

Illus. 2. Chao Meng-fu, Autumn Colors on the Ch'iao and Hua Mountains, *dated 1296. National Palace Museum, Taipei.*

mountains in the background, separated by streaks of mist and clouds. In the final section, this combination continues with variations. The background is still occupied by a range of high mountains painted in washes, while the middle ground, by the addition of a medium-high mountain range, forms a fascinating contrast to the village on the water, surrounded by interesting willows and other trees. The village, the low hills, and most importantly, the land strips at the end form a series of steps that lead our eyes into the distance.

The entire composition of this twelve-foot-long handscroll is thus divided into six movements, which can be characterized as, from right to left, an open-close-open-close-combination-variation sequence. This is very much in line with the basic conception of Chinese painting as that which possesses a strong parallel to music. The dramatic development is quite apparent. The repetition of motifs, the variation of themes, and the relationship of sequences all give the painting a very rich symphonic quality. This is one of the most distinguishing characteristics of Chinese painting, of

which the Wang Chien work is an outstanding example. In this way, Chinese painters in the seventeenth century are more interested in an abstract visual composition in a time sequence rather than in realistic depiction. In this form of intimate, personal, and individual expression, the handscroll is best to be viewed by one single person seated at a table, unrolling it section by section (about two feet at a time), to enjoy the excellence of the composition.

As its title suggests, this scroll is a landscape based on the manner of Chao Meng-fu, a painter active in the early Yüan period, around the year 1300. The inscription written by Wang Chien himself at the end of the scroll tells about the circumstances leading to its creation:

In the year *ping-tzu* [1636] when I visited the venerable Tung Wen-min [Ch'i-ch'ang] at his home in Yün-chien [Sung-chiang, near Shanghai] he showed me Chao Meng-fu's *The Autumn Colors on the Ch'iao and Hua Mountains* handscroll from his collection. Looking at the painting together, we marveled at the roundness and fullness of Chao's handling of the brush and the elegance and richness of his use

Illus. 3. Chao Meng-fu, The Water Village, *dated 1302. Palace Museum, Peking.*

of colors, which were far beyond what later people could dream to have achieved. Since then time went fast and now it has been almost thirty years. Last winter, when I visited Chin-ch'ang [Suchou], a friend from Hsin-an [in Anhwei Province] brought Chao Meng-fu's *Water Village* for me to see. It turned out to have come from the collection of my ancestor Kung-pao [Wang Shih-mou, 1536-1588, his great-granduncle]. At the end of the painting there are more than sixty colophons written by Yüan Dynasty connoisseurs; all greatly praised it. His painting method was so good that it was as if it was executed by a divine hand. His brushwork was distinguished by a heaven-inspired spontaneity and freedom, totally free of any bad habits of mediocre painters. Both of these scrolls were greatly treasured by Hsiang Yüan-pien [1525-1590, the most famous collector in the sixteenth century]. This spring, when I happened to stay at the White Crane Villa in Nan-hsiang [near Shanghai], I found myself enjoying the quietude and seclusion by the window under the sun and in the right mood. Getting up I prepared ink in my inkwell. Recalling these two paintings as my models, I completed this picture. I regret that I am not able to capture one out of ten-thousandths in the quality of Chao's paintings, but only hope to show that even in my declining years I am still able to study his works earnestly.

In the early spring of the year *jen-yin* (1662), by Wang Chien.

Here, the important part of this inscription is the indication that Wang Chien did not paint this picture from nature, but from his

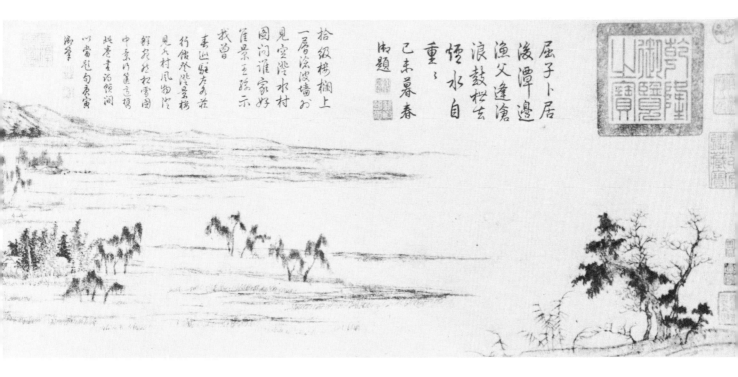

memories of the two famous scrolls by the early Yüan (late thirteenth and early fourteenth centuries) master Chao Meng-fu, which
inspired him to create his own. Thus this painting is basically
abstract in approach, for the artist thinks mainly in terms of arrang-
ing lines, colors, shapes, textures, and movements to achieve a
composition analogous to music or drama. The painting thus can
be called, in musical terms, "an improvisation (or variation) on the
theme of Chao Meng-fu's works."

That Chao Meng-fu was Wang Chien's model in this painting
is already clearly indicated in the inscription on the scroll quoted
above. Both as a high official and a scholar-calligrapher-painter in
the early Yüan period, Chao was the most influential artist during
his own time. Of Chao's landscape paintings, the two most famous
handscrolls are the two mentioned by Wang Chien in his inscription, the *Autumn Colors on the Ch'iao and Hua Mountains* of 1296
(illus. 2) and the *Water Village* of 1302 (illus. 3).[2] Luckily, both of
these paintings survived not only to the seventeenth century for
Wang Chien to see but also to the present day. The *Autumn Colors*
is now in the Palace Museum in Taipei, and the *Water Village* is in
the Palace Museum in Peking. A comparison between these two
paintings and that of Wang Chien will provide some idea of what

Illus. 4. Wang Chien, Landscape in the Manner of Chao Meng-fu *(detail 1).*

Illus. 5. Wang Chien, Landscape in the Manner of Chao Meng-fu *(detail 2).*

the artist has accomplished in his variation on the theme of Chao Meng-fu's works.

Actually, a general look at both of the Chao scrolls does not seem to convince people that Wang Chien modeled his painting on them, for in those two works can be found neither the kind of strange, distinctive, and almost animated mountains nor the dazzling interplay of color dots on their peaks which are prominent throughout the entire composition. On a closer inspection, however, one can begin to discover some of the indebtedness of Wang Chien to the Yüan painter. Indeed, almost the whole composition of the *Autumn Colors* is inserted into the painting to become the third movement of Wang Chien's scroll. There, in the middle ground, is a village surrounded by groves of trees similar to those in the middle section of the Yüan painting (illus. 4). Behind the village rise two mountains, whose pointed shape is reminiscent of Chao Meng-fu's Mount Hua (or Hua-fu-chu). Nearby to the right is another hill in the shape close to Mount Ch'iao. The V-shaped composition, the landspits, the assorted tree groups, the pine groves, and other smaller details are all derived from those in Chao Meng-fu's work. Although, as indicated in the inscription, Wang Chien had seen Chao's painting in 1636, twenty-six years before he painted the present scroll, he seems to have had a good memory of many of the details in the Yüan painting. Thus the insertion of this detail derived from the composition of the *Autumn Colors* has a certain effect of a pleasant surprise. After moving through the first two movements, one comes to the third to discover that he is in the secluded dreamland of Chao Meng-fu. In the mind of Wang Chien and in those connoisseurs who were familiar with Chao's scroll, this almost came as a vision.

In the same way, in a general look at the whole painting one finds it difficult to find any trace of Chao Meng-fu's *Water Village,* which was done on paper and in pure ink. But again, when one comes to the very last movement of Wang Chien's long scroll, there the motifs of the *Water Village* appear in various combinations (illus. 5). There is a group of trees in the foreground and, though more complex, the tree types and the land forms are all similar. In the whole stretch of land strips in the lake from the foreground to the far distance, the same willows, bridge, houses and rolling hills are present. Even the basic shapes of the high mountains in the *Water Village* are echoed in the group of mountains just right of the final scene in this scroll. Again, it provides the same impression to one who is familiar with Chao's work. After the encounter with the reminder of the *Autumn Colors* in the third movement, here in the sixth and final section one comes to another dreamland created by the Yüan painter in the form of the *Water Village*.

Thus it is significant that Wang Chien, in using motifs from the earlier painter, places these two scenes in the third and sixth sections of the painting. Moreover, in the other sections, images from these two Yüan works are also found. Similar tree types, landspits, and houses occur here and there. The only major difference is that the mountain forms are not so familiar in the existing works of Chao Meng-fu. Did Wang Chien try to add many more of his own original elements to the painting, rather than to derive everything from the Yüan painter?

It is well known that Wang Chien, as a pupil and young friend of the great master and connoisseur, Tung Ch'i-ch'ang (1555-1636), was mainly interested in the Yüan painter Huang Kung-wang, and through Huang, also in the tenth-century artist, Tung Yüan.[3] Both of these painters were known for a manner that emphasizes the pure quality of brushwork and freedom of expression. Tung Ch'i-ch'ang, in developing his taste for the old masters, was more or less responsible for raising Huang's works to the pinnacle of artistic expression. Tung Yüan, as a source of inspiration for Huang, was also an important link.[4] Through Tung Ch'i-ch'ang's theories and influences, a whole generation of late Ming and early Ch'ing painters became strong followers of Huang Kung-wang.[5] Among them, Wang Chien, and his close friend who was six years his senior, Wang Shih-min (1592-1680), were most interested in this idea. A large number of their paintings are thus painted in the manner of Huang Kung-wang.

Another side of Wang Chien's approach is not much known, that is, Wang's interest in Chao Meng-fu. Among the existing and recorded paintings of Wang Chien are a considerable number done in the manner of Chao Meng-fu, with dates ranging from 1643 to 1677, the last year of his life.[6] Furthermore, in each of the many albums of Wang Chien, there are usually one or two leaves in the manner of Chao Meng-fu.[7] This means that, while Wang Chien is quite interested in the so-called Four Masters of Late Yüan (Huang Kung-wang, Wu Chen, Ni Tsan and Wang Meng), he is also very much attracted by Chao Meng-fu as a model.

One special aspect emerges concerning Wang Chien's interest in Chao Meng-fu. In almost all of Wang Chien's paintings in the manner of this Yüan painter that are still known in either extant or recorded works, the blue-and-green manner is the rule. That means, in the eyes of Wang Chien, that Chao Meng-fu was mainly an artist in the blue-and-green style. Among the two works that Wang Chien used as models for the handscroll in the Spencer Museum, the *Water Village* is a pure ink painting, which has no connection with the blue-and-green tradition, whereas the *Autumn Colors,* though often mentioned as blue-and-green, is only lightly done in those colors, unlike the major paintings in that manner.[8] Nevertheless, it is interesting that in Wang Chien's own painting, the whole scroll can definitely be characterized as blue-and-green, with the heavy use of those colors in mountains and rocks. Again, it is an indication of Wang Chien's basic concept of Chao Meng-fu's paintings.

In order to clarify this issue, we must look into the whole body of Chao Meng-fu's landscapes. It is known that both Chao and his senior friend, Ch'ien Hsüan, painted in the blue-and-green manner, a term that came into general use in the Yüan period to designate the kind of landscape painting based on models from the T'ang Dynasty.[9] As indicated in both written sources and in the wall paintings at Tun-huang of T'ang date, landscapes in that period were at that point of development from the use of alternate colors to denote a number of mountains to the application of *ts'un* (textures) to describe mountains. The practice of utilizing ts'un may have begun toward the end of T'ang, but was certainly perfected during the Five Dynasties period. In that transition during T'ang, a general use of blue-and-green was most common.[10] Then, during the Sung and Yüan periods, a number of painters, notably Chao Po-chü of early Southern Sung (mid-twelfth century), were known to have imitated the T'ang manner as a way of showing their interest in the past.[11] This idea became a strong force in the art circles during the early Yüan period, led by Ch'ien Hsüan and Chao Meng-fu. Most of Ch'ien's surviving landscapes are in this manner.[12] Among Chao Meng-fu's extant paintings, a considerable body can be characterized in this manner. They include the *Tzu-kung Visiting Yüan Hsien in a Humble Hut* in the Palace Museum, Taipei,[13] the *Pavilion under the Wu-t'ung Tree* in the Shanghai Museum,[14] the *Mind Landscape of Hsieh Yu-yü* in the Princeton Art Museum,[15] and the *Landscape of Wu-hsing* in the Shanghai Museum,[16] all considered earlier works, with rather heavy use of blue-and-green in mountains and rocks. Although, with the exception of the last one, all are generally regarded as figure paintings, their elaborate landscape background is nevertheless relevant in this context. Next is a group of paintings in which the blue-and-green is still used but much more toned down, including the *River Village—Fishermen's Joy* in the Cleveland Museum,[17] the *Autumn Colors* of 1296 in the Palace Museum, Taipei,[18] and the pair of hanging scrolls entitled the *East and West Mountains of Tung-t'ing,* of which only the East one is still extant in the Shanghai Museum.[19] These seem to belong to the middle period of his artistic activity. Many other landscapes in blue-and-green are, of course, attributed to his name, but the ones named are sufficient to suggest why Wang Chien developed this image of Chao Meng-fu as basically a blue-and-green painter.

As in the case of his *Landscape in the Manner of Chao Meng-fu* in the Spencer Museum, there seems to be an attempt on the part of Wang Chien to identify Chao Meng-fu with the landscapes containing heavy blue-and-green. As we have seen, it is only the manner of Chao's very early years. In fact; this style is more typically identified with Ch'ien Hsüan, but we have no knowledge of Wang Ch'ien's works modeled after Ch'ien. This means that somehow Wang Chien seemed to have taken Chao as the representative of this whole genre and conveniently attributed all the manners of blue-and-green to Chao. Indeed, Chao became the basic model for Wang Chien's blue-and-green manner.

It must be pointed out here that Chao Meng-fu was a very complex personality and artist during a period of great transition. Nowadays, because of modern means of reproduction and the widespread practice of publication, a much better image of Chao as an artist has been formed. In the Yüan texts, Chao was mentioned as a painter of figures, horses, birds and flowers, bamboos, and landscapes. Actually, his versatility not only is not limited to subject matter, but also is seen in his manner and style. As a highly intellectual artist who had the first opportunity to break away from the rather confining atmosphere of the Southern Sung academy through his travels between his native Chekiang and northern China, he constantly broadened his approaches and changed his manner. As a result, there is no one single image of Chao Meng-fu's art. Rather, he shows a most remarkable development in his works, absorbing many major elements from the past, from the Six Dynasties to Sung, and anticipating the many achievements of the late Yüan. Consequently, during the Ming and Ch'ing periods, there were not many followers of Chao Meng-fu. While the Four Masters of Late Yüan had their own familiar images to inspire a great number of followers in those periods, Chao had very few. During the Ming period, the two artists most affected by Chao were Yao Shou of the fifteenth century and Wen Cheng-ming of the sixteenth. Between them each had his own image of Chao. As the painter in the seventeenth century most interested in Chao, Wang Chien also had an image of the Yüan artist which was quite different from that of either Yao Shou or Wen Cheng-ming. Perhaps this was a result of the fact that each was acquainted with different works by the Yüan master. Yao's image of Chao was that of a painter of the hermit-fisherman type of landscape, usually in ink;[20] Wen's suggested paintings such as the *Autumn Colors* and some related pieces in his middle period;[21] and Wang Chien's came mainly from the heavily colored blue-and-green manner of Chao's early period. Since most of the painters in the Ch'ing period were more interested in the pure ink manners of some late Yüan masters, especially Huang Kung-wang, Wu Chen, Ni Tsan, and Wan Meng, the blue-and-green style which became associated with Chao Meng-fu did not seem to have many followers.[22]

Returning to the Spencer museum's painting by Wang Chien, we find that, although the work was based on Chao Meng-fu's *Autumn Colors* and *Water Village*, the elements of these two paintings have been merged together with Wang's general image of the blue-and-green into one basic idea of Chao. As a result, this composite manner does not exactly reflect any one of Chao's works or stages, but only Wang's total concept of the Yüan master's style.

Originally, in Chao Meng-fu's own attempt to return to the manners of earlier periods, he aimed at recapturing the spirit of ancient masters, as noted in one of his well-known statements:

> What is precious in a painting is the spirit of antiquity; without it, skill is wasted. Nowadays men who know how to draw at fine scale and lay on rich and brilliant colors consider themselves competent. They totally ignore the fact that a lack of the spirit of antiquity will create so many faults that the result will not be worth looking at. My own paintings seem to be quite simply and carelessly done, but connoisseurs will realize that they are close to the past and so may be considered superior. This is said for cognoscenti, not for ignoramuses.[23]

This return to the past varies with different paintings among Chao's works. For example, in the *Tzu-kung Visiting Yüan Hsien in a Humble Hut* which is based on a subject of the fifth century B.C., his treatment of the landscape elements is extremely archaic, although it is hardly based on any model from the Chou Dynasty. In the *Mind Landscape of Hsieh Yu-yü,* which deals with a scholar of the early fourth century, he painted in the manner of the Six Dynasties. Then, in such works as the *Autumn Colors,* which is based partly on Wang Wei's ideas, he adopted some elements of the T'ang, but also combined them with some concepts of his own. In both the *Water Village* and the *East Mountain of Tung-t'ing,* because of the more contemporary subject, the approach is less archaic, more his own. This complexity in Chao's approach to the past seems to be not exactly understood by Wang Chien, perhaps partly due to his lack of a coherent idea of Chao's development based on a series of works available to him. In Wang's own scheme, he drew constant inspiration from Sung and Yüan masters, and seemed to have placed each of the artists into a category. As a result, he had set types for Li Ch'eng, Fan K'uan, Tung Yüan, Chü-jan, Huang Kung-wang, Wu Chen, Ni Tsan, and Wang Meng. But for Chao Meng-fu, he also seemed to have in his mind only one single type, the blue-and-green manner. Since there was no one single standard image of Chao, and some of Chao's manners had become part of the other masters' styles, such as the dry brush technique in *Water Village* and the hermit-fisherman theme, his stylistic image was relegated to the blue-and-green manner. This is one of the main reasons why Chao's influence was rather limited in the later periods.

One positive reason for this identification of the blue-and-green manner with Chao Meng-Fu is that in his approach to the past, there were symbolic overtones of nostalgia for a long-gone period or for dreamland. As a matter of fact, after the Yüan period, the blue-and-green manner, as utilized by a few artists such as Shih Jui in early Ming and Ch'iu Ying in middle Ming, came to be applied more often for paintings depicting such subjects as the Isles of the Immortals, the Peach Blossom Spring, and some T'ang stories such as the Lute Song.[24] Wang Chien, in working Chao Meng-fu's ideas, must also have had similar ideas, for example a similar whimsical approach. In the landscape handscroll at the Spencer Museum, the blue-and-green itself, the arbitrary shapes of the mountains, the archaic cloud patterns, the lack of a consistent horizon line, the paths and streams that lead in and out of the picture, and the various motifs based on particular paintings all reflect this archaic and whimsical attitude.

There is no one single treatise from Wang Chien which deals with his basic ideas on painting.[25] Among the inscriptions he wrote on some of his paintings, however, a few general ideas can be noted. In an album of *Landscape after Ancient Masters* in the Palace Museum, Taipei, dated 1660,[26] two years before the handscroll at the Spencer Museum, he wrote: "I do not seek for form likeness, in order to avoid the bad habits of ordinary painters." Actually, this statement is repeated quite often in his inscriptions. In another, he wrote: "When I first began to study painting, I followed Huang Kung-wang. With all my faults, I was fortunate enough to attract the attention of the Venerable Tung [Ch'i-ch'ang]. In my middle years I wandered all around the country, with not much time devoted to the serious study of painting, thus not able to achieve much. Now in my declining years I am not able to do a lot, but am filled with many regrets."[27] This was written on a painting of 1676, the year before his death, and represents his humble means to outline his own life. In several paintings he characterized the quality he was seeking as "something quiet and secluded, simple but subtle."[28] To this end, he chose models from many of the Sung and Yüan painters. As indicated in the inscription of the Spencer Museum scroll, he found in Chao Meng-fu "the roundness and fullness of Chao's handling of the brush and the elegance and richness of his use of colors" in the *Autumn Colors,* and the "brushwork . . . distinguished by a heaven-inspired spontaneity and freedom, totally free from any bad habits of mediocre painters" in the *Water Colors.* All of these seem to agree with his basic approach to painting, which came from his mentor, Tung Ch'i-ch'ang, who was also mentioned by Wang in the inscription on the Spencer painting.

In fact, some history of the paintings *Autumn Colors* and *Water Village* can be mentioned here since it will cast some light on the relationships among Wang, Tung, and Chao. In the history of the *Autumn Colors,* which I have published, it came into the collection of Wang Shih-mou (1536-1588), brother of Wang Chien's great-grandfather, Wang Shih-chen, and then into the famous collection of Hsiang Yüan-pien (1525-1590), whose many seals are found on the scroll. Among the many colophons on the *Autumn Colors* are five written by Tung Ch'i-ch'ang, who mentioned that he had seen this painting in the Hsiang family in 1582, and later was given the painting by Hsiang Mei-po, possibly one of the sons of Hsiang in 1602.[29] Then, according to Wang Chien's own inscription on the scroll in the Spencer Museum, Tung showed Wang this scroll in 1636, the year of the former's death. The *Water Village,* according to a colophon by Tung Ch'i-ch'ang, was also in the collection of Wang Shih-mou, and later passed into the hands of Tung himself. Since the two brothers Wang Shih-chen and Shih-mou were very close to each other, both works may have been considered as having been in the family. This is why Wang Chien himself refers to the painting as having been in the hands of his ancestor, Kung-pao, here referring to Shih-mou.[30] Because Tung Ch'i-ch'ang knew both of the Wang brothers in his youth, he became interested in the art of their descendant, Wang Chien, and taught him some of the ideas he had formed. As a result, after Tung's death, Wang Chien and his friend Wang Shih-min became the champions of his theories on art.[31]

As a member of a typical literati family in T'ai-ts'ang, near both Suchou and Shanghai, Wang Chien followed the standard life of a literatus.[32] Between Wang Shih-chen and Shih-mou, it was said that there was a library of more than 10,000 volumes.[33] Thus, in Wang Chien's youth a thorough education in the classics was already assured. Because of his interest in painting, his family must have made sure that he received the instruction of the greatest connoissseur, calligrapher, and painter of that time, Tung Ch'i-ch'ang. In 1633, Chien passed the provincial examination to become a *chü-jen.* In 1635, he was appointed prefect of Lien-chou, in Kwangtung Province, not far from the Vietnam border. The next year, probably when he returned to visit his home area, he went to see Tung, who showed him the *Autumn Colors.* Tung died during the autumn of that year. The next year, Wang resigned from his post to retire at the age of forty. After renovating the Yen-chou Garden first developed by his great-grandfather, he remained back at T'ai-ts'ang for the rest of his life. At home he became a close friend of Wang Shih-min who, like him, was a pupil of Tung Ch'i-ch'ang. Together they became the leaders of a school in T'ai-ts'ang and carried on many of the theories of Tung.[34]

In T'ai-ts'ang, Wang Chien had another close friend, Wu Wei-yeh (1609-1671), who was also a painter but much better known as a poet and essayist.[35] For their strong friendship and for their attachment to Tung Ch'i-ch'ang, Wu wrote a poem called "The Nine Friends of Painting" which referred to the painters in Tung's circle. Besides Tung, the group included Li Liu-fang, Yang Wen-tsung, Shao Mi, Chang Hsüeh-tseng, Pien Wen-yü, Ch'eng Chia-sui, Wang Shih-min, and Wang Chien.[36] Among them, Wang Chien was the youngest. This clarifies the way Wang was regarded by his friend. Later, when Wu became a high official in Peking, he invited Wang Chien to go there, perhaps with the intention of introducing him to the court. After spending some time there, Wang returned to his hometown without taking any official post, devoting himself entirely to painting, and continuing the ideas and practices of Tung Ch'i-ch'ang.[37]

One of Tung's basic ideas was the importance of the intensive study of the works of ancient masters as a way to learn the secrets of painting. This was quite in line with the literary theory held by Wang Chien's great-grandfather, Wang Shih-chen, that one must return to the simplicity and directness of the essays of the Ch'in and Han Dynasties and the poetry of High T'ang. In painting, the masters of the Sung and Yüan Dynasties would serve as models along this line. With the help of Tung Ch'i-ch'ang and their own reputation as painters, both Wang Shih-min and Wang Chien were able to see a considerable number of paintings by the masters of earlier periods in the collections of famous connoisseurs. Every time these artists saw some exciting paintings, they would copy, imitate, and paint variations on their themes. As a result, they became well learned in the artistic traditions of the past, and were probably among the most learned in the history of Chinese painting. So filled with admiration of the past were they that their whole approach to painting was based on the works of the masters. Thus, almost their entire body of work can be characterized as "variations on the themes of" certain old masters. Among them was Chao Meng-fu, who seemed to have appealed to Wang Chien more than to Wang Shih-min.

Through this kind of approach, the artist can express his own ideas in the manner of certain masters already noted for some specific characteristics. Thus, Li Ch'eng was known for his grasp of the magnificent shapes of mountains; Fan K'uan for the powerful structure of his mountains; both Tung Yüan and Chü-jan for their free brushwork and spirited expression;[38] Huang Kung-wang for the continuation of Tung and Chü with greater simplification; Wu

Chen for his dark, free, and somber brushwork; Ni Tsan for his dry brush technique and pure quality; and Wang Meng for his complex brushwork and nervous energy. Each of these types was used by later artists as a vehicle for expressing similar ideas.

In his interest on Chao Meng-fu, Wang Chien seems to have shown that, more than any other artists in his generation, he had a better understanding of Yüan art history and the role Chao played in that crucial period. But because of the limited amount of Chao's works known to him in different stages of his life, he was not able to grasp fully the whole range of Chao's development. Following the practice of his own time in which each master was regarded as representing a certain type rather than someone with a long development, Wang Chien seems to have seen Chao as a painter of blue-and-green manner, manifested in two different types.

As noted before, the first type, in heavy blue-and-green, is an archaic feature, most commonly used in the T'ang Dynasty in the depiction of mountains. By using this T'ang element in his own works, Chao Meng-fu in the early Yüan period attempted to bring about a feeling for a past that was the embodiment of an ideal, especially one related to some of the most famous hermits of the past, such as Hsieh Yu-yü and T'ao Ch'ien, both nature lovers, and Wang Wei, a poet-painter. To Wang Chien, however, this type of blue-and-green manner evoked some idea of fantasy and imagination. In his paintings on this theme, he often imitated some of Chao Meng-fu's works. This treatment of the blue-and-green style reflected the change in its associations and connotations which took place in the Ming period. Among the works attributed to Chao Meng-fu is one entitled the *Abode of the Immortals,* published earlier in the *Paintings and Calligraphy of the Palace Museum.*[39] The painting, signed and dated 1319 but not generally accepted as his work, is done in blue-and-green and may have been seen by Wang Chien. After Chao, the association between the blue-and-green manner and the theme of the Isles of the Immortals became almost standard. In late Yüan, Ch'en Ju-yen did a painting of this subject in blue-and-green, now in the Cleveland Museum.[40] In middle Ming, Ch'iu Ying was the artist who painted in blue-and-green extensively, sometimes on subjects which refer to T'ang or before, such as the *Farewell at Hsün-yang* scroll at the Nelson Gallery in Kansas City and two scrolls depicting the *Peach Blossom Spring* in the Boston and Chicago Museums.[41] Wen Po-jen, in the late sixteenth century, also painted a number of blue-and-green works in the Isles of the Immortals theme, now in the Palace Museum, Taipei.[42] Thus Wang Chien seems to have followed this trend, but mainly in connection with Chao Meng-fu.

The second type of blue-and-green manner which Wang Chien found in Chao Meng-fu was that in light blue-and-green, as exemplified in *Autumn Colors,* which was supposed to have come from Tung Yüan. Although all the extant attributions to Tung Yüan at present are mainly in ink with very little color, it was recorded by Sung writers that he painted in two manners, one in pure ink and the other in colors.[43] Among the colophons on the *Autumn Colors,* several mentioned Tung Yüan as the model for Chao. In his middle period, Chao's works did show that he depended less on the colors and more on ink in much freer brushwork. Since Tung Yüan was regarded as one of the great masters of literati painting, especially by many leading Yüan painters and by Tung Ch'i-ch'ang and his followers, it was natural for the late Ming and Ch'ing painters to take him as a model not only in ink but also in colors. Since his image in ink far overshadowed the one in colors, it seems that they saw his landscapes in colors through the works of Chao Meng-fu. This kind of painting, in light blue-and-green and free brushwork, conveyed to the Ch'ing literati a similar feeling as that in the *Autumn Colors,* namely a kind of nostalgic and dreamy effect on the one hand and a sense of free and natural brushwork so much loved by the literati on the other.

In the *Landscape in the Manner of Chao Meng-fu,* Wang Chien actually combined both types of blue-and-green from the Yüan master into one long scroll. The high mountain ranges in the first, second, fourth, and fifth sections are mainly based on the T'ang type, while the pastoral scenes showing villages against a flat, low-lying background in the third and sixth sections are based on the Tung Yüan type, all seen through Chao Meng-fu's works. As a composite work of these elements from Chao, the scroll conveys a feeling of dream and fantasy with respect to the past not usually found among the typical works of Wang Chien, and exemplifies one aspect of literati painting, either rightly or wrongly, as the Chao Meng-fu tradition.

NOTES

[1] See *Catalogue of the Oriental Collection,* ed. Stephen Addiss and Chu-tsing Li, Lawrence, Kansas: Helen Foresman Spencer Museum of Art, 1980, pp. 115-117.

[2] These two paintings are the subject of my *The Autumn Colors on the Ch'iao and Hua Mountains: A Landscape by Chao Meng-fu,* Artibus Asiae Supplementum XXI (Ascona, Switzerland, 1965).

[3] For basic biographical materials on Wang Chien, see A. W. Hummel, *Eminent Chinese of the Ch'ing Period* (Washington, 1943), p. 812; O. Sirén, *Chinese Painting: Leading Masters and Principles* (New York, 1956-1958), V, 104-109.

[4] On the influence of Tung Yüan on later painters, see Li, *Autumn Colors,* pp. 60-69 and Richard Barnhart, *Marriage of the Lord of the River: A Lost Landscape by Tung Yüan,* Artibus Asiae Supplementum XXVII (Ascona, 1970).

[5] See Shen Fu, "A Study of the Authorship of Hua-shuo," in *Proceedings of the International Symposium of Chinese Painting* (Taipei: National Palace Museum, 1972, pp. 85-140, and Wai-kam Ho, "Tung Ch'i-ch'ang's New Orthodoxy and the Southern School," *Artists and Traditions,* ed. Christian F. Murck (Princeton, 1976), pp. 113-130.

[6] There are at least seventeen paintings by Wang Chien in the manner of Chao Meng-fu among those recorded or still extant. Among them, eight are listed in Hsü Pang-ta, *A Chronological List of Dated Paintings and Calligraphy from Various Dynasties* (Shanghai, 1963) and nine are still extant in collections ranging from China, Taiwan, and Japan to America. Among them the best known are *White Clouds over Hsiao and Hsiang Rivers* dated 1668, now at the Freer Gallery of Art, Washington, D.C., and *Landscape in the Manner of Chao Meng-fu* dated 1677, in the Palace Museum, Taipei.

[7] Among the Wang Chien albums that are known in both recorded and extant sources, there are at least seven, with dates ranging from 1660 to 1676, that have at least one leaf based on Chao Meng-fu. The best known is the one in the Palace Museum, Taipei, dated 1660.

[8] Some discussion of the "blue-and-green" tradition, especially in connection with Chao Meng-fu, can be found in my paper, "The Role of Wu-hsing in Early Yüan Artistic Development under Mongol Rule," first read in the Symposium on Yüan Culture held at Bowdoin College, Maine, in the summer of 1976 and recently published in *China under Mongol Rule,* ed. John D. Langlois, Jr. (Princeton, 1981), pp. 331-370. A discussion of this problem can also be found in two recent publications, Richard Vinograd's *"River Village—The Pleasures of Fishing,* and Chao Meng-fu's Li-Kuo Landscapes," *Artibus Asiae,* XL, 2/3 (1978), 124-142, and Sherman E. Lee's *"River Village—Fisherman's Joy,"* Bulletin of the Cleveland Museum of Art, LXVI (October 1979), pp. 270-288.

[9] For a discussion of the use of the term "blue-and-green" in the history of Chinese painting, see publications in preceding note.

[10] Most typical examples of the landscape elements in blue-and-green manner can be found in Caves 217, 172, and 103 in Tunhuang, all considered to be from the High T'ang period (712-763). This manner is only slightly touched upon in Michael Sullivan's recent book, *Chinese Landscape Painting in the Sui and T'ang Dynasties* (Berkeley and Los Angeles: University of California Press, 1980), p. 110. Since he developed a more detailed classification of Sui and T'ang landscape painting into the boneless, linear, and painterly styles, all having something to do with the blue-and-green manner, he did not have to emphasize this idea. As indicated in my paper "The Role of Wu-hsing," the whole term of "blue-and-

green" was developed by later critics, especially in Yüan, to refer to a manner that was used in T'ang, though the writers in T'ang did not see it as a special manner.

[11] Chao Po-chü was first mentioned as a painter of blue-and-green landscape in an early Yüan text, the *Hua-chi pu-i* (Supplement to the *Hua-chi* of Teng Ch'un of the 12th century) by Chuang Su (late 13th century).

[12] There are several articles on Ch'ien Hsüan's bird and flower and figure paintings, but as yet no extensive treatment of his landscapes. One such study is now being undertaken by Robert Mowry. So far, treatment of Ch'ien's landscapes can be found in some general discussions of his works, such as James Cahill's section on him in *Hills Beyond the River* (New York, 1976), pp. 19-37, and my paper "The Role of Wu-hsing."

[13] Published in the *Ku-kung ming-hua* (Taipei: National Palace Museum, 1966), V, 3, and in *Ku-kung shu-hua-lu* (Taipei: National Palace Museum, 1965), IV, 110-113.

[14] Published in Hsieh Chih-liu, *T'ang, Wu-tai, Sung, Yüan ming-chi* (Shanghai, 1957), No. 93, and *T'ang Sung Yüan Ming Ch'ing hua hsüan* (Canton, 1963), No. 14.

[15] Published in several places, including Barnhart, *Marriage of the Lord of the River*, Fig. 24; Sherman E. Lee and Wai-kam Ho, *Chinese Art under the Mongols: The Yüan Dynasty (1279-1368)* (Cleveland: Cleveland Museum, 1968), p. 90; Cahill, *Hills Beyond the River*, Figs. 10 and 11; Murck, *Artists and Traditions*, p. 82. However, none of these reproduces the complete composition.

[16] *The Landscape of Wu-hsing (Wu-hsing ch'ing-yüan t'u-chüan)* was never published in any of the major publications except in the newspaper, *Ta-kung-pao*, May 23, 1979, p. 8.

[17] Two long articles on this painting have appeared recently, including one by Richard Vinograd and another by Sherman E. Lee, both listed in n. 8 above.

[18] This painting has been one of the most published works of Chao Meng-fu. See especially my *Autumn Colors*.

[19] According to a number of traditional catalogs, there was a pair of paintings on silk and in color on this subject. But at present only the *East Mountain of Tung-t'ing* is left, in the Shanghai Museum. Wang Shih-min, however, made a copy of both in an album, which is published in *Yün-hui-chai ts'ang T'ang Sung i-lai ming-hua chi* (Shanghai, 1948).

[20] See, for example, Yao Shou's *Angling on a River in Autumn, after Chao Meng-fu*, published in Siren, *Chinese Painting*, Vol. VI, pl. 142. In his own inscription, Yao wrote: "In my later years I loved the painting methods of Sung-hsüeh, Chao Ch'eng-chih . . ."

[21] On the impact of Chao on Wen Cheng-ming, Anne de Coursey Clapp in her book, *Wen Cheng-ming: The Ming Artist and Antiquity*, Artibus Asiae Supplementum XXXIV (Ascona, 1975), has documented some of these in detail, with some references to the *Autumn Colors* and other works in blue-and-green, on pp. 20-24.

[22] One of the reasons Chao's influence did not extend beyond Wang Chien was that during the eighteenth century most of the important works of Chao Meng-fu gradually went into the imperial collection, thus were no longer available to painters except those serving in the court.

[23]This statement, originally in a painting, now lost, is recorded in Chang Ch'ou, *Ch'ing-ho shu-hua-fang* (preface dated 1616), Vol. yü, p. 19b. It has been translated a number of times by various scholars. The present translation is based on O. Sirén, *The Chinese on the Art of Painting* (Shanghai, 1936), p. 110, with revisions by Alexander Soper.

[24]This was the general use of the blue-and-green in Ming and early Ch'ing. A number of paintings connected with this development are mentioned below. Some of them are included in the recent exhibition, "Eight Dynasties of Chinese Painting," at the Nelson Gallery of Art in Kansas City. See the catalog, *Eight Dynasties of Chinese Painting* (Cleveland Museum of Art, 1980), Nos. 80, 114, 136, 137, 142, 164, and 257.

[25]Although sometimes a book with the title *Jan-hsiang-an hua-po* is listed under Wang Chien's name, it is hardly a book, for it includes only four short colophons by him. There is no other writing listed under his name.

[26]See *Ku-kung shu-hua-lu,* VI, 105-106. It is an album in the manner of ancient masters, including Tung Yüan, Chü-jan, Mi Fei, Chao Meng-fu, Huang Kung-wang, Wang Meng, Wu Chen, and Ch'en Ju-yen.

[27]This is found in *Chung-kuo ming-hua-chi,* (Shanghai: Yu-cheng Book Co., 1909), II, pl. 67.

[28]See, for example, the inscription he wrote on the *White Clouds over Hsiao and Hsiang Rivers* at the Freer Gallery mentioned in n. 6 above.

[29]According to Pan Kuang-tan, *Famous Clans of Chia-hsing in Ming and Ch'ing Dynasties* (in Chinese) (Shanghai, 1947), p. 42, Hsiang Yüan-pien had five sons. Mei-po could have been Hsiang Te-ming, the eldest son, who usually inherits the major share of the family fortune. Unfortunately he is not recorded.

[30]The term "Kung-pao" in the inscription refers to an official at the service of a prince, sometimes as his teacher. Between the two Wang brothers, it seems that Shih-mou was closer to the court than Shih-chen and thus was the person referred to in Wang Chien's inscription. Since Shih-mou's seals are on the *Water Village,* this should be the case.

[31]Both of them adhered to Tung's ideas very closely, though emphasizing the imitation of ancient masters more than other aspects. Through them, Tung's ideas were transmitted to the two later Wangs, Wang Hui and Wang Yüan-ch'i, whose successful career at the court of K'ang-hsi helped make Tung's ideas most influential in the Ch'ing period.

[32]For a good summary of Wang Chien's life, see Wen Chao-t'ung, *Ch'ing-chu liu-ta hua-chia* (Hong Kong, 1960).

[33]Ibid., p. 2.

[34]The School of T'ai-ts'ang, after the first two Wangs, was continued by the grandson of Wang Shih-min, Yüan-ch'i, and then by many generations of the latter's descendants into the Ch'ien-lung period, all following Tung's ideas and practices, but with more emphasis on the imitation of old masters than creation of their own.

[35]A good summary of Wu Wei-yeh's life and literary works can be found in Hummel, *Eminent Chinese of the Ch'ing Period,* pp. 882-883.

[36]Because of Wu's poem, this group is constantly referred to as the "Nine Friends of Painting" in later writings on art.

[37]This decision in Wang Chien's later life made it possible for him to devote himself entirely to art. Because of it, the younger generation of the "Four Wangs," especially Wang Hui, seemed to have benefited a great deal from his association with Wang Chien, for some of the younger artist's best works were done during the late 1660s and the 1670s, during the last years of Wang Chien's life.

[38]This idea of the three (or four) masters of early Sung is based on the Yüan critic, T'ang Hou's idea: "Those Sung painters who excelled T'ang in landscape painting are only three: Li Ch'eng, Fan K'uan and Tung Yüan. Tung Yüan captures the spirit of the mountains; Li Ch'eng, the shape and appearance; and Fan K'uan, the bone structure. These three masters shine brightly over old and new to become the models for a hundred generations." *(Hua-chien,* annotated ed. [Peking, 1959], p. 37).

[39]*Ku-kung shu-hua-chi,* XLIV. The painting is signed and dated 1319.

[40]See *Eight Dynasties of Chinese Painting,* no. 114.

[41]For the *Farewell at Hsün-yang,* see *Eight Dynasties of Chinese Painting,* no. 164.

[42]Cf. his two scrolls, the *Yüan-chiao Studio* of 1550 and the *Fang-hu Island* of 1563, both in the Palace Museum, Taipei. See *Ku-kung shu-hua-lu,* V, 398-399.

[43]This is mentioned in Kuo Jo-hsü's *T'u-hua chien-wen-chih.* See the translation by Alexander Soper, *Kuo Jo-hsü's Experiences in Painting* (Washington, 1951), p. 19.

FRAGMENTS: TWO SCULPTURES OF THE INFANT CHRIST

Marilyn Stokstad

University of Kansas

Illus. 1. Infant Christ, *Helen Foresman Spencer Museum of Art, University of Kansas, Lawrence, Kansas.*

THE SEATED *Infant Christ* in the Helen Foresman Spencer Museum of Art at the Univeristy of Kansas, Lawrence, Kansas, and the Helen Spencer *Virgin and Child* in the William Rockhill Nelson Gallery of Art and Atkins Museum of Fine Arts, Kansas City, Missouri, represent the quality of art works, and suggest the facilities for students and the public, which Dr. Franklin Murphy has been instrumental in developing in the part of the country he always romantically referred to as "the trans-Mississippi West." As a trustee of the Nelson Gallery and the Chancellor of the University of Kansas for nine years, Dr. Murphy delighted in casting the pebbles of art and scholarship into university and museum ponds. He still enjoys the results produced by the ever widening ripples of his pioneering efforts. Thus fragments of two monumental devotional images have found a home in midwestern museums through the work begun by Dr. Murphy and continued by his friends, Dr. W. Clarke Wescoe and Mrs. Helen Foresman Spencer.

The *Infant Christ*,[1] seated on His mother's knee—He now armless; she represented only by a broken hand on His thigh and a bit of drapery—such is the fragment that must once have been part of a monumental image of the *sedes sapientiae*, the Virgin as throne of Wisdom (illus. 1). A product of the Mosan school under the inspiration of Nicholas of Verdun, the sculpture embodies the ideal of Gothic Humanism as it was manifest in sculpture during the early years of the thirteenth century. The erect, poised Infant is a memorable image in spite of its fragmentary state. The fine proportions and sturdy body modeled with rich, flowing drapery, the delicately carved toes and hand, the subtle planes of the face and careful structure of the head with its close-cropped hair all suggest an artist well aware both of Nicholas' work in enamel and metal and of the classical sources of the Mosan school. The breadth and freedom of movement achieved by the sculptor surpasses more famous though comparable images, such as the Virgin and Child in St. John's Church in Liège. An unusual detail, which suggests a date of about 1210, is the mantle that the sculptor has drawn around the torso high under the arms like a cummerbund. This bundle of drapery emphasizes the horizontality of the composition by repeating the deep looping arcs over the legs. The fall of the drapery over the Virgin's arm suggests that a mantle lying in horizontal arcs covered her figure too. The Child must originally have had a metal crown supported on the fillet above the curls that frame His face. In spite of the sculpture's small size the *Infant Christ* reflects the monumen-

Illus. 2. Virgin and Child, *William Rockhill Nelson Gallery of Art and Atkins Museum of Fine Arts, Kansas City, Missouri; Kenneth A. and Helen F. Spencer Foundation Acquisition Fund.*

Illus. 3. Virgin and Child, *side view.*

tal art of cathedral portals, and the image when complete must have been one of the grandest conceptions of the *sedes sapientiae* in later Mosan sculpture.

Another type of image favored by sculptors in northern and eastern France, Flanders, and the Rhineland is one in which the Infant stands on His mother's lap to bless worshipers or to receive the three Magi. The theme occurs regularly in the fourteenth century; however, it appeared earlier where the cult of the three kings inspired great popular devotion. Thus, it is not surprising to find these images in wood and stone prevalent in the region around Cologne where the relics of the Magi had been brought to the cathedral and were housed in a magnificent shrine made by Nicholas of Verdun and his shop.

Was the Nelson Gallery's *Virgin and Child*[2] (illus. 2) a simple devotional image or could it have been part of an Epiphany scene? When the figures were complete with arms, hands, and attributes, and enriched with colors and gold, they would have presented a marvelous vision of the Queen of Heaven and her Son which could have stood as an independent cult image. William Forsyth has shown that in sculptures of the Virgin with the standing Child, the Child usually holds a ball and a bird while the Virgin commonly holds a book.[3] In the Nelson Gallery's sculpture, however, the position of the Child's shoulders suggests that he gestured toward an unseen worshiper and probably extended His right hand in blessing. The Virgin's arm was free from the rest of her body, and no indication remains of a book or any other object which might have rested on her knee. Mary probably held a scepter or another of her attributes—the lily, the rose, or a rose branch. On the other hand, if the figures came from an altarpiece dedicated to the Epiphany, the slight turn of the Child to His right could be accounted for by the presence of figures of the three Kings.[4] Late thirteenth- and fourteenth-century French ivories,[5] as well as altarpieces spread from Covarubbias in Spain to Aachen in Germany, provide models on which to reconstruct the scene. As the central figures of the altarpiece, the Virgin and Child would have been high above the viewer (illus. 3, 4). The visual distortion caused by such placement would have been compensated for by the extreme foreshortening of Mary's legs and the elongation of her torso. The forward inclination of the heads would have made Mother and Child all the more visible.

The serene image of the *Virgin and Child* in the Nelson Gallery combines a mood of quiet introspection with awareness of the worshiper. Mother and Son do not react to each other but instead gaze out and downward. Mary sits on a simple bench whose box-like form is enriched by moldings but whose front terminations are lost. She holds her Child firmly as He stands with His left foot still on the throne beside her thigh although He has placed His right foot on her knee. Mother and Child are united in an essentially vertical composition, both drawing back and then forward. Naturally, the original extension of the arms would have broken the compact form. As Gothic figures they partake of both the monumentality of the early thirteenth century and the relaxed elegance associated with the Court Style.

The Christ Child, like the Spencer Museum *Christ*, is an idealized youth; however, here at the end of the thirteenth century the sculptor has further refined the features—almond eyes under slanted brows, slender nose, and delicate almost smiling mouth—in contrast with the sturdy, rounder forms associated with sculpture from the circle of Nicholas of Verdun. Like many figures of the Christ Child from northern France, He is alert, gracious but dignified and, as William Wixom has said, "affable." The Virgin's face is an elongated oval poised on a long neck and framed by softly waving hair as well as encircling veil and (lost) crown. Her dainty narrow features, with eyes, lips which hint at a smile, and high arched brows carved in a continuous line with her nose, give a piquancy to an otherwise idealized face and reflect the courtly elegance of the later Gothic style.

An ample veil covers Mary's head and shoulders, lies in horizontal arcs across her breast and falls over her left shoulder. This arrangement of the veil is found in early Gothic sculpture, and continues in the thirteenth century tombs in St. Denis. (By the end of the thirteenth century the Child, in playing with His mother's veil, may pull it across her breast, thus creating a similar horizontal movement of drapery.) The fine sharp folds of the veil contrast with the broader treatment of the tunic, an unadorned garment belted high with a maiden's long dangling belt. A long tunic also covers the Child from neck to toes and falls in vertical folds which repeat the lines of His mother's dress. A mantle falls symmetrically over Mary's shoulders, is pulled under one arm and envelops the lower part of her body to break in sharp angular pockets around broadly modeled knees. Carved in fine, precise folds, the drapery falls in narrow vertical panels emphasizing the extraordinary elongation of the torso, the slight inclination of Mary's short lower

Illus. 4. Virgin and Child, *side view from viewer's level.*

legs, and the striding pose of the Child. Mary's crown would have further increased the verticality of the composition, for it must have been a tall, elaborate metal and jeweled creation. It would have extended the already long face and balanced the breadth of the veil whose circular form now contrasts with the otherwise strong rising movement of the sculpture as a whole. The extraordinarily compact and harmonious composition uniting the two figures in sweeping arcs also suggests a date still in the thirteenth century.

Clearly, the style of the *Virgin and Child* derives ultimately from Reims, Amiens, and the courtly art of the Ile-de-France—from Vierge Dorée and all her sisters and daughters. Among Parisian sculpture the gisants of Constance of Arles and Hermintrude, commissioned by St. Louis for the pantheon in St. Denis (1263-1264), provide the most striking parallels;[6] while among figures inspired by the Vierge Dorée the standing Virgin from the Chapel of the cemetery in Saint Amand-les-Pas, attributed to Amiens at the end of the thirteenth century, repeats the facial type although not the drapery which resembles the Nelson Virgin.[7] The redating of the ivory Virgin of the Ste.-Chapelle in the Louvre to 1265-1279[8] suggests that fourteenth-century ivories to which the Nelson Gallery figures may be compared may also be somewhat earlier. The Virgin and Child in the Musée des Arts Décoratifs, Paris,[9] attributed to the fourteenth century, bears a superficial resemblance to the Gallery's sculpture although the heads of both Mother and Child lack the finesse, the figures are broader, and the drapery more flaccid. The distinctive veil across the breast and the long fingers gripping the Child across the upper torso, although similar, are summarily carved. This sculpture may be a workshop copy inspired by the Nelson Gallery image. M. Didier, while arguing for a date of 1330-1340 for the Nelson Gallery Virgin, compared the carving of the Virgin's face to late thirteenth-century figures from Ypres and suggested that the sculpture might come from the general area of northern France, Ypres and Tournai.[10]

While the delicacy and precision of the carving of the Virgin and Child suggest the courtly art of Paris and the inspiration of Reims, the most direct comparisons seem possible with the angels now in the Cloisters, New York.[11] These angels have been associated with angels in the churches in the villages of Audemont and Humbert in Artois, dated in the last quarter of the thirteenth century.[12] A date late in the thirteenth century for the Virgin and Child also seems possible, for the figures retain the severe verticality and monumentality of conception of the thirteenth century without either the breadth of face and figure or the self-conscious elegance of the fourteenth century. Angels, Virgin, and standing Child, and the seated Christ Child are all part of that sphere of reciprocal influence, extending from Paris and Reims to Liège and Tournai, which made northern France and Flanders the major center of art at the end of the Middle Ages, a center whose influence was as important for the development of late Gothic and Renaissance culture as Byzantium had been to the early Middle Ages. The sculptures now stand in museums as fragmentary survivors of the rich heritage destroyed by the wars and pollution of the nineteenth and twentieth centuries, a heritage kept alive in educational institutions and by enlightened patrons.

NOTES

[1] *Infant Christ*, 1200-1210, Franco-Flemish (Mosan), wood with traces of polychrome, height 31.7 cm./12½ inches. Acquired from Edward R. Lubin, New York, by the Kansas University Museum of Art during the chancellorship of Dr. W. Clarke Wescoe. Provenance: Helen F. Spencer Museum of Art, University of Kansas, Lawrence, Kansas, number 61.2. Exhibited: New York, Metropolitan Museum of Art, "The Year 1200," 12 Feb.-10 May, 1970, catalogue by Konrad Hoffman, number 37, pp. 30–31, illustrated; Houston, Texas, Museum of Fine Arts, "From the Collection of the University of Kansas," 15 April—13 June, 1971, catalogue by Jack Schrader, number 13, illustrated; Tokyo, Japan, National Museum of Western Art, "Masterpieces of World Art from American Museums," 11 Sept.-17 Oct., 1976, and National Museum, Kyoto, 2 Nov.-5 Dec., 1976, number 11, illustrated.

[2] *Virgin and Child*, end of the thirteenth century, northern France (Artois?), wood with traces of polychrome covered with brown stain, height 101.6 cm./40 inches. Acquired from Edward R. Lubin, New York through the Kenneth A. and Helen F. Spencer Foundation Acquisition Fund; said to have come from a private collection in Paris. William Rockhill Nelson Gallery of Art and Atkins Museum of Fine Arts, Kansas City, Missouri, number F74-7. No record of previous exhibition or publication.

[3] William H. Forsyth, "The Virgin and Child in French Fourteenth Century Sculpture," *Art Bulletin*, 39, 3 (1957), 171–182.

Author's Note. The directors and curators of the Spencer Museum and the Nelson Gallery, Dr. Wescoe and Mrs. Helen Spencer, join in congratulating Dr. Murphy.

[4]Ursula Nilgen, "The Epiphany and the Eucharist: On the Interpretation of Eucharistic Motifs in Mediaeval Epiphany Scenes," *Art Bulletin*, 49, 4 (1967), 311-316, discussed development of the drama of the kings in the West as part of the liturgy for the feast of the Epiphany. Eilene Forsyth, ("Magi and Majesty: A Study of Romanesque Sculpture and Liturgical Drama," *Art Bulletin*, 50, 3 [1968], 215–222, and *The Throne of Wisdom* [Princeton University Press, 1970]), has shown how in the twelfth century portable images of the Virgin and Child played a role in these dramas. For a study of the Virgin and Child in French sculpture see R. Suckale, *Studien zu Stilbildung und Stilwandel der Madonnenstatuen der Ile-de-France zwischen 1230 und 1300* (Munich, 1971); W. Sauerlander, *Gotische Skulptur in Franreich* (Munich, 1970), also English edition; Forsyth, *Virgin and Child . . .*; and the catalogues P. Brieger and P. Verdier, *Art and the Courts: France and England from 1259 to 1328*, National Gallery of Canada, Ottawa, 1972; and "Transformations of the Court Style, Gothic Art in Europe 1270-1320," prepared by the Department of Art, Brown University and the Museum of Art of the Rhode Island School of Design, Providence, Rhode Island, 2-27 Feb., 1977.

[5]Raymond Koechlin, *Les ivoires gothiques français*, 3 vols. (Paris, 1924). Note, for example, the tabernacle of the Virgin, Metropolitan Museum of Art, Acc. no. 17.190.270, gift of J. Pierpont Morgan, 1917, Koechlin no. 142; reproduced and discussed in "Transformations of the Court Style," no. 16.

[6]Georgia Sommers Wright, "A Royal Tomb Program in the Reign of St. Louis," *Art Bulletin*, 56, 2 (June, 1974), 224–243.

[7]D. Kimpel and R. Suckale, "Die Skulpturenwerkstatt der Vierge Dorée am Honoratus portale der Kathedrale von Amiens," *Zietschrift für Kunstgeschichte*, 36 (1973), 217–268; Hervé Oursel, *Sculptures romanes et gothiques du nord de la France* (Lille, 1978-1979).

[8]D. Gaborit-Chopin, "La Vierge a l'enfant d'ivoire de la Sainte-Chapelle," *Bulletin monumental*, 130 (1972), 213–224.

[9]Koechlin gift, 1902.

[10]Robert Didier, letter to Ralph T. Coe, Aug. 8, 1974. Jan Steayart (letter to Ralph T. Coe, 1974) dated the figures about 1320 and suggested that they are French "without the refinement of Paris." A. Erlande-Brandenburg expressed the opinion, verbally, 1980, that the sculpture is thirteenth-century northern French work.

[11]Acc. no. 52.33.2. James Rorimer, "Two Gothic Angels for the Cloisters," *Metropolitan Museum of Art Bulletin*, 11 (1952), 105 ff., and *The Cloisters* (New York: Metropolitan Museum of Art, 1963), p. 155. Similar angels may be seen at Princeton and in the Louvre. See also Richard H. Randall, "Thirteenth Century Altar Angels," *Record of the Art Museum* (Princeton University), 18, 1 (1959), 2–16.

[12]Vera K. Ostoia, *The Middle Ages: Treasures from the Cloisters and the Metropolitan Museum of Art*, Los Angeles County Museum of Art, 18 Jan.-29 Mar., 1970, and the Chicago Art Institute, 16 May-5 July, 1970, number 66.

DANTE AND THE HISTORY OF ART
REFLECTIONS INSPIRED BY DANTE GABRIEL ROSSETTI'S PAINTING, "LA PIA DE' TOLOMEI"

Edward A. Maser

The University of Chicago

IT IS DIFFICULT FOR someone who spent seven exciting and rewarding years working under the direction and inspiration of the man whose personality and accomplishments are celebrated by this group of studies, to select from among the many problems in the history of art and the many works of art with which that time was filled, something to present appropriate to this occasion and worthy of it. Franklin Murphy's interest in the history of art ranges very wide—the secular art of the Middle Ages; bronze sculpture, medals, and plaquettes from the Renaissance to the present; the sculpture of the Italian Renaissance and the German Baroque and Rococo; the prints of Albrecht Dürer; Romantic painting, American Regionalist painting, primitive art—to name but a few. His tastes are catholic and informed. He often seems to prefer, however, works of art in their historical or cultural context more than those whose greatness lifted them out of it. He apparently believes that the arts are one of the most important aspects of life, if not the most important, and with missionary zeal and an evergreen enthusiasm tries to make them so in his own and in that of others. This being the case, it seems fitting to offer here in his honor and for his delectation, some observations related to a painting in whose acquisition and study he was more or less intimately involved.

The painting is Dante Gabriel Rossetti's oil depicting the ill-fated *La Pia de' Tolomei*,[1] a subject taken from Dante (Purgatorio, Canto V) which the painter began in 1868 and only completed in 1880. The circumstances of its acquisition by the Museum of Art of the University of Kansas in 1956 (the museum is now called the Helen Foresman Spencer Museum of Art), the role it played in the life of the museum and the university, as well as the scholarly studies inspired by it, interdisciplinary ones as well as in the history of art, make it appropriate for consideration here. It can thus serve as an example (and it is only one among many) of how through Franklin Murphy's encouragement and guidance a work of art, its intrinsic quality aside, could also become a part of the lives of many people.

Brought to the attention of the museum by the late Ellen Lamble Werner in 1955, who had seen it in London, the painting was acquired the following year. After cleaning and restoration, it was presented to the public in an exhibition on Rossetti and the Pre-Raphaelites at the museum[2] and was simultaneously published in the museum's bulletin in an article by a distinguished member of the university's department of English.[3] Details related to the presentation and publication of the painting also formed part of a paper read on May 26, 1969, at the 55th annual meeting of the

Illus. 1. Dante Gabriel Rossetti (1828-1882), La Pia de' Tolomei. *The Helen Foresman Spencer Museum of Art, The University of Kansas, Lawrence. Accession no. 56.31.*

American Association of Museums in Boston, which was published by that organization later in the year.[4] Caught up, one might say, by this flurry of activity and study related to the painting, I became interested in the whole problem of the relation of Dante to the visual arts in general, the results of which are presented here.[5]

There were, primarily, three different ways to approach the age-old question of what Dante's relation to the visual arts actually was, each pertinent to the understanding of the man, his work, and its significance as well as to the arts themselves. Only one of them, the second, is directly related to Rossetti's painting, yet the others are not without interest considered in relation to it. Dealing with them in their chronological order, the first is, of course, the consideration of the poet's personal connections with the arts and with contemporary artists during his own lifetime. The second, no less important, is the study of how the poet's personality and works influenced and inspired subsequent generations of artists, providing them, as they did Rossetti, with, above all, subject matter and with poetic imagery. The third, perhaps of special significance to us in the United States, is the consideration of how Dante and his concern with, and influence on, the arts brought art critics and historians to a fuller appreciation and understanding of the art of the past, particularly that of his own day.

It is, of course, a commonplace that Dante, in the *Divina Commedia,* summed up the thought of his age and in doing so opened the way for the new age upon whose threshold he stood. It is not surprising then, that he also concerned himself with the visual arts, besides poetry the other great vehicle for the communication of ideas and images, the only other artistic medium able to crystallize, and to present with directness and impact, those images and concepts which Dante evoked so sublimely with the written word.

That Dante himself was intimately concerned with the visual arts of his day seems borne out in his writings. That he was actually a practitioner of one of them is also possible, for in the *Vita Nuova,* as is well known, he says: "Da quel giorno nel quale si compiva l'anno che quella Donna era fatta delle cittadine della vita eterna, io mi sedeva in parte nella quale ricordandomi di lei io disegnava un angelo sopra certe tavolette."[6] In this passage, so often cited in proving Dante's many-sided genius, his statement that he drew a picture of an angel, whether meant literally or not, is, nevertheless, suggestive, for he apparently felt it to be a very appropriate means of expressing his love for the departed Beatrice and for commemorating her.

Even more indicative of his great concern with the arts is the fact that, in the *Commedia,* he selected one of their practitioners as his vehicle for discussing something as important to the thought of his time as the transitory nature of earthly fame. When, with Virgil, he approached the first circle of Purgatory, he met there among the Proud, the manuscript illuminator and miniaturist, Oderisi of Gubbio. Recognizing him, he said:

> *"O!" diss'io lui, "non se'tu Oderisi,*
> *l'onor d'Agobbio, e l'onor di quell'arte*
> *che alluminar chiamata è in Parisi?"* [7]

While it is certainly not surprising that a man of letters should have been familiar with a decorator of books, it still suggests a great love and respect for these ornaments and visual amplifications of a text that he considered Oderisi an honor to his native city, at a time when artists were not considered much more than artisans. Ostensibly still concerned with the theme of human vanity, he then had Oderisi reply:

> *"Frate," diss' elli, "più ridon le carte*
> *che pennelleggia Franco bolognese:*
> *l'onore è tutto or suo, e mio in parte."* [8]

While the fact that Franco Bolognese's colored pages "laughed" more and were more admired than his own was Oderisi's way of showing how quickly earthly fame in the arts passes away; it was also Dante's way of revealing to us his awareness of a change in artistic taste that was taking place in his own day. This is borne out even more in the lines which continue the artistic discussion—for the history of art, perhaps the most famous three lines in the *Commedia:*

> *"Credette Cimabue nella pintura*
> *tener lo campo, e ora ha Giotto il grido,*
> *sí che la fama di colui è scura."* [9]

In these few lines Dante described, clearly and unmistakably, the artistic revolution which took place during his lifetime. He revealed his own insight into not solely the problem of artistic fame but also the marked difference between two different modes of painting, that of Cimabue, who, in spite of his great achievements, was recognized as an artist rooted in past traditions, and that of his pupil, Giotto, whose manner of painting not only "put in the shade" that of his master, but was such that even contemporaries like Oderisi, who also represented the old style, and Dante, the enlightened layman, could recognize that a new epoch in the development of painting was beginning with him.

Just as Dante made the *Divina Commedia* more vivid and alive through his use of the vernacular, a down-to-earth Tuscan pulsating with vitality, so did Giotto achieve the same effect in his work. The *maniera greca* of Cimabue, an expression of the medieval Italian concern with the Byzantine tradition of forms into patterns and its subjugation of all forms to the two-dimensional, gave way, in the work of Giotto, to a totally new approach, to a new naturalism. He endowed his painted figures with a three-dimensionality so striking that one seems to see solid and tangible forms existing in space and not designs applied to a two-dimensional surface. His figures were arranged on the painting surface in order to heighten this illusion and not to form a decorative pattern on it; they were made to live and breathe and move in a space provided for them which receded back into the picture. What his works lacked in transcendental mystery was compensated for by a monumental solidity and a new majestic humanity. What was sacrificed in exquisite details of surface decoration, was gained in creating a picture that was a coherent and unified entity, filled with carefully coordinated and seemingly solid forms. In other words, Giotto presented the supernatural in human terms—and this was the revolution which had taken place—for it was felt that by depicting it according to the laws which governed the real world, it was enhanced, not diminished.

By thus comparing these two masters, Dante, while ostensibly talking about fame, contrasted the old and the new styles in painting as a device for recording the fact that the art of his time was undergoing a radical change. What Dante saw happening, and he was obviously aware of it, was the emergence of what is called, for want of a more precise term, the Italian Gothic style. The national qualification of the stylistic term is to suggest, not that the art of this period was simply an Italian borrowing of a style from the North—from the "Goths"—but rather to emphasize the individual nature of Italian art at this time, which seems to have been a fine blend of the new style from France and the classic tradition of the Mediterranean world, made up of Roman memories and Romanesque achievements.

Although the *Commedia* had not yet been written when they were painted, Giotto's frescoes in the Scrovegni Chapel in Padua are, perhaps, the greatest contemporary parallel exposition of its ideas in another medium. This is not to say that Dante had any direct influence on them. Although Benvenuto da Imola told of Dante's visit to the artist in Padua, there is probably more poetry than truth in the event. That Dante respected Giotto, however, we know from the poem and it is not inconceivable that the two Florentines knew each other, particularly as involuntary and voluntary exiles from their city. Whatever the contacts, that the two men shared the same spirit is evident in a comparison of their work, for Giotto, like Dante, took the traditional images of his world and lifted them onto a new plane of reality, at once general and ideal, yet filled with an earthly flavor which related them to human experience and thus made them more comprehensible.

Cesare Gnudi, in his beautiful book on Giotto in which he draws sensitive and fascinating parallels between the great poet and the great painter, points out that for Giotto's career as a painter, the frescoes in the Arena Chapel represented the culmination of his life's work, just as the *Commedia* did for Dante.[10] What one might call Giotto's "vernacular" treatment of the sublime stories such as those of the Virgin and Her Son or of Joachim and Anna, can be considered to be, moreover, the visual equivalents of Dante's use of the vernacular in his poem, and his use of known personages from his own society as characters in it. He thereby lifted the real language and the real people of his day to a new level of significance by using them to tell the most sublime of stories, the great Christian scheme of the universe and its meaning. Gnudi conceives too, of the pictorial series in the Scrovegni Chapel as so many "cantos," each scene a part of a connected narrative, but each, like the cantos in the *Commedia,* a single striking expression of a great concept, told with a great economy and mastery of means.[11] By means of the new plasticity of forms, by the use of easily comprehended dramatic gesture, by realistic touches of detail, Giotto brings down to earth, and thereby glorifies, such lofty concepts as the betrayal of love, renunciation, hope, and its fulfillment. This then is the real essence of Dante's relation to the visual arts of his day. It was not the mere fact that he knew and appreciated artists, but that he shared with them new modes of thought and new ideas on expressing them.

Once written and well enough known to exercise a direct influence on the literary and artistic world, the *Divina Commedia* became something more than simply one further manifestation of the *Zeitgeist* of the Italian Middle Ages, of which Giotto's paintings was another. As well as being the greatest literary achievement of Italy, it became the richest source of inspiration and subject matter for generations of artists. It was no longer solely the lofty idealism, the grand manner, and the noble humanity of the poet's thought which was mirrored in their work, as it was in Giotto's, but the more specific images, the narrative elements, the individual problems or incidents, which became not so much the source of inspiration as the actual subject matter of the visual arts.[12]

Illustrations of the Comedy appeared soon after its completion, but overwhelmed and enthralled by the richness and variety of Dante's vision, they rarely achieved anything like the lofty, universalizing tone of the literary masterpiece. Often very beautiful in their own right, they nevertheless remained little more than illustrations of Dante's ideas. Even such an appealing artist as Botticelli, who in his later years turned to illustrating the *Commedia*,[13] was able to capture little of the grandeur of the poem. It was not the vehemence and power of the *Inferno* which seems to have struck a cord in Botticelli's soul, moreover, but rather the gracefulness and feminine charm of Beatrice's realm, the *Purgatorio* and the *Paradiso,* which truly inspired him. These he treated with an elegance of line and a lyrical, Spring-like quality which is typical of him and the late *Quattrocento* in Florence, but which seems to have little to do with Dante. Conversely, it was just the *terribiltà* of the *Inferno* which inspired such artists as Luca Signorelli, or his pupil, Michelangelo. They, while never specifically illustrating scenes from the poem, certainly reveal in their work, particularly in the Orvieto frescoes of Signorelli and the Sistine Chapel frescoes of Michelangelo, a grasp of the magnitude of the great drama of man's destiny as the Middle Ages saw it and as Dante expressed it. Concentrating almost exclusively on the human actors in the drama, as did Dante and as did Giotto, they achieve the same degree of universality of meaning and strength of emotion—be it horror or beatitude—as did their great predecessors. Michelangelo's image of Renaissance man, filled with pride, suddenly confronted, as he is in the Sistine's Last Judgment fresco, with the horrible consequences of the neglect of his soul, is, indeed, one of his greatest. It calls to mind in its power such a tragically heroic figure as Farinata degli Uberti in the poem. Although they came long after him, such paintings as those of these two great artists, connected by that shining thread which binds the history of Italian painting together, do lead back, in that they owe him so much, to the monumental forms of Giotto, and in doing so also derive, as does he, from the spirit which permeates Dante's poem. They are not mere illustrators of his stories, but much more the direct heirs of his spirit.

While the seventeenth and eighteenth centuries were (with some notable exceptions) less interested in Dante's imagery (and his poetry), the romantic nineteenth century saw the great revival of appreciation of his work as the subject for works of art.[14] From Flaxman to Delacroix, from Rossetti to Rodin, the immortal images of the *Commedia*—Paolo and Francesca, Conte Ugolino, Farinata degli Uberti, La Pia de' Tolomei—stirred the imagination of artists and provided them with the subjects of thrilling works of art. It is in this context that the painting by Rossetti should also be seen and further understood. It can, for the purposes of this study, serve as representative of the many other examples which could be mentioned.

Yet Dante's continued significance for the visual arts cannot be limited to that of being merely a storehouse of images and ideas to which artists up to our own day could turn when in need of inspiration or exciting subject matter. There is yet another way in which he and his work remained important for the visual arts up to our own time. As has been mentioned, Dante's poetry, while still respected as one of the great monuments of the literary history of Europe, no longer pleased as poetry. It suffered, as monuments tend to, a certain degree of neglect as the centuries passed. It was not until the eighteenth century that such men as Giovanni Battista Vico began to point out qualities within it worthy of appreciation. In his *Giudizio sopra Dante*, Vico, who felt that the source of poetry was not in the ingenuity of reason but in the excited imagination and in strength of feeling, considered Dante to be "il nostro Omero."[15] Through such praise and reappraisal as this, and through the great increase in the scholarly investigation of the Italian past taking place during the century, the study of Dante, his great work, and his age began to flourish. In works such as those of Ludovico Antonio Muratori and Girolamo Tiraboschi,[16] Alighieri and the culture of his time received increasingly sympathetic scrutiny. Indeed, Muratori (whose publication of Benvenuto da Imola's Dante commentary is the source of the story of Dante's visit to Giotto in Padua) became, in his discussion of the fine arts of the Middle Ages, one of the earliest apologists for medieval art,[17] considered to be, since Vasari's time, the art of the *tempi bassi,* the centuries of barbarism between the end of the glorious ancient world and its revival in the Renaissance.

Led, then, from their philological and critical study of Dante, scholars also began to investigate the art of his age. Under the aegis of the great Alighieri, the art of the illuminators of manuscripts, of Duccio and Cimabue, of Giotto and his followers, began to be understood to be something more than the well-intentioned but inadequate work of mere precursors of Raphael. Over this eighteenth-century world of diligent scholarly research, rediscovery, and growing appreciation, the great spirit of Dante loomed, like a beneficent protective genius over the revival of interest in the so-called "primitives."[18]

When Seroux d'Agincourt, who wished to be known as the "Winckelmann of the Dark Ages," published his great picture book, *L'Histoire de l'art par les monuments,* he did not neglect to include several in which Dante figured prominently.[19] When Giotto's primacy as the "restorer of painting" was contested by the Sienese historian Guglielmo della Valle, who chauvinistically believed that it was in Siena, of course, and not in Florence, that the revival of painting took place, he grudgingly said of the Padua frescoes that they had the same irregularities and the same beauties which were scattered through the *Commedia* of Dante.[20] Thus there developed a constant reference back to Dante whenever medieval art came under discussion. Indeed, one of the first non-Italian writers on medieval art, a collector of "primitives" in his own right, actually began his interest in the Italian Middle Ages as a Dante scholar.

Alexis-François Artaud de Montor (1772-1849)[21] was a French aristocrat who served his country as a diplomat in Italy during the Empire, first at the Holy See and later in Tuscany. He was an ardent student of Italian history and letters and, as a complement to his historical and literary studies, he also began to search out and acquire medieval paintings. He discussed them in a book on early Italian art[22] which he published in 1808, and later republished with sixty engraved plates after paintings in his collection in 1841-1843, under the title *Peintres primitifs.*[23] Apparently working on it simultaneously, he also published a translation of the *Divine Comedy* in 1811-1813,[24] which was destined to be the most frequently reprinted translation of Dante in the history of French Dante studies. Artaud de Montor also wrote on Pius II, on Machiavelli, and, after the revolution of 1830 when he retired from the diplomatic service to dedicate himself to letters, he wrote, in 1841, a *Histoire de Dante,* republishing in the same year the illustrated edition of his earlier work of medieval art. This, then, is an example of how Dante remained related to the art of his time, as a general influence on the growing appreciation of medieval art and as the author through whose work it was felt that the modern world could best arrive at an understanding of the art of his day.

To bring the importance of Dante's influence on the study of medieval art even closer to home and to our own time, it is interesting to note that the first organized teaching of the history of art in our own country was also inextricably connected with Dante scholarship. When, in the fall of 1874, President Eliot of Harvard appointed Charles Eliot Norton as the first annual lecturer on the "History of the Arts of Construction and Design" in the new department he was creating, the formal teaching of the history of art in the United States can be said to have begun.[25] As Professor of Fine Arts, which he became the following year, Norton, in his twenty-three years of teaching at Harvard, established art history there as an academic discipline—and what he taught was the history of the art of the age of Dante, for he thought of himself first and foremost as a student of the Divine Poet. He came to his position at Harvard as an established expert on the age of Dante, as a translator of the *Vita Nuova,* as the author of a book on his travels and studies in Italy, and as a frequent contributor to periodicals on things Italian, artistic, and Dantean.[26] When James Russell Lowell resigned in 1877, Norton also took over his course on Dante and continued to teach it along with his courses on art. He became president of the Dante Society in 1891, the year in which his own prose translation of the *Divine Comedy* appeared, and held the post until his death in 1908. The growth and development of Dante studies in the United States is due largely to his efforts,[27] as is the study in our country of the history and appreciation of the art of any age, not solely that of Dante. It is an aspect of Dante's relation to the visual arts which we are still experiencing today.

Thus, the whole matter of Dante and the visual arts has a three-fold nature, based on that magic number which figures so prominently in the *Commedia.* First, as a manifestation of a new spirit, which Dante expressed in literature, but which also was expressed visually in the art of such a man as Giotto, whose relations with the poet are so covered with legend and wishful thinking that they represent a veritable *Inferno* for the scholar. Second, as the subject of the art of his day and of succeeding centuries during which the images of the man and his creations become transformed and sublimated in the *Purgatorio* of the artistic imagination until they were purged of the shackles of time and place and became the spiritual property of the world. And lastly, as Beatrice was to him among the ineffable wonders of Heaven, Dante has served as a sort of spiritual guide to later searchers after the truth, to the explorers venturing into the uncharted empyrean realms of scholarly research devoted to his time, resulting in, among other things, a better understanding of what the visual arts meant to him and his age and continue to mean to us in our own, which constitutes, one might say, the *Paradiso* of the history of art we enjoy today.

NOTES

[1] Dante Gabriel Rossetti (1828-1882), *La Pia de' Tolomei,* painted between 1868 and 1880. The Helen Foresman Spencer Museum of Art, The University of Kansas, Lawrence. Accession no. 56.31. Oil on canvas, 41½ × 47½ inches (104.8 × 120.6 cm). Signed lower right: D. G. Rossetti. Acquired from Leger Galleries, London in 1956.

[2] *Dante Gabriel Rossetti and His Circle,* The University of Kansas Museum of Art, November 4–December 15, 1958.

[3] W. D. Paden, *"La Pia de' Tolomei* by Dante Gabriel Rossetti," *The Register of the Museum of Art,* The University of Kansas, Lawrence, 2, 1 (November 1958), 3-48.

[4] Edward A. Maser, "A College Bulletin For, By, and In Spite of a College Faculty," *Midwest Museums Quarterly,* 20, 3 (Summer 1960), 23-26.

[5] Some of the material included here was first presented in an illustrated public lecture entitled "Dante and the Art of His Time" given to open the Dante Centennial celebration held at the University of California, Los Angeles, on May 5, 1965, again under the aegis of our *festeggiato.*

[6] *Vita Nuova,* XXXIV, 1.

[7] *Purgatorio,* XI, 79-81.

[8] *Ibid.,* 82–84.

[9] *Ibid.,* 94-96.

[10] Cesare Gnudi, *Giotto* (Milano, 1958), 9-34, 110.

[11] *Ibid., 134-164.*

[12] For further information on this matter, the reader is referred to such well-known works as Ludwig Volkmann, *Iconografia dantesca* (Leipzig, 1897); Salviati, *Iconografia dantesca* (Bologna, 1911); and R. Altrocchi, "Present State of Dante Iconography," *Italica,* 12 (1935), 106-115.

[13] See Adolfo Venturi, *Il Botticelli interprete di Dante* (Florence, 1921), and Lamberto Donati, *Il Botticelli e le prime illustrazione della Divina Commedia* (Florence, 1962).

[14] Volkmann, 95-159.

[15] Giambattista Vico, *Opere* (Naples, 1860), VI, 24.

[16] Ludovico Antonio Muratori, *Antiquitates italicae medii aevi . . .* (Milan, 1738-39); Girolamo Tiraboschi, *Storia della letteratura italiana,* (Venice, 1782-1785), III, 66 ff.

[17] Muratori, Ch. VIII.

[18] For a further discussion of the revival of interest in the "primitives" and an extensive bibliography, see: Giovanni Previtali, *La fortuna dei primitivi* (Turin, 1964).

[19] Jean Baptiste Louis Georges Seroux d'Agincourt, *Histoire de l'art par les monuments depuis sa décadence au IVe siècle jusqu'à son renouvellement au XVIe* (Paris, 1823).

[20] Guglielmo della Valle, *Lettere Sanesi sopra le Belle Arti* (Venice, 1782-1786), I, 4.

[21] *La grande Encyclopédie* (2d ed.; Paris 1886-1902), III, 1175. Another Dante translator who was also an art collector was the Englishman Charles Rogers (1711-1784), who produced the first complete English translation of the *Inferno* in blank verse in 1782.

[22] Jean-Alexis François Artaud de Montor, *Considérations sur l'état de la peinture dans les trois siècles qui ont précédé Raphaël* (Paris, 1808).

[23] *Peintres primitifs. Collection de tableaux apportée de l'italie et publiée par M. le chevalier Artaud de Montor* (Paris, 1843). Interestingly enough, a large part of Artaud de Montor's collection passed into the Bryan collection and eventually ended in the collections of the New York Historical Society, where it still is today.

[24] *Le Divine Comédie di Dante Alighieri traduite en français par M. le chevalier Artaud de Montor* (Paris, 1811-1813; 2d ed., 1836).

[25] Kermit Vanderbilt, *Charles Eliot Norton* (Cambridge, Mass., 1959), 121-123.

[26] *Ibid., passim.*

[27] Angelina La Piana, *Dante's American Pilgrimage . . .* (New Haven, Conn., 1948), 130.

FRENCH MARKET HALLS IN TIMBER
MEDIEVAL AND POSTMEDIEVAL

Walter Horn and Ernest Born

University of California, Berkeley

FROM THE TWELFTH to the sixteenth centuries the kings of France and their provincial feudatories, impelled by the desire to increase their revenue in taxes, erected in cities whose land they owned large timbered halls in which peasants from the surrounding countryside as well as traveling merchants from close and distant lands found protective shelter for the sale and exchange of produce and goods.

The majority of these buildings—most notable among them the famous medieval market halls of the city of Paris—have disappeared, victims of urban congestion. The few that remain, primarily in cities not exposed to urban sprawl, have not received the attention they deserve, a sin of omission springing from a deep-seated and not easily eradicable prejudice against the study of vernacular architecture current among architectural historians on this as well as on the other side of the Atlantic.

One of the most striking victims of this neglect is the market hall on the small city of Méréville in the department of Seine-et-Oise, France, located at about 70 kilometers southwest of the city of Paris (illus. 1-10).

To the best of our knowledge this structure has never been recorded in architectural drawings worthy of its beauty and historical importance, nor placed in its proper historical perspective. The plans, sections and elevations here published for the first time (illus. 3-5) are based on measurements taken by Ernest Born and myself in the summer of 1960, in the context of a broader inquiry into buildings of this construction type—a study disrupted, unfortunately, by other unavoidable tasks.

In essence this hall is but a large pitched roof supported by a slender frame of timber that divides the space internally into a multitude of separate bays without obstructing the totality of its view. It has no load-bearing walls to close it off from the busy world outside, nor curtain walls to disassemble it internally into disjointed units of space. It is open to the eye all the way through. Its magnificent inner frame of timber discloses instantly the nature and function of each of its component members: their compressive and tensile strength, their ability to support, to brace, to hold apart and to tie together—and in this manner to unite their forces in the creation of a skeletal system of supports capable of holding up a roof of considerable weight without at any place obstructing the full and continuous flow of the space that roof shelters.

Illus. 1. Méréville (Seine-et-Oise) France. Market hall built by Bertrand de Reilhac in 1512. Exterior from northeast. Photo by James W. Roberts.

Illus. 2. Méréville (Seine-et-Oise) France. Market hall built by Bertrand de Reilhac in 1512. Interior looking east. Photo by James W. Roberts.

Because of its monolenticular limitations, the photographic camera does not capture these qualities to their full extent. We are inviting our readers, nevertheless, to absorb as much of these distinctive spatial and structural characteristics as can be done under these limitations by examining the photographs reproduced in illus. 1, 2, 7 and 8, before turning to the descriptive and historical parts of this study.

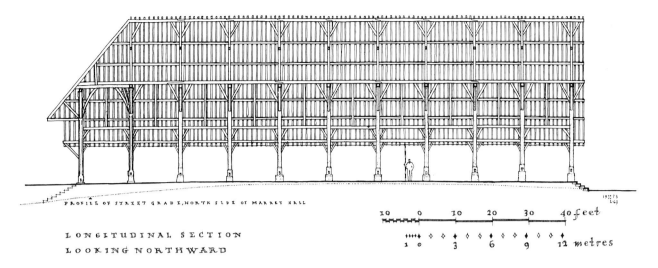

PROFILE OF STREET GRADE, NORTH SIDE OF MARKET HALL

LONGITUDINAL SECTION
LOOKING NORTHWARD

Illus. 3. Méréville (Seine-et-Oise) France. Market hall built by Bertrand de Reilhac in 1512. Longitudinal section by Ernest Born.

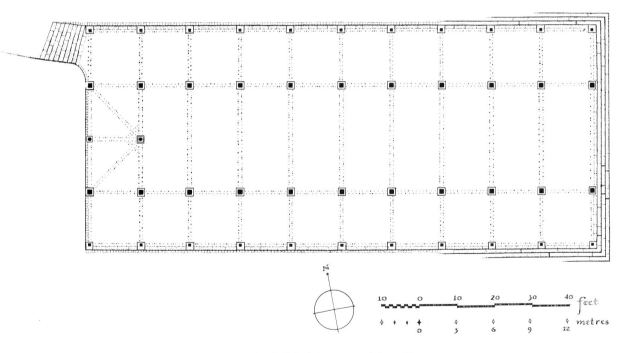

Illus. 4. Méréville (Seine-et-Oise) France. Market hall built by Bertrand de Reilhac in 1512. Plan by Ernest Born.

Illus. 5. Méréville (Seine-et-Oise) France. Market hall built by Bertrand de Reilhac in 1512. Transverse section by Ernest Born.

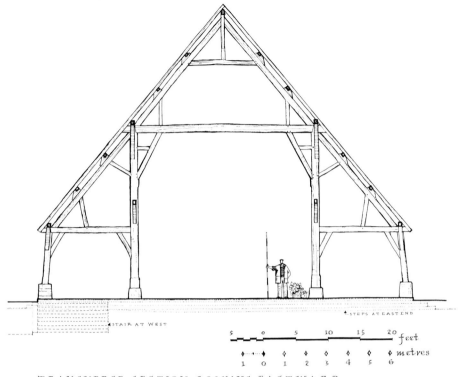

STAIR AT WEST

STEPS AT EAST END

5 0 5 10 15 20 *feet*

1 0 1 2 3 4 5 6 *metres*

TRANSVERSE SECTION LOOKING EASTWARD

THE MARKET HALL OF MÉRÉVILLE (SEINE-ET-OISE)

LAYOUT AND STRUCTURE

The market hall of Méréville is 134 feet, 4 inches long, 56 feet, 7 inches broad, and measures from floor to ridge 44 feet and 4 inches. Its vast, impressive roof, hipped in the west but straight at its principal entrance side in the east, rests on a frame of eleven trusses of timber so constructed as to divide the interior crosswise into a nave and two aisles and lengthwise into a sequence of ten bays. The trusses are fairly evenly spaced and each nave bay appears to be twice as wide as it is deep, while the bays in the aisles in turn are half the surface area of the nave bays. Our measurements were taken with a tape graduated into modern English feet on which one foot is the equivalent of 30.48 centimeters. The builder of the market hall of Méréville probably availed himself of the *pied royal*, which was the equivalent of 32.484 centimeters. It is possible that his structure was conceived within a grid of 40 squares, each measuring 12 by 12 royal feet.

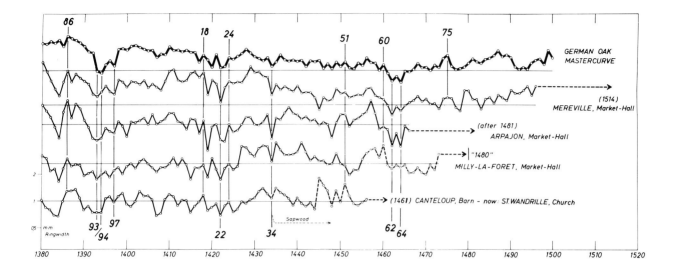

Illus. 6. Tree ring analysis by Veronika Giertz of the timbers of the market halls of Méréville, Arpajon, Milly-la-Forêt and the tithe barn of Canteloup (now serving as church for the Abbey of St. Wandrille). This analysis was the first to demonstrate that French medieval oak can be dated with the aid of dendrochronological master charts worked out for German oak.

Each truss of the hall consists of two principal inner and two shorter outer posts, framed into a triangular system by means of tie beams and principal rafters (illus. 5). None of the roof-supporting timbers is in direct contact with the ground, since each post is placed upon a strong block of stone, thus protecting its fibers from direct exposure to the moisture of the ground. The outer posts lean strongly inward and were originally intended to lean inward, as can be deduced from the design of the joints which are cut to conform with this inclination (illus. 5 and 8). The tie beams are slotted into the posts and stiffened in the corners with strong diagonal braces (illus. 5). Similar braces stiffen the frame in the aisles, the corners between the aisle ties, and the aisle rafters as well as the corners between the main posts and these rafters. The feet of the principal rafters which form the triangular upper tier of the trusses are tenoned into the upper surface of the nave tie beams, while at the top they butt against a king post that rises from a collar beam located 35 feet above the principal tie.

Along the longitudinal axis of the building (illus. 2, 3, and 7) the trusses are consolidated by:

1. four full courses of longitudinal plates resting on the upper surface of the tie beams, directly over the head of the posts;
2. two courses of longitudinal rails butted into the principal posts on either side of the nave about halfway up these posts, and braced against the latter with the aid of angle struts;
3. eight courses of purlins, fastened to the back of the principal

Facing page
Illus. 7. Méréville (Seine-et-Oise)
France. Market hall built by Bertrand
de Reilhac in 1512. Interior looking
east along southern row of supporting
posts. Photo by Philip Spencer.

Illus. 8. Méréville (Seine-et-Oise)
France. Market hall built by Bertrand
de Reilhac in 1512. Exterior, looking
east along the outer posts of the north
aisle. Photo by W. Horn.

rafters (and held in place by shoeblocks), two over each aisle rafter and two over each of the upper rafters;

4. a full-length course of ridge beams tenoned into the head of the king posts and braced from them by means of angle struts.

The roof itself is covered by small tiles (surely not the original skin) on lathwork pegged to the outer rafters (ten to each bay, not counting the ones that lie in the plane of the principal rafters) rising

Illus. 9. Méréville (Seine-et-Oise) France. Market hall built by Bertrand de Reilhac in 1512. Head of center post in hipped portion of hall. Photo by James W. Roberts.

Illus. 10. Méréville (Seine-et-Oise) France. Market hall built by Bertrand de Reilhac in 1512. Joinery of principal posts at level of tie-beam. Photo by Walter Horn.

in two tiers, the lower one from the wall plate to the roof plates, the upper tier from the roof plate to the ridge beam.

One of the most extraordinary components of the carpentry of the roof is the post in the center of the westernmost bay of the hall, that receives the load of the hipped portion of its roof (illus. 9).

The hall is not built on level ground but on the convex surface formed by the top of the hill, on which it stands, as is strikingly shown in illustration 8, a condition to which the carpenter builder adjusted with ingenious simplicity and elegance by lengthening and shortening the outer posts of the hall as required or by modifying the height of the bases from which they rise. Building structures of this kind on sloping ground was standard procedure in the Middle Ages, because of the advantages this condition offers for easy drainage.[1]

The floor of the hall is formed by stamped clay, the natural surface of the ground on which the building stands, and it is framed all around its edges by fine curbstones and, on the entrance side, to a depth of two-and-a-half bays, by three courses of steps that compensate for the sloping surface of the hill, which gives to the otherwise light and transparent structure an unexpected touch of monumentality (illus. 1, 3 and 8).

The scarfing of all the longitudinal courses of timber (plates, purlins, and ridge beams) suggests that the hall was built from west to east. The plates over the principal posts are laid in two-bay spans, the ridge piece in one-bay spans. All timbers are pegged from east to west. There is no evidence to suggest that the trusses were reared as fully assembled frames. The details of joinery suggest that the building was raised in open piece-by-piece assembly.

SEQUENCE OF ERECTION

All posts are standing in their natural upright positions. Heartwood almost all the way up, they only sparingly show waney edges toward their upper ends. Most of the base blocks from which the posts rise are renewed and there is evidence in many places (especially among the two outer rows of posts) that the feet of the posts have been cropped. Otherwise the entire system is old and in good condition, except for the common rafters and the roof skin, which have been renewed, as well as one post in the southeast corner of the hall. All trusses show a slight westward tilt, perhaps caused by aerodynamic stresses: the full force of the wind strikes the open east side while the hipped roof at the western end arrests its flow, thus causing the wind to push the fabric westward. In the westernmost bay the trusses, in addition, list slightly toward south.

CONDITIONS OF TIMBERS AND STATE OF PRESERVATION

The early historians of the old duchy of Etampes to which Méréville belonged assigned the construction of its hall to the year 1511.[2] This view was based on a letter patent of King Louis XII, dated November 14, 1511, which granted to Bertrand de Reilhac, seigneur and Vicomte of Méréville (1503-1522) the right to establish fairs and markets at Méréville.

The full text of this letter patent, dated Blois 14 Novembre 1511, is known through a handwritten copy now kept in the Archives Departémentales of Versailles (*Manuscrit du Instituteur Mulart, École*

HISTORY AND DATE OF THE HALL

Communale de Méréville, 20 Septembre 1899), from which I quote the introductory paragraph:

> We, Louis by the Grace of God [= Louis XII, king of France from 1499-1515] make it known to all present now and in the future, that we have received the humble supplication of our beloved Bertrand de Reilhac, lord and vicomte of Méréville, to the effect that said place of Méréville is located in good and fertile country, where grain and wine are grown, and where daily several merchants pass through coming from all regions. On account of this as well as for the embellishment and future growth of said place, for the profit and utility of the public cause and of the country around it, it would be much required and necessary that there be held in the said place four fairs per year and a market each week, if it were our pleasure that these fairs and markets be established. Wherefore, We, in consideration of all these matters . . .

(There follows in equally convoluted language the official grant of the right to hold the requested fairs and markets.) The letter patent stipulates that these privileges be granted on condition that no other fairs and markets be held on the same days within a distance of four miles around the city. It does not mention the construction of a new hall; and the dating of the surviving structure is complicated by the fact that the fairs and markets of Méréville, a city in a locality that had been heavily damaged during the Hundred Years' War (1338-1453)— and with particular severity during the bitter struggles that preceded the termination of that war!—had in fact already been reinstated by Étienne le Fèvre, Vicomte of Méréville from 1456 to 1472 as can be inferred from an *aveu et dénombrement* of Pierre V de Reilhac, dated June 27, 1482.[3]

On the basis of radiocarbon measurements undertaken by the Isotope Laboratory of the University of California, Los Angeles in 1962 and 1967, we were inclined to ascribe the construction of the market hall of Méréville to Étienne le Fèvre (1456-1472) rather than to Bertrand de Reilhac (1503-1522).[4] A dendrochronological analysis, however, of the timbers of the existing structure, undertaken two years later by Veronika Giertz, under the joint auspices of the University of California at Los Angeles and Berkeley, and the University of Munich, did not confirm this view but disclosed that the trees from which the timbers of the hall were fashioned were felled in 1516 $\pm$ 4 (illus. 6).[5] This established with finality that it was Bertrand de Reilhac and not Étienne le Fèvre who built the present hall. Since the charter entitling the vicomte to "establish fairs and markets" in Méréville was issued on November 14, 1511[6], the spring or summer of 1512 turns out to be the earliest possible time for the construction of the hall.

In the Middle Ages, and until the time of the French Revolution, the right to establish markets and to construct halls to attract and protect trade was held by the local lord or delegated to the local lord by his suzerain, the king. It was from the ownership of the land and the building where merchandise was displayed and sold that the lord derived his prerogative to levy taxes, to control weights and measures, and to lease to merchants the benches and stalls of his hall.

There is no doubt that the cost for the two halls that Phillipe Auguste erected for the market of Champeaux in Paris, in 1183, was carried by the treasury of the Crown,[7] but there existed also toward 1183 a royal market at Roye-en-Vermandoix, where the king considered it advantageous to share the cost for the construction and maintenance of the hall with the burghers[8]—an arrangement which cost the Crown the loss of half of the revenues of the market.[9] Where the volume of trade was immense, as in Paris, sharing the initial costs of construction with others was not to the king's advantage.

The history of the markets of Paris show, however, that once the halls were built, the kings sought to divest themselves of the obligation to keep their halls in good repair, and to transfer this responsibility to the merchant guilds to whom the halls had been leased. It was in this manner that in 1263 St. Louis rid himself of one of his halls in the market of Champeaux in favor of the merchants, although not without conditions: The merchants had to pay an annual rent, carry the financial burden for major and minor repairs, and even take it upon themselves to rebuild the hall, should it be destroyed in its entirety.[10] In adopting agreements of this sort the Crown merely followed the example of the Church, which had made use of similar arrangements at earlier periods. The cartulary of Notre Dame de Paris includes a contract of March, 1216, made between the chapter of the cathedral and one Master Aubry Cornu, according to which the latter was held to pay an annual rent of 30 livres for the lease of a market hall which the chapter had built at Rozoy-en-Brie.[11] In return, the chapter conceded to Master Aubry all revenues derived from the trade carried on in this hall and the right to dispose of these revenues as he saw fit. Master Aubry was held responsible for the maintenance of the hall but the chapter remained responsible for the reconstruction of the hall "in case of a fire—which God forbid—or some other unpredictable event."[12] In this case the hall was not directly leased to the merchants, but to an intermediary who took it upon himself to supervise the

THE RIGHT TO ESTABLISH FAIRS AND MARKETS

smooth conduct of the affairs of the market, to receive the rights attached to it, and keep the buildings in good repair.

The lords of the secular world were not in need of any such intermediaries since they could lean upon the power of their military and juridical organizations for such purposes. Their chatelain and his armed men, as well as a variety of other local functionaries, formed a reliable cadre of men to take care of such matters, should they themselves live at places too distant to be in personal control. There is good documentary evidence to attest this fact.

THE NATURE OF REVENUES FROM MARKET HALLS

An account of revenues *(compte de hallage)* of the year 1320, gives an idea of the size and importance of the taxes the kings levied from their market halls in Paris.[13] Other accounts not as easily accessible furnish us with equally valuable and even more detailed information about the taxes imposed upon their citizenry by the king's vassals in other parts of the country. In 1321 Jean II, dauphin and comte de Savoie erected a market hall in Crémieu, a small urban settlement in Haute Savoie. Article 10 of the foundation charter of this structure dated December 11, 1321, stipulates that the citizens of Crémieu were not obliged to pay any taxes to the dauphin's chatelain as long as they sold their merchandise in their own homes or on benches set up in front of them; but if they took their goods to the market they were obliged "to pay the customary price for the lease of the bench in the hall."[14] According to the official accounts of the Chatellénie of Crémieu for the year 1139 the charge "for small transportable benches rented for the days of the market only" *(parvis benchis minutis, que recipientur die fori)* amounted to 8 florins, whereas the lease of the permanent benches in the interior of the hall *(bancs alberges)* for the entire year amounted to 15½ florins.[15] Article 48 of the charter of 1321 obliges the butchers of the town to surrender to the lord "the tongues of the beef" they had slaughtered as well as the "nombles" of the pigs they offered for sale.[16]

Similar charters define the dauphin's right of ownership and taxation for other market halls in the county, such as that of Montmélian (charter of 1233), St. Symphorien d'Ozon (charter of 1274), Côte-St. André and Roussillon.[17]

By far the most detailed document of this kind, however, is the aforementioned *aveu et dénombrement* of Pierre V de Reilhac, dated June 27, 1482,[18] listing the taxes levied for the market hall of

Méréville, the predecessor of the hall discussed in this paper. The test of this document, which is of prime importance for the study of the jurisdictional and economic structure of the medieval institution of markets and fairs in France, has so far been published only in brief excerpts (not free of errors)[19] and for that reason is here given almost in its entirety, in a transliteration of the original as well as in a translation into English; both versions we owe to the skill and kindness of our colleague Leonard Johnson:

Transliteration

Item les foires et les marches et la coutume dudit marche, lequel marche se commence le lundy a Nonne et dure le mardy tout le jour, et ceux qui vendent aucune denree depuis lad. heure de nonne du lundy et le mardy tout le jour tant au marche comme ailleurs partout la paroisse de Méréville ou venants vendre led. jour et lad. denree se vend sur sepmaine doivent aussy la coustume en laquelle coustume le vicomte souloit prendre sur aucunes denrees la moitie de lad. coustume et sur le autres denrees le tiers denier, de laquelle coustume la declaration sensuit.

Et premierement tous les boulangers qui vendent pain en charette chacun an chacune charette doit un denier et les autres qui vendent hors chareete doivent maille.

Item chacun mercier vendant au jour du marche doivent chacun mardy maille.

Item tous les minages de tous les grains qui sont vendus de tous ceux de la paroisse de Méréville qui vendent au jour du mardy et du lundy pois lad. heure de nonne ou offrent vendre aud. marche comme dessus est dit parmy la paroisse de Méréville doivent de vingt-quatre muids unce, et du plus plus et du moins moins. Item tous les hanages du sol nouveaux. Item la coutume des lins et chanvres faulx et serpes pots verres et hanaps qui sont vendus a chacun marchand dan en an vendus aud. marche doivent six deniers. Item une charette un cheval charge a somme de sel peut devoir au cas qui vend en gros lesquels doivent chacun an une mine de sel pour toute lanne si vend aud. marche. Item tous les marchands vendans gresses cest asscavoir oings remieux chandelles et autres gresses doivent chacun un denier. Item aussy les vendeurs de souliers neufs doivent aussy un denier a chacun marche. Item tous less bouchers vendans chair en la halle de Méréville doivent chacun an chacun une jambe de porc ou le poids quelle est prisee. Item tous les bouchers vendans chair en lad. ville et tous les drapiers doivent chacun mardy trois mailles. Item tous ceux qui vendent souliers repareillez doivent chacun mardy [blank in text]. Item chacun poulaillet doit deux deniers pour toute lannee. Item tous les regrestiers qui vendent et acheptent doivent chacun marche un denier. Item tous vendeurs de fer, de clou, happes et autres denrees et ferrerie doivent au marche chacun maille. Item tous vendeurs de souliers de bazanne megissiers et autres denrees doivent chacun poitevine. Item chacun sellier doit maille chacun an.

Translation

Item, the fairs and markets and the tax on the said market, which begins on Mondays at nones[20] and lasts all day on Tuesdays; and those who sell any merchandise from the said hour of nones on Mondays and all day on Tuesdays in the market as well as everywhere else throughout the parish of Méréville; or those who, coming to sell on the said day, sell their wares during the week, also owe the tax; on which tax the viscount was accustomed to take half of the said tax on some merchandise and on others the third *denier*.[21] The declaration of this tax follows.

And first, all the bakers who sell bread in carts: each year each cart owes one *denier*, and the others, who sell without a cart, owe a *maille*.[22]

Item, each peddler selling on market day owes a *maille* each Tuesday.

Item, all the measures of grain which are sold by all those of the parish of Méréville who sell on Tuesdays and on Mondays after the said hour of nones or who, from the said market, sell within the parish of Méréville, as said above, owe one ounce out of twenty-four *muids*,[23] and proportionately more or less. Item, all new harvests.

Item, the tax on flax and hemp, scythes, and billhooks, pots, glasses and goblets, which are sold to each merchant yearly in the said market, owe six *deniers*. Item, a horse with a load of salt can owe each year a *mine*[24] of salt for the whole year if it is sold at the market. Item, all the sellers of fats, that is, unguents, tallow, candles and other fats, each owe one *denier*. Item, all the shoemakers selling cowhide each owe a *denier*. Item, also, the sellers of new shoes owe a *denier* at each transaction. Item, all butchers selling meat in the market building of Méréville owe each year a leg of pork or the equivalent of its weight. Item, all the butchers selling meat in the said city and all the drapers owe three *mailles* every Tuesday. Item, all those who sell mended shoes owe [blank in text] each Tuesday. Item, each poulterer owes two *deniers* for the whole year. Item, all the second hand dealers who buy and sell owe one *denier* at each transaction. Item, all ironmongers and hardware salesmen each owe one *denier* at the transaction. Item, all sellers of shoes made of sheep's leather, tawers, and the like each owe *poitevine*.[25] Item, each saddler owes a *maille* each year.

OTHER MEDIEVAL AND POST-MEDIEVAL MARKET HALLS OF FRANCE

When, precisely, the need arose to display for sale agricultural produce and other goods of trade under the roof of large aisled halls is not known, but it is reasonable to assume that this was one of the consequences of the general commercial prosperity that reigned in Europe after the reconquest in the eleventh century of Mediterranean sea-lanes by the merchant fleets of Pisa and Venice. The market hall is one of the signal architectural expressions of that prosperity.

The earliest halls of France of which we have positive documentary evidence are those which Philippe Auguste erected in 1183 on the market of Champeux in Paris.[26] Under St. Louis (1226-1270) their number was increased by two further halls, specifically for

Illus. 11. St. Pierre-sur-Dives (Calvados) Normandy, France. Market hall, thirteenth-fourteenth century. Exterior from southwest. Photo by Philip Spencer.

the fishery trade, and 1278 Philip the Bold added another one for the skin-dressers and shoemakers.[27] Subsequently, each guild or corporation built its own hall and the number of halls owned by the merchants of Paris was further increased by those which other towns maintained in Paris. By the end of the fourteenth century the agglomeration of halls in the market of Paris had become so great that instead of employing the word *"halle"* in the singular as was previously done, the plural form *"halles"* was employed even when meant to refer to only a single building—a designation rarely abandoned in any subsequent period.

The medieval market halls of Paris have disappeared. They were torn down in the course of far-reaching modifications of the Quartier des Halles undertaken between 1543 and 1572. In the large cities of France, which continued to grow after the Middle Ages, the old market halls, in like manner, were wiped out by the exigencies of more complex ways of living. Only in quiet places of the country such as Méréville, where past traditions are more

Illus. 12. St. Pierre-sur-Dives (Cal-vados) Normandy, France. Market hall, thirteenth-fourteenth century. Interior looking east, rebuilt after fire of 1944. Photo by Philip Spencer.

purely preserved, do we still find the living record of those vast shadowy halls which in former days sheltered so much of Europe's commerce and wealth.

The oldest, perhaps, and certainly the largest among the surviving market halls of France is the hall of St. Pierre-sur-Dives in the department of Calvados in Normandy (illus. 11-14).[28] Unlike Méréville, and virtually all the other market halls of France, the roof-supporting timber-frame of this hall is encased in a monumental shell of masonry. In this respect the hall looks more like a medieval tithe barn (illus. 37-39). The style of its masonry suggests a thirteenth- or fourteenth-century date.

The hall has a clear inner length of 225 feet, a clear inner width of 64 feet, and rises at its ridge to a height of 42 feet. Its vast and commanding roof is carried by thirteen widely spaced trusses at intervals varying between 16 feet 1 inch and 18 feet 6 inches. These trusses are connected by a system of longitudinal timbers in essence identical with that of Méréville. The hall was shelled and severely

Bouet del.

ENTRÉE PRINCIPALE DES HALLES DE SAINT-PIERRE-SUR-DIVE.

Illus. 13. St. Pierre-sur Dives (Calvados) Normandy, France. Market hall, thirteenth-fourteenth century. Exterior of northern gable wall (after M. de Caumont, Statistique Monumentale du Calvados, *vol. 5 [Paris-Caen 1867], p. 563).*

Illus. 14. St. Pierre-sur-Dives (Calvados) Normandy, France. Market hall, thirteenth-fourteenth century. Plan by Ernest Born.

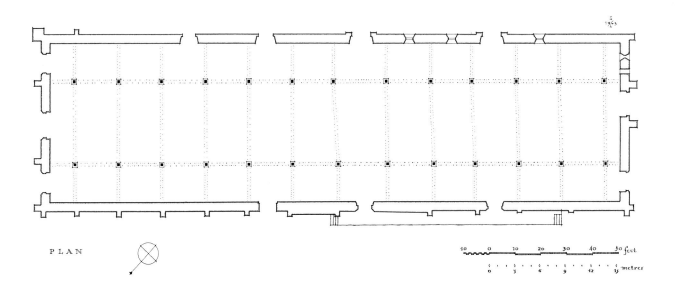

PLAN

Illus. 15. Crémieu (Isère) France. Market hall, 1314. Exterior from northwest. Photo by André Leconte.

Illus. 16. Crémieu (Isère) France. Market hall, 1314. Interior view looking west. Photo by W. Horn.

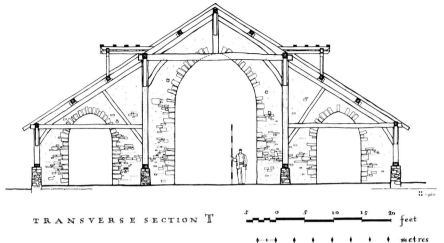

Illus. 17. Crémieu (Isère) France. Market Hall, 1314. Transverse section by Ernest Born.

Illus. 18. Crémieu (Isère) France. Market hall. Plan and longitudinal section by Ernest Born.

TRANSVERSE SECTION T

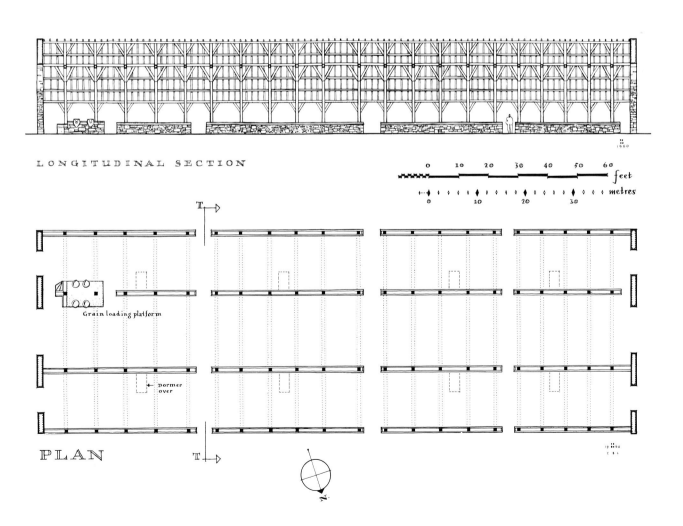

LONGITUDINAL SECTION

Grain loading platform

→ Dormer over

PLAN

damaged by the retreating German army in World War II (1944), but skillfully restored after termination of hostilities and formally re-inaugurated in 1949.

Second in age, presumably, as well as in length is the market hall of Crémieu, Isère (illus. 15-18). It was erected between 1315 and 1321 by the dauphin Jean II.[29] Its gables are built in masonry and pierced by large pointed arches. On the sides the hall is open. Its outer posts rise from low masonry walls—not high enough to visually disassociate inner and outer space. The hall is 200 feet long, 64 feet wide, but only 28 feet high. Its roof is supported by 22 trusses (a numerical record for this type of construction) spaced at the unusually short distance of only 9 feet. The low pitch of the roof discloses that the hall was built on territory where Roman and northern influences intermix.

Next in line chronologically are the market halls of the city of Milly-la-Forêt (illus. 19-22) and of Arpajon (illus. 23-26).[30] These two buildings are so similar in design and structural detail that one is tempted to ascribe them to the same master carpenter. Both are of virtually the same dimension. Milly is 145 feet long, 52 feet wide, and 40 feet high. The corresponding dimensions of Arpajon are 142 feet by 56 feet by 40 feet. In both cases the roof is carried by twelve aisled trusses raised at an average distance of 13 feet. Both halls are open on all four sides. There are minor differences in the design of the terminal bays. In Milly the southern gable end is straight while the northern end is hipped over the terminal bay. By contrast in Arpajon the roof of the hall is hipped over both of its terminal bays. The most striking similarity between the two structures is to be found in the design of the nave trusses in the triangular area above the tie beam (illus. 20-21). This part of the truss is formed, in each case, by two principal rafters rising from opposite ends of the tie beam to converge in the head of a tall king post that carries the ridge beam. The king post exerts no pressure whatsoever upon the tie beam on which it appears to stand.[31] It is held suspended by the two converging principal rafters which in discharging their roof load on the outer ends of the tie beam put the latter into tension, thus counteracting any tendencies it might have toward sagging in the middle in response to either its own or any superincumbent weight. The ridge beam is fastened to the king posts by mortice and tenon joints. It keeps the trusses equidistant and in this manner protects the roof from tilting in the longitudinal sense. In both, Milly-la-Forêt and Arpajon the main ridge is sup-

Illus. 21. Milly-la Forêt (Seine-et-Oise) France. Market hall, shortly after 1479. Transverse section by Ernest Born.

Illus. 22. Milly-la-Forêt (Seine-et-Oise) France. Market hall, shortly after 1479. Plan by Ernest Born.

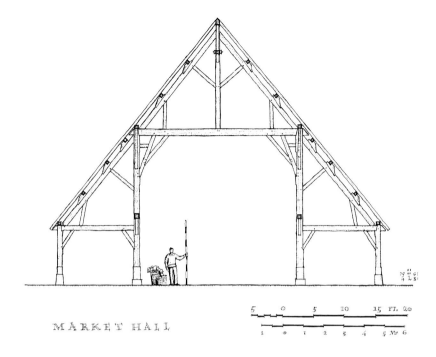

MARKET HALL

TRANSVERSE SECTION LOOKING NORTHWARD

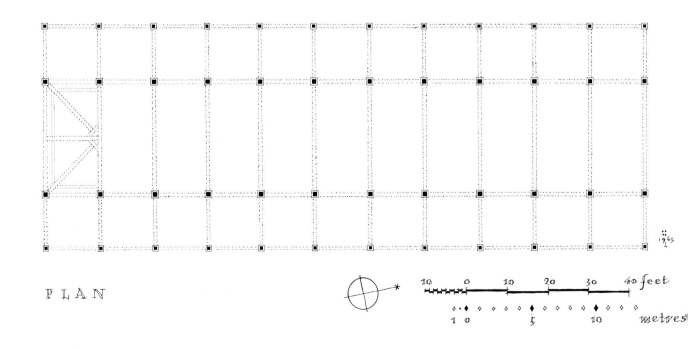

PLAN

Illus. 23. Arpajon (Seine-et-Oise) France. Market hall, shortly after 1481. Exterior view from southeast. Photo by Rameau.

Illus. 24. Arpajon (Seine-et-Oise) France. Market hall, shortly after 1481. Interior looking west. Photo by Rameau.

Illus. 25. Arpajon (Seine-et-Oise) France. Market hall, shortly after 1481. Transverse section by Ernest Born.

Illus. 26. Arpajon (Seine-et-Oise) France. Market hall, shortly after 1481. Plan by Ernest Born.

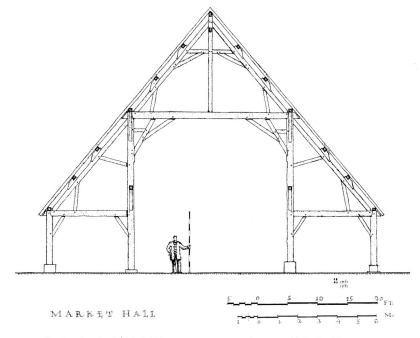

MARKET HALL

TRANSVERSE SECTION LOOKING NORTHWARD

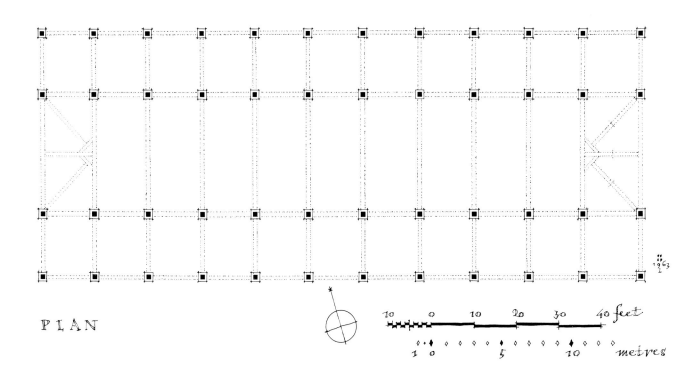

PLAN

ported in this task by a subridge, the component members of which are tenoned longitudinally into the king posts a short distance below the main ridge.

The date of construction of the hall of Milly-la-Forêt can be established with full accuracy by an undisputable document: a *lettre patente* of Louis XI, issued on May 5, 1479, written in the pompous and convoluted language characteristic for this type of document. In this letter the emperor authorizes his cousin Louis Mallet de Graville, Amiral de France, to establish markets and fairs in the city of Milly and to construct a hall for that purpose.[32] The decisive phrase as far as the construction of the hall is concerned is: "Voulons et nous plaist Que Notre Dit Cousin et sesd. successeurs puisse faire et faire faire Bastir [halle] et construire et edifier [Halle]." Veronika Giertz's dendrochronological analysis of the timbers of the existing hall is in full accord with this testimony (illus. 6). It discloses that its timbers were felled in 1480.

A poster affixed to one of the posts of the hall of Arpajon proclaims that this building was erected by that same Amiral Louis Mallet de Graville between 1450 and 1470. Our tree ring analysis of this structure did not confirm this date but yielded the term "shortly after 1481" as the most likely date of construction (illus. 6). This supports our hypothesis, based on structural observations, that the two halls were designed by the same master and built at more or less the same time. The hall of Méréville comes next in date.

Further, extremely well preserved, but considerably later in date are the halls of the city of Richelieu, built between 1631 and 1640 by Cardinal Richelieu,[33] and the hall of the city of Questembert in the department of Morbihan in Brittany (illus. 27–30) built in 1675.[34] There are many more[35]—none of them properly investigated.

ORIGINS

Until a few decades ago we knew virtually nothing about the origins of the type of construction employed in the French market halls discussed in this paper, but recent discoveries made in The Netherlands, Germany, the Scandinavian countries, Iceland, and England have made it clear that they descend from a type of timber building that was in general use throughout vast stretches of northwestern Europe during prehistoric, protohistoric, and medieval times. In all of these periods its primary function was to serve as

Illus. 27. Questembert (Morbihan) France. Market hall. Exterior from southeast. Photo by Jos.

Illus. 28. Questembert (Morbihan) France. Market hall, 1675. Interior looking west. Photo by James.W. Roberts.

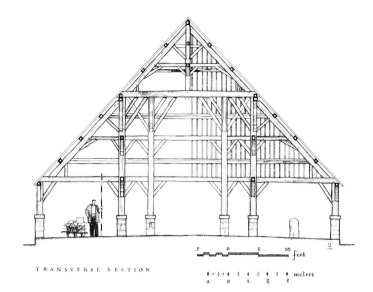

TRANSVERSE SECTION

Illus. 29. Questembert (Morbihan) France. Market hall, 1675. Transverse section by Ernest Born.

Illus. 30. Questembert (Morbihan) France. Market hall, 1675. Plan and longitudinal section by Ernest Born.

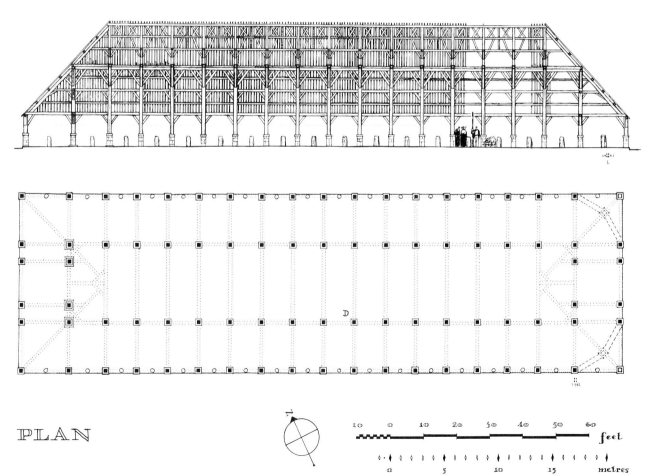

PLAN

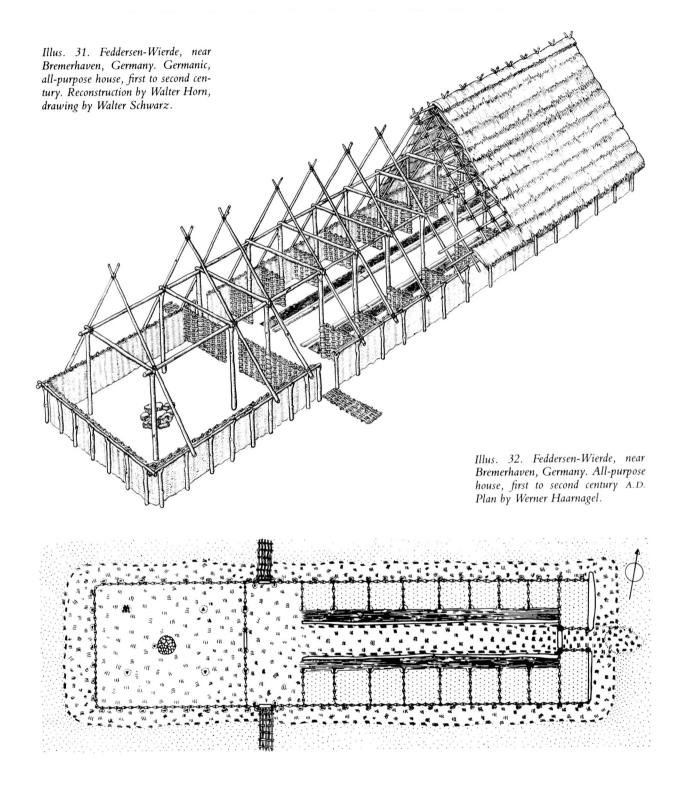

Illus. 31. Feddersen-Wierde, near Bremerhaven, Germany. Germanic, all-purpose house, first to second century. Reconstruction by Walter Horn, drawing by Walter Schwarz.

Illus. 32. Feddersen-Wierde, near Bremerhaven, Germany. All-purpose house, first to second century A.D. Plan by Werner Haarnagel.

a dwelling for landholders, accommodating, often under a single roof, both a family and their livestock.

We have a typical example from the first and second centuries B.C. in a farmstead excavated in 1955, at a place called Fedderson Wierde in northern Germany (illus. 31 and 32).[36] The presence of an open fireplace in the southeastern end of the building make it clear that the first three bays of the house were used by the farmer and his family, while the layout of the remaining bays leave no doubt that the principal part of the house was used for the stabling of livestock, two heads of cattle being accommodated in each bay of the aisles.

When the first continental examples of the house type were excavated in 1934-1936, at Ezinge, Province Groningen,[37] The Netherlands, they were a unique phenomenon, but in the three decades that followed more than two hundred houses of the same construction type were discovered in The Netherlands, northern Germany, Scandinavia, Saxon England, Iceland, and even Greenland.[38] Later excavations brought the even more startling discovery that this same type was a standard construction form in the Lowlands as early as 1250 B.C. and perhaps even in the fourteenth century B.C.[39] It is clear, therefore, that the aisled medieval timber hall, as well as its urban derivative the aisled market hall, were descendants of a building type which by the end of the Middle Ages had already reached a life-span of close to three thousand years, and which in The Netherlands and in northern Germany continues to be used even today, with only minor modifications, for the same purpose for which it was originally conceived, in the form of the Frisian *Los Hus* and the Lower Saxon *Wohnstallhaus.*

The famous Plan of St. Gall (a copy made around 820 of a masterplan for a monastic settlement worked out we believe in the course of two reform synods held in the Palace of Emperor Louis the Pious at Aachen in 816 and 817) attests that this type of building was in the ninth century a common form of house construction employed on both the highest and lowest levels of Frankish society.

We are reproducing in illustrations 33 and 34 the outline and a reconstruction of the House for Distinguished Guests shown in the Plan. It consists of a central hall for dining *(domus hospitum ad prandendum)* which had its tables and benches peripherally ranged around an open fireplace *(locus foci).* A subsidiary suite of outer spaces accommodated the traveling emperor and his court *(caminatae cum lectis)* as well as his servants and horses *(cubilia servitorum;*

Illus. 33. Plan of St. Gall, c. 820. House for Distinguished Guests. Author's reconstruction, drawn by Ernest Born.

stabula caballarum). The reader will observe that the horses, to reach their stables in the rear of the house, had to be guided through the dining room.

The Plan of St. Gall shows ten more houses of precisely that same design although not quite as elaborately drawn: a House for the Emperor's Vassals, a Hospice for Pilgrims and Paupers, a Great Collective Workshop (where the monastery's workmen and craftsmen were housed), a House for Servants of Outlying Estates, a great Granary for storage of the annual harvest, plus three to five houses for the monastic livestock and their keepers.

Since the scheme delineated on the Plan of St. Gall is not the image of an existing monastery site, but a prototypal plan that shows of what buildings a Benedictine monastery should be com-

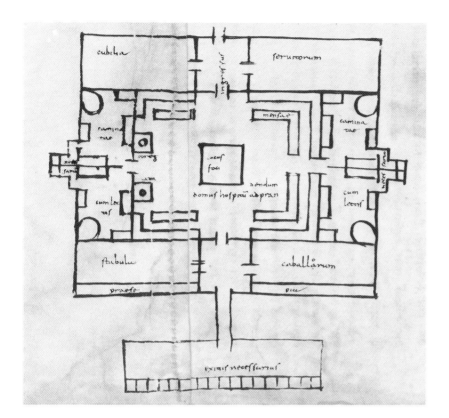

prised and how these should relate topographically to one another, it offers us in these drawings nothing less than a cross section of the architecture of the entire Carolingian countryside.[40]

As everywhere else in the Germanic territories of medieval Europe so in England, after its conquest by the Anglo-Saxons—and increasingly so with the arrival of the Normans—this building type must have had a phenomenal density of distribution. Hall Heorot of the famous Beowulf epic belonged to this tradition.[41]

Other royal audience halls of this design have been excavated at Old Yeavering, Northumbria (616-932),[42] and at Cheddar, Somerset (1100-1135).[43] The earliest surviving examples are the Great Hall of the castle of Leicester, Leicestershire, ca. 1150 (illus. 35),[44] and the Great Hall of the Bishop's Palace at Hereford, Herefordshire, ca. 1180.[45]

The spacious interior of Leicester Hall was ruined in the nineteenth century when it was divided into three separate courtrooms

Illus. 35. Leicester Castle, Leicester, England. Interior of the Great Hall. Reconstruction by T. H. Fosbrook (after Fox, 1942/43).

by internal wall partitions. The majestic quality and spaciousness of its original appearance are faithfully and convincingly rendered in a woodcut by Thomas Fosbrooke, made in 1919. The Hall of Hereford had been struck by a similar misfortune as early as the eighteenth century when the bishops, in search of privacy and greater comfort, encased its magnificent timber frame in a jumble of inner subdivisions which forever destroyed its structural beauty.

The largest and most celebrated extant example of this genre of building is Westminster Hall (illus. 36, *A* and *B*), principal audience hall of the kings of England, which in its original form as built by William Rufus (1097-1099), must have had the appearance of a market hall of colossal dimensions. Today this hall is covered by a single span, a masterpiece of hammerbeam construction, which Richard II raised at the end of the fourteenth century.[46] But prior to the invention of the arch-braced hammerbeam, a hall of this enormous width could not have been spanned in single trusses and could only have been supported by two rows of freestanding inner timber or masonry posts dividing the structure lengthwise into a nave and two aisles and crosswise into a sequence of bays. We can make a convincing picture of what that system must have appeared

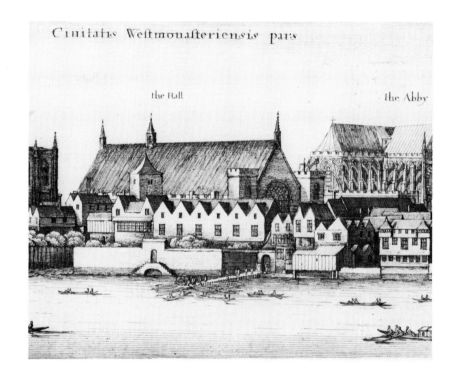

Cuitatis Westmonasteriensis pars

the Hall   the Abby

*Illus. 36,*A. *Westminster Hall, England. Exterior View of Royal Hall built by William Rufus (1079-1099). Engraving by W. Holland, 1647.*

*Illus. 36,*B. *Westminster Hall, England. Plan of original hall schematically reconstructed by W. R. Lethaby (redrawn by Ernest Born).*

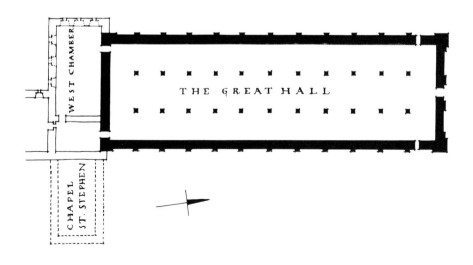

WEST CHAMBER

CHAPEL ST. STEPHEN

THE GREAT HALL

in its original form by stepping into one of the monumental tithe barns of the great monastic orders, such as the thirteenth-century barn of Great Coxwell in Berkshire (illus. 37–40). This is, in its essential lines, what the royal hall in the palace of Westminster must have looked like from the time of William Rufus to that of Richard II when it was the administrative center at which a major portion of the political history of England was forged.

In medieval England, hall and barn were structurally interchangeable, and if there were any difference between the two, it was that the barns in general were considerably larger and infinitely more numerous than halls. Few medieval manors were in need of more than one hall, but every medieval manor needed three or four barns on its scattered holdings.

The need was even greater for the large monastic orders whose land holdings, in general, exceeded those of the average secular feudatory, as is put into powerful visual relief by a glance at the monumental tithe barn of Great Coxwell (illus. 37–40) whose timber frame and striking external building masses are of cathedral-like beauty.[47] Among comparable continental structures are the large monastic barn of Ter Doest in Belgium or the vast roof of the Abbey grange of Parçay-Meslay, Department of Indre-et-Loire, France.[48]

SUMMARY AND CONCLUSIONS

Our analysis shows that the medieval and postmedieval market halls of France, with their impressive timber frame dividing the interior crosswise into a nave and two aisles and lengthwise into a continuous sequence of rectangular bays, has its origin in the Germanic all-purpose house which, in a multitude of different functional applications, forms one of the principal features of rural and manorial architecture of the Middle Ages.

The most distinguished trait of this type of structure is that with only a minimum of materials it offers an ingeniously simple method of covering large spaces beneath a vast roof carried by a frame of relatively thin yet strong timbers which divide the whole into a modular sequence of subordinate spaces without in any manner marring the totality of its visual appearance. It is to this extraordinary ability to offer simultaneously spatial unity and spatial divisibility that this building owes its longevity and its unusual flexibility.

By origin almost exclusively confined to dwelling, the sheltering of animals, and harvest storage, in response to the growing com-

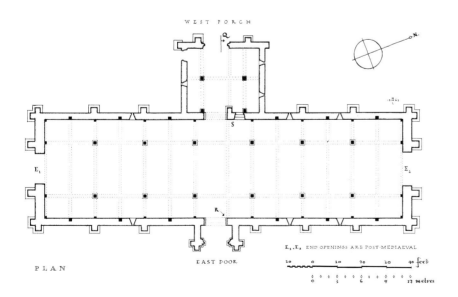

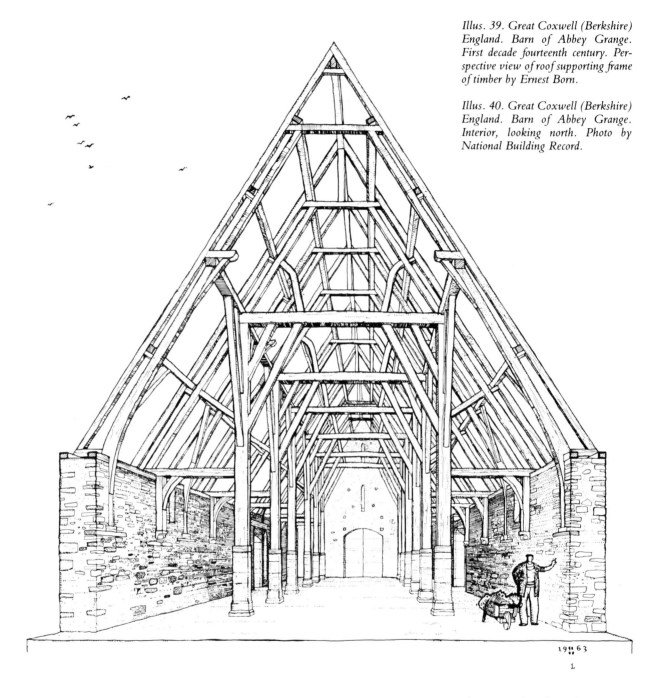

Illus. 39. Great Coxwell (Berkshire) England. Barn of Abbey Grange. First decade fourteenth century. Perspective view of roof supporting frame of timber by Ernest Born.

Illus. 40. Great Coxwell (Berkshire) England. Barn of Abbey Grange. Interior, looking north. Photo by National Building Record.

BARN, ABBEY GRANGE, GREAT COXWELL, BERKSHIRE, ENGLAND
VIEW LOOKING NORTHWARD

plexities of medieval life and social organization the structure entered into a virtually explosive phase of functional variability. On the highest level of society it appeared as a residential and administrative seat for feudal lords and their retainers including the king himself (illus. 35 and 36). In the country it was used as a church; in the town as a hospital for the sick and infirm, and as a meeting and council hall for guilds. It reached its peak of constructional beauty both in England and on the continent in the great monastic tithe barns, an outstanding example of which appears in illustrations 37–40. From the twelfth century onward, in response to the rise of international trade, it became in Paris and countless smaller towns of France the standard form for urban market halls under whose protective roof the local peasantry and traders from distant lands would sell their produce and goods in rented stalls (illus. 1-30).

The history of this important building type is as yet unwritten. In the pursuit of an intense, yet highly unilinear preoccupation with the history of ecclesiastical architecture, our profession has fallen into the grip of a prejudice against the study of vernacular architecture that not only has kept us ignorant of the greatness of our own architectural past, rural and feudal, but also has retarded our understanding of the impact this building tradition had on the shaping of two of the greatest ecclesiastical styles of the West, the modular, skeletal, and bay-divided architecture of the Romanesque and Gothic.

NOTES

[1] For other occurrences of similar conditions; see Walter Horn and Ernest Born, *The Barns of the Abbey of Beaulieu at Its Granges of Great Coxwell and Beaulieu St. Leonard's* (Berkeley and Los Angeles, 1965), p. 3; Walter Horn and F. W. B. Charles, "The Cruck-built Barn of Middle Littleton in Worchestershire, England," *Journal of the Society of Architectural Historians*, XXV (1966), 224–226; and F. W. B. Charles and Walter Horn, "The Cruck-built Barn of Leigh Court, Worcestershire, England," ibid., XXXII (1973), 11–12.

[2] For a partial publication of this text see Abbé C. Bernois, "Histoire de Méréville," *Annales de la Société Historique et Archéologique du Gâtinais*, XX (1902), 339.

[3] For a fuller treatment of this document see below, pp. 208–210.

[4] For a summary of the radiocarbon measurements of the timber of the market hall of Méréville, see Walter Horn, "The Potential and Limitations of Radiocarbon Dating in the Middle Ages: The Art Historian's View" in Rainer Berger, ed. *Scientific Methods in Medieval Archaeology* (Contributions of the UCLA Center for Medieval Studies, Berkeley and Los Angeles, 1970), pp. 31–35; and Rainer Berger, "The Potential and Limitations of Radiocarbon Dating in the Middle Ages: The Radiochronologist's View," ibid., pp. 110–111.

[5]Veronika Giertz's dendrochronological findings have so far only been announced in the paper presented by me for the team at the London meeting of the Vernacular Architecture Group in December 1970, and published in a preliminary form in *Vernacular Architecture*, II (1971), 3–6, which also contains a summary by F. W. B. Charles of the research of the continuation of this work in England.

[6]Bernois, "Histoire de Méréville," p. 339.

[7]Leon Biollay, "Les Anciennes Halles de Paris," *Mémoires de la Société de l'Histoire de Paris et de l'Ile de France,* III (1877), 297.

[8]Ordonnances des rois de France, vol. XI, p. 230. Cf. Victor Mortet and Paul Deschamps, *Recueil de Textes relatifs à l'Histoire de l'Architecture* (Paris, 1929), p. 145.

[9]Ibid.: "Nos autem medictatem sumptuum ad predictam halam faciendam et reparandam apponemus et medictatem proventuum precipiemus, et burgenses similiter medictatem apponent et medictatem percipient."

[10]Biollay, "Les Anciennes Halles de Paris," p. 297.

[11]The document is quoted by Mortet and Deschamps, *Recueil de Textes,* pp. 223–224.

[12]Ibid: "Ex tunc autem modicos sumptus, si qui faciendi essent, teneor (sc. magister Albericus Cornutus) de meo facere, et tam halas quam cellarium in bono stato conservare; magnos verosumptus qui forte, quod Deus avertat, ex lucendio vel alio infortunio contingeret, capitulum de suo facere teneretur."

[13]"Produit de hallage de Paris," published by George Bernhard Depping, in "Regelements sur les Arts et Métiers d'Étienne Boileau" (Collection de documents inedits sur l'histoire de la France, 1st series, III,4 (Paris, 1837), pp. 433–436. For the date of his compte, cf. Biollay, "Les Anciennes Halles de Paris," p. 294.

[14]Roland Delachenal, *Charte de Crémieu,* p. 41: (Extrait du Bulletin de l'Académie Delphinale, 3e ser., XX, Grenoble, 1886, pp. 1–70): "Quicumque bancham suam vel habebunt propriam in dicta villa ante domum suam, vel conductam, nichil debeant domini usagii pro illa bancha, sed si deportent res sual venales, quecumque fuerint, ad mercatum domini, debent domino pro locacione banche prout ibidem consuetum est."

[15]Ibid., n. 4.

[16]Ibid., p. 54: "Nombles" from Latin *umbilicus*; Low Latin *numbulus* or *lumbulus*; German *Lende*; the inner part of the thigh of a pig. See Fréderick Godefroy, *Dictionnaire de l'Ancienne Langue Française du XVe Siècle,* V, Paris, 1888, s.v. (where *"nomble"* is also interpreted as "echinel de porc").

[17]For references to these sources see Horn and Born, "Les Halles de Crémieu, Isère, France," pp. 23–25.

[18]*Aveu et dénombrement de al baronnie de Méréville, rendu par Pierre Reilhac, echanson du roi, à Jean de Foix, Comte d'Étampes, 27 Juin 1482.* Archives Départmentales de Versailles.

[19]For a partial publication of this text see Bernois, "Histoire de Méréville," p. 339.

[20]Nones: the canonical hour, varying between about two-thirty P.M. in the winter and three-thirty in the summer.

[21]*Denier*: a small coin, the weight of one two-hundred-fortieth of a pound of silver. For this term and the terms listed in notes 22-25 see *A Dictionarie of the*

French and English Tongues, compiled by Randle Cotgrave. Reproduced from the first edition, London 1611, with introduction by William S. Woods, (Columbia University of South Carolina Press, 1950).

[22]*Maille*: half a *denier*. (Cotgrave, *s.v.*)

[23]*Muid*: a measure of weight, used for grain, coal, and so on. Cotgrave, *s.v.* defines a *muid de blé* as "contaures twelve *Septiers* (the *Septier* two *Mines*, the *Mine* six *Boisseaux*; the *Boisseau* fours Quarts) which come to about five Quarters, a Combe, and a Bushell of London measure."

[24]*Mine*: a measure of weight; "half of a *Sextier*, and 24 part of a *Muid*" (Cotgrave, *s.v.*).

[25]*Poitevine*: "a French farthing, or the fourth part of the *Denier Tournois*" (Cotgrave). It is easy to read "poitrine" instead of "poitevine," but that makes no sense (Cotgrave, *s.v.*).

[26]The construction of these halls is mentioned in the *Chronicon Guillelmi de Nangis* (see *Recueil de Historiens de Gaule et de la France*, vol. XX (Paris, 1840), and in H. François Delaborde ed., *Gesta Philippi Augusti de Rigord* (Paris, Société de l'Histoire de France, 1882), p. 30.

Parisius in platea quam Campelles nominant hallas construi et mercatum in eis fieri instituit (Guilelmus de Nangis): Parisius . . . duas magnas domos, quas vulgus halas vocat, edificari fecit (Rigord)

[27]For the history of Les Halles of Paris, see Henri Sauval, *Histoire et Recherches des Antiquités de la ville de Paris*, vol. I (Paris, 1724), pp. 647–648; and Biollay, "Les Anciennes Halles de Paris," pp. 293–355.

[28]For the market hall of St. Pierre-sur-Dives, see Raymond Queneday, *Les Provinces de l'Ancienne France, La Normandie, Calvados*, vol. II (Paris, 1929), p. 2 who assigns the hall to the thirteenth century. Camile Enlart (*Manual d'Archéologie Française*, 2d augmented ed., vol. II, part I [Paris, 1929], p. 380 n. 3) dates the hall to the fourteenth or fifteenth century.

[29]For Crémieu see Horn and Born, "Les Halles de Crémieu, Isère, France," pp. 66–90.

[30]Monographic studies of these two important buildings are as yet wanting.

[31]In the trusses, designed along similar lines, but at a considerable lower pitch, of the roof of the church of the Monastery of Saint Catherine at Mount Sinai the king post does not even reach down to the level of the tie beam, but is freely suspended in the air. The roof of this church, built between 548 and 565, is the earliest Christian church roof known. Although hidden from sight by wooden panels which were not part of the original fabric, the timbered trusses of this roof survive in pristine condition. For more detail see George H. Forsyth and Kurt Weitzman, *The Monastery of Saint Catherine at Mount Sinai, The Church and Fortress of Justinian* (Ann Arbor, 1965), p. 8 and Plates LXXXII–LXXXIII.

[32]This *lettre patente* of Louis XI authorizing the construction of the hall of Milly is to be found in the archives of the city of Milly under the listing *Registre des Titres de la Baronnie de Milly* D:I P:I. It is a document of prime importance, not only because of the certainty of its date but also for the light it sheds on the economy and privileges associated with such grants.

This letter (to the best of my knowledge never published) was brought to my attention by the late Comte de St. Périer de Morignon. A transcript has been made available to me Mr. Raymond Geber of Milly, member of the Commission des Antiquités et des Art de Seine-et-Oise, to whom I feel deeply indebted for that courtesy.

[33]For Richelieu see Henriette de Chizeray, *Le Cardinal Richelieu et son Duché-Pairie* (Paris, 1961); Gabriel Hanotaux, *Histoire du Cardinal de Richelieu*, vol. VI (Paris, 1947), pp. 327–382 ("Le chateau et la ville du Richelieu"); and L. A. Bosseboeuf, "Histoire de Richelieu et des environs au point de vue civil, religieux et artistique," *Mémoires de la Société archéologique de Touraine*, XXXV (1890), 266–290 (Création et organization de la ville, duché"). A good architectural survey of this building is still wanting. Radiocarbon measurements are discussed on pp. 38 and 113 of the articles by Walter Horn and Rainer Berger cited in note 4, above.

[34]For Questembert see Walter Horn, "Les Halles de Questembert," *Bulletin de la Société Polymathique du Morbihan* (1963), pp. 1–16, and M. E. Marquer, publishing under the pseudonym of Bleignen, *Au Coeur de Haut-Varmetias*, Questembert (Rennes), pp. 113–115.

[35]Immediately to mind come the market halls of (in alphabetical order): Beaumont-du-Gâtinais, Brançion (Seine-et-Loire), Dives-sur-Mer (Calvados), Égréville (Seine-et-Marne), Étrétat (Seine Maritime), La Faouet (Morbihan), La Côte St. André (Isère), Nolay (Côte d'Or), Seihnelay (Yonne).

[36]For Feddersen-Wierde see Werner Haarnagel, "Vorläufiger Bericht über die Wurtengrabung auf der Feddersen-Wierde bei Bremerhaven," *Germania*, XXXIV (1956), 123–141, and *Germania*, XXXV (1957), 275–317; *Neue Ausgrabungen in Deutschland* (Berlin, 1958), pp. 215–228; as well as other articles by the same author in *Germania*, XXXIX (1961), 42–65; XLI (1963), 42–65; also *Ausgrabungen in Deutschland* (Mainz, 1975), II, 10–29.

[37]For Ezinge see Albert Egges van Giffen, "Der Warf Ezinge, Prov. Groningen, Holland und seine Westgermanischen Häuser, *Germania*, XX (1936), 40–47; and idem, "Die Siedlungen in den Warfen Hollands, besonders in dem Dorfwarf Ezinge," *Forschungen und Fortschritte*, XII (1936), 189–191.

[38]For a summary review of this material, based on the literature then available, see Walter Horn, "On the Origins of the Medieval Bay System," *Journal of the Society of Architectural Historians*, XVII (1958), 1–23.

[39]For the earliest Germanic Bronze Age settlements with houses of this construction type, see H. T. Waterbolk, "The Bronze Age Settlement of Elp," *Helinium*, IV (1964), 96–131.

[40]My theory that the guest and service buildings of the Plan of St. Gall belong to the family of the Germanic all-purpose house was first expressed on pp. 5-16 of my article "On the Origins of the Medieval Bay System."

It was visually implemented by Ernest Born and myself in a model reconstruction of the buildings delineated on the Plan of St. Gall, which was displayed at the Council of Europe Exhibition Karl der Grosse, held in Aachen in the summer of 1965. A brief description of the rationale that led to this reconstruction is given in the German and French editions of the Catalogue published in conjunction with this exhibition. See Wolfgang Braunfels, ed., *Karl der Grosse, Werk und Wirkung*, Zehnte Ausstellung unter den Auspizien des Europarates (Düsseldorf, 1965), pp. 402–410, and same editor under the title *Charlemagne, Rayonnement et Survivances* (Düsseldorf, 1965), pp. 391–400.

For a fuller treatment of this subject see Walter Horn and Ernest Born, *The Plan of St. Gall: A Study of the Architecture and Economy of, and Life in a Paradigmatic Carolingian Monastery*, Vol. II (Berkeley, Los Angeles, London, 1979).

[41]Attempts to graphically reconstruct Hall Heorot have been made by Moritz Heyne, *Über die Lage und Konstruktion der Halle Heorot in Angelsächsischen Beowulfliede* (Paderborn, 1864); by K. G. Stephani, *Der älteste deutsche Wohnbau und*

seine Einrichtung, Vol. I (Leipzig, 1902), pp. 401 ff; and Suse Pfeilstücker, Spätantikes und Germanisches Kunstgut in der Frühangelsächesischen Kunst (Berlin, 1936). Also to be consulted, the more recent study by· Rosemary J. Cramp, "Beowulf and Archaeology," Medieval Archaeology, I (1957), 57–77.

[42] On Yeavering, "One of the finest excavations ever undertaken" and "under conditions of considerable difficulty" (Philip Rahtz, "Buildings and Rural Settlements," in David M. Wilson, ed. The Archaeology of Anglo-Saxon England [London, 1976], p. 65), unfortunately twenty years later not even a preliminary report is available. Brief notices are to be found in David M. Wilson and John C. Hurst, "Medieval Britain in 1956," Medieval Archaeology, I (1957), 148–149; H. M. Colvin, ed., The History of the Kings Work (London, 1973), pp. 2–3 and 5–6; and the article by Philip Rahtz, quoted above, pp. 65–68.

[43] For Cheddar see the excellent preliminary report by Philip Rahtz, "The Saxon and Medieval Palaces at Cheddar, Somerset: An Interim Report of Excavations, 1960-1962," Medieval Archaeology, VI-VII (1962-1963), 53–66.

[44] The best and most recent summary of the history of Leicester Castle is to be found in Levi Fox, "Leicester Castle," Leicester Archaeological Society Transactions, XXI, 2 (1942-1943), 127–170; James Thompson (An Account of Leicester Castle [Leicester, 1859], p. 10) attributes the hall to Robert "le Bossu," Second Earl of Leicester; G. T. Clark, (Mediaeval Military Architecture in England, Vol. II [London, 1884], p. 183) to Robert de Beaumont, Count of Merlan and subsequently first Earl of Leicester (d. 1118); Margaret Wood ("Norman Domestic Architecture," Archaeological Journal, XCII [1935], 190) dates the hall "c. 1150"; Fox (Leicester Castle, p. 135) to "about the middle or between the middle and the last quarter of the 12th century." For a brief summary of recent opinions on the date and later alterations of Leicester Hall see Walter Horn, "The Potential and Limitations of Radiocarbon Dating in the Middle Ages: The Art Historian's View," in Rainer Berger ed., Scientific Methods in Medieval Archaeology, Center for Medieval and Renaissance Studies, University of California, Los Angeles (Berkeley, Los Angeles, London, 1970), pp. 56–66.

[45] The hall was first described by John Clayton in a paper read to the Royal Institute of British Architects on January 25, 1847, extracts of which were published by the Rev. Francis T. Havergal in Fasti Herefordenses and other Antiquarian Memorials of Hereford (Edinburgh 1896), pp. 138–140. The following year the hall was described in a more comprehensive article by Charles Henry Hartshorne, "The Hall of Oakham," Archaeological Journal, V (1848), 124–142. For subsequent literature see Wood, "Norman Domestic Architecture," pp. 202–203. The editors of the Royal Commission on Historical Monuments, Herefordshire I (London 1931), where the hall is dealt with on pp. 116–117, date it into "the late 12th century." Wood in her "Norman Domestic Architecture," p. 188, dates the hall "c. 1160." Havergal, in Fasti Herefordenses, p. 136, attributes the hall to Bishop Robert Folliot or Bishop William de Vere (i.e., between 1174 and 1199). No record as to the name of the builder of the hall or its exact date of construction exists.

In its present state the hall is severely defaced. Between 1713 and 1721 under Bishop Bisse, the entrance bay of the hall was severed from the remaining work by two masonry walls which cut transversely across the hall (Havergal in Fasti Herefordenses, p. 145). On this occasion also the long walls were redone in brick. Between 1868 and 1895 Bishop Atley then subdivided the two remaining bays by longitudinal wall partitions, creating on either side of a central corridor under lowered ceilings the bishop's present drawing room, a library, and a chaplain's room (ibid.). The site of the original fireplace appears to have been retained for the chimney in the bishop's drawing room, and bedrooms were established on the upper level.

The hall was at least three bays long and possibly five if, as Clayton and the editors of the Royal Commission on Historical Monuments conjecture, the bay at each end of the building now occupied by cross wings originally formed part of the hall. In the latter case it would have had the extraordinary length of 120 feet (46 feet longer than the Leicester hall!); in the former, 74 feet (1 foot shorter than Leicester). Its width was 50 feet, and its height which can only be estimated perhaps in the order of 44 feet (almost identical with Leicester). The construction of Hereford Hall has been ascribed to the time of Bishop William de Vere (1186-1200), but judging by the character of its scalloped capitals it might have been erected at any time during the second half of the twelfth century.

[46] Westminster Hall is dealt with in W. R. Lethaby, "The Palace of Westminster in the Eleventh and Twelfth Centuries," *Archaeologia*, 60 (1906), 131–141, and by the Royal Commission on Historical Monuments, *London(West)* (London, 1925), pp. 121–123. For the roof specifically cf. Herbert Cescinski and Ernest R. Gribble, "Westminster Hall and Its Roof," *Burlington Magazine*, 40 (1922), 76–84.

The belief that Westminster Hall in its original state must have been divided into a nave and aisles by two rows of intermediary supports was first expressed by Sidney Smirke in 1836, "Remarks on the Architectural History of Westminster Hall," *Archaeologia*, 29 (1836), 416. Smirke's opinion is shared by every authoritative student of the subject including the late Director of Works, Sir Franck Baines. Cf. Lethaby, pl. 136; Cescinski and Gribble, p. 76; Royal Commission on Historical Monuments, p. 121; and Geoffrey Webb, *Architecture in Britain, The Middle Ages* (Baltimore and Harmondsworth, 1956), pp. 66–67, fig. 38.

[47] For Great Coxwell and Ter Doest, see the study of Horn and Born, *The Barns of the Abbey of Beaulieu* cited above in n. 1, and Horn and Born, *The Plan of St. Gall*, vol. II (1979), p. 107 and figs. 349–351 on pp. 102–106.

[48] The abbey grange of Parçay-Meslay is briefly dealt with on pp. 12–14 of my article "On the Origins of the Medieval Bay System" cited above in n. 38 and in Horn and Born, *The Plan of St. Gall*, vol. II (1979), pp. 107–113 and figs. 352–355.

A PORTRAIT IN SEARCH OF IDENTIFICATION

John Walker

National Gallery of Art, Washington, D.C.

EXCEPT WHEN AN historical character has been portrayed so often that his features are stereotype, a positive identification of a sitter is nearly impossible. Yet in this respect museums often label portraits with unquestioning dogmatism. To prove my point I have chosen to investigate a particular painting in the Mellon Collection, and my research, I believe, held up a mirror to some of my own iniquities in the past and threw light on how two well-known authorities in the field of Flemish painting, Gustave Gluck and Ludwig Burchard, reached some of their conclusions. This is my excuse for so detailed an inquiry into the identification of the sitter in one portrait (illus. 1).

The painting in question was purchased by Andrew Mellon in 1930 from the Soviet Union. It had been bought by Catherine the Great from Heinrich von Bruhl.[1] I was puzzled by it all the time I was at the National Gallery of Art and on my retirement I decided I would do some research on this baffling but very beautiful portrait which is now labeled Henry Duke of Gloucester and attributed to Adriaen Hanneman. Perhaps the most intriguing part of my investigation was the correspondence I came across between Gluck and Burchard. Their letters irradiate that umbrageous world of certificates and attributions. They were accepted as supreme in their field, and their judgments were, when free from outside influence, precise and intuitive. In the case of the Mellon picture I discovered there had been some monetary considerations.

My studies also showed me the determination of museum authorities to make the labels of works of art conclusive and to suppress any doubts they may have had about identification and attribution. I do not exempt myself from these strictures. How hard I fought on behalf of certain of our paintings to make a dubious ascription stick when a question mark was called for! There was the *Madonna and Child* by Masaccio, which I knew from photographs had been reworked by Duveen to try to make it prettier. I stuck by Berenson's attribution, though I knew in my heart of hearts that only the Madonna's toes were still as the master left them. And there were two Vermeers, which I defended for years, but which are now rightly in storage. Let him who is free from sin cast the first stone. Nevertheless, I am going to throw a few.

The picture I investigated now appears under a lesser attribution and identified as portraying a more obscure person than was the case when it was purchased by Mr. Mellon. I do not object to this, but I do demur to the certainty that is implied by the label, when

Illus. 1. A Young Prince *by Sir Anthony van Dyck or a Follower, probably Adriaen Hanneman. Andrew W. Mellon Collection. Labeled at the National Gallery:* Henry, Duke of Gloucester, *by Adriaen Hanneman.*

an intense study of some months forced me to conclude that certainty is impossible. Here a modest question mark would be desirable, and perhaps more wisely the identification and attribution I shall suggest.

The picture hung in the Hermitage Gallery from the time of its acquisition by Catherine the Great. It was first labeled, with the assurance typical of museum curators, *William II of Nassau and Orange* by Van Dyck.[2] This identification and attribution Knoedler and Co. told Mr. Mellon were facts which could be relied on. The firm expressed no reservations, nor did they submit more recent Hermitage catalogs. In the last of these their client would have seen that, although the identification as William II was maintained, the artist was downgraded to Adriaen Hanneman. Mr. Mellon paid $102,060 for the painting, at that time a small price for a Van Dyck but a great deal for a Hanneman.

This obvious fact worried Herr Zatzenstein, the principal negotiator for the syndicate behind the Russian deal, and it caused anxiety to his partners. They had paid only $55,000 for a work believed to be by Hanneman, and they stood to make a handsome profit. Naturally they wanted the original attribution to Van Dyck sustained. We now enter the shadowy world of the "experts." At the time the best authenticators of anything by Van Dyck were the two celebrated catalogers of his paintings I have mentioned. The elder, Gustave Gluck, was the accepted authority on his work, and the younger, Ludwig Burchard, the rising connoisseur destined for still greater fame. I was fortunate enough to be allowed to see the notes and letters they exchanged on this subject. Their correspondence throws light on a murky aspect of connoisseurship.

For a modest fee of 20,000 marks Zatzenstein succeeded in having the Van Dyck attribution sustained by these two distinguished critics, but not without considerable soul searching on the part of Gluck. The time is the winter of 1931 and Gluck has already returned the proofs of his book on Van Dyck, which he had written for the Klassiker der Kunst series. Burchard, egged on by Zatzenstein, wishes him to include the recently purchased Hermitage portrait, which depicts a young boy with brown eyes and brown hair (illus. 1). Gluck is reluctant and writes, "The Russian picture presents scientific difficulties, for, while I attribute it to Van Dyck, I have not seen it personally. It seems to me an iconographic problem. Is it the same person as in the double portrait in Amsterdam? [the portrait of William II and Mary, daughter of Charles I, painted

Illus. 2. Studio of Sir Anthony van Dyck. William II, Prince of Orange and Mary, Princess Royal, 1641. The Rijksmuseum, Amsterdam.

in 1641 at the time of their marriage, illus. 2]. I cannot believe this. The features are different and the fundamental difference in ages cannot be accounted for. For these reasons I would rather not mention the picture."

This was a discouraging beginning for Burchard who was forty-five and on the threshold of his brilliant career. He was, however, undaunted. He answered that the subject of the Hermitage picture had occupied his thoughts long before he saw the actual painting. He had discussed it with Hofstede de Groot, who assured him it could not be William III as Cust thought (see n. 7) both because of the features of the sitter and his costume, which Burchard correctly says dates from the 1640s and not the 1660s. Having ruled out the picture being the future king of England, Burchard decided it must be his father William II.

His principal argument is a letter from Jane Drummond, Countess of Roxburghe, the governess of Princess Mary, to Count Brederode at The Hague. The letter was transcribed and printed in *De Navorscher*, Amsterdam, 1872.[3] Burchard concentrated on two sentences in particular, which read: "Le malheur m'en a tant voulu que monsieur Van Dyck a presque toujours este malade, depuis vostre depart de ce Pays, tellement que je n'ay pu avoir le portrait qu'il faisoit de monsieur le prince jusqu'a ceste heure. Mais il a promis asseurement a la Reyne qu'il auroit le vostre prest, dans huict jours, et qu'il desiroit le porter lui-mesme avec un autre qu'il faisoit pour madame la princesse d'Auranges."[4] This Burchard paraphrased:

> Van Dyck has not yet finished the portrait of the Prince of Orange ordered by Count Brederode but he has promised the English Queen to finish it in eight days. She says that Van Dyck wants to bring it himself to the Hague. At the same time he wants to bring another portrait of the same prince which he painted for the Prince's mother, the Princess Amalie von Solms. Van Dyck is to leave in ten or twelve days and will bring to Count Brederode, in addition to the portrait painted for him, "le portrait de Madame," for someone else, and the beforementioned "autre qu'il faisoit pour Madame la Princesse d'Auranges."

Burchard concludes from this letter that Van Dyck painted a single portrait of the Prince of Orange, apparently in duplicate, one for Count Brederode, which was near completion the thirteenth of August 1641, and the second for the mother of the young prince, which Van Dyck had already finished at that time.

Many years later Burchard made a transcript of the same letter for Miss Margaret Toynbee, the distinguished authority on the

Stuarts, and found to his chagrin that the operative phrase reads "le portrait qu'il faisoit *pour* Monsieur le Prince" and not "*de* Monsieur le Prince."[5] This greatly weakens Burchard's case that it is a portrait of William II. Puyvelde in a letter to the *Burlington Magazine* later pointed out, however, that this does not necessarily exclude William II. "It might equally mean a portrait of the prince made for himself."[6] On the other hand, Gluck was not impressed by Burchard's communication. He wrote, "I am convinced that the letter [from Jane Drummond] has nothing to do with the portrait of William. No doubt it refers to the portrait of Princess Mary, which was ordered in duplicate."

His obstinacy over Jane Drummond's letter must have been disheartening. Moreover, Burchard faced a further difficulty. He had to explain the difference in looks between William as he appears in the double portrait of 1641 in Amsterdam where he is shown with his bride (illus. 2) and the portrait from the Hermitage (illus. 1). This he does by attacking the attribution of the Amsterdam canvas. He explains to Gluck in a rather poetic passage that Van Dyck's late portraits have a special quality, "like dust on a silk material aetherial and fluid, as it were dry cigarette ashes blown over the rustling folds of silk draperies." In contradiction to this the painting of the textiles in the portrait of the prince in Amsterdam, also his hair and flesh, appear quite drab and heavy, "greasy like alabaster, flat like a *marron glacé.*"

We have no record of Gluck's reaction to his protégé telling him how to recognize an autograph Van Dyck! One can imagine his anger at such insolence. But whether the Amsterdam picture is or is not by the master, it must be acknowledged that the sitter is considerably plumper than the narrow-faced youth in the Hermitage portrait. As Van Dyck died in 1641, the two paintings must be dated at latest from that year if the attribution of the Hermitage picture is to stand. Nevertheless, Gluck seems to have been so persuaded by cigarette ashes in contrast to *marron glacé* that in spite of rejecting the applicability of Jane Drummond's letter and in spite of seeing no resemblance between William in his marriage portrait and the Hermitage sitter, he accepted Burchard's identification and attributed and listed the portrait in the Klassiker der Kunst as William II by Van Dyck.[7] It is curious that Burchard and Gluck overlooked a strong argument in their favor. William II did have a long, narrow face. In another portrait at Windsor, almost certainly of him, there is in my opinion a strong resemblance to the youth in

Illus. 3. Gerrit van Honthorst. William II, c. 1641. Windsor Castle.

the Mellon portrait (illus. 3), certainly far closer than to known portraits of Henry Duke of Gloucester which is the identification accepted by the National Gallery of Art for the Mellon portrait. In this painting William II has none of the chubbiness of the youth to be seen in the Amsterdam double portrait; nor are his features fleshy in other likenesses known to be of him: neither in the painting belonging to the Prince of Hanover (illus. 4), nor when he was painted subsequently with his bride, a picture now in the Rijksmuseum (illus. 5), nor in the later portrait in the collection of the Earl Fitzwilliam at Wentworth Woodhouse (illus. 6). All these have a long, straight face. These likenesses prove how differently the features of the same person can be presented by painters working almost at the same time. The perils of portrait identification are, or should be, awesome; but it is hard to awe a museum curator!

I admit that I was so prejudiced by the 20,000 DM paid to Burchard that I was skeptical of the conclusion reached by these two experienced experts, the ablest that the field of seventeenth-century Flemish painting has known. But I now think the chances are good that they were on the right track. The portrait may well be of William II and by Van Dyck, or it may be of Charles II and also by Van Dyck, as I shall point out. My change of opinion is based on a number of factors. But a principal point is my discovery that there are at least three copies of the Mellon picture dating probably from the seventeenth century. One belongs to Lord Fitzwilliam, who died recently, one to Lord Bristol, and one to Mrs. Baden Powell. The Bristol and Baden Powell replicas have always been identified as portraits of Charles II. For so many copies of a portrait to have been made, two criteria are obvious. Either the subject of the painting was famous, or the artist responsible was an outstanding master, or both. The Mellon painting is now labeled at the National Gallery of Art *Henry, Duke of Gloucester* by Adriaen Hanneman, thus meeting neither of the criteria. What a demotion the Mellon picture has suffered! It is now looked on as a portrait of a somewhat dim princeling by a relatively unrenowned artist. Has it not sunk so low that three copies are improbable? With three preserved, one wonders how many more have vanished. If considered to be by Van Dyck of William II or of Charles II, the copies are explicable. But to copy several times a portrait by Hanneman of Henry Duke of Gloucester as a boy violates the law of probability. Henry accomplished very little in his short lifetime, and at the age of the youth in the Mellon portrait he had accomplished

Illus. 4. Gerrit van Honthorst. William II, Prince of Orange. *H.R.H. The Prince of Hanover.*

Facing page
Illus. 5. Gerrit van Honthorst. William II and Mary Stuart. *The Rijksmuseum, Amsterdam.*

Illus. 6. Unknown Artist. William II, Prince of Orange. *Wentworth Woodhouse.*

nothing. Van Dyck, who painted both William and Charles in their youth, could not have painted a portrait of Henry dressed up in armor, for the third son of Charles I was only a baby when the artist died. So if it is a portrait of this obscure prince, who rates only half a dozen lines in the *Encyclopaedia Britannica*, even in the eleventh edition, it must have been painted by a follower of Van Dyck, and Adriaen Hanneman is the most likely candidate. But as I suggest at the end of this article, the superior quality of the Mellon picture would seem to rule out so pedestrian and uneven a painter.

It is only in recent times that anyone has questioned the identification of the Mellon portrait as being of William II, father of the

Illus. 7. Sir Peter Lely. Three Children of Charles I, *1647. Egremont Collection, Petworth. The National Trust and H. M. Treasury. The Duke of Gloucester is on the extreme left.*

future King of England. Even when the attribution to Van Dyck was doubted the paiting was still thought to be the likeness of the stadtholder. This has remained unchallenged from the days of the earliest provenance we can trace, the collection of Count von Bruhl in the mid-eighteenth century, until very recently.[8] Such reliance has been placed on this identification that the Belgian government, admittedly no iconographic expert, in 1964 issued a postage stamp reproducing the portrait to honor William II. A tradition so unquestioned and so venerable must be carefully weighed against any contrary evidence. What is this evidence? Not the features of William II compared to those of Henry Duke of Gloucester. The Windsor portrait of William II (illus. 3) shows him at about the same age as the boy in the Mellon painting with the same long, narrow face. The resemblance is striking. By contrast Gloucester in his portrait at Petworth standing beside his sister and brother reveals a rotund, dimpled face (illus. 7). The same rounded chin and heavy lidded eyes appear in the rather effeminate portrait at Hampton Court (illus. 8) and in the triple portrait by John Hoskins at the Fitzwilliam Museum, Cambridge (illus. 9).[9]

Illus. 8. Sir Peter Lely. Henry, Duke of Gloucester. *Hampton Court.*

Illus. 9. John Hoskins. Three Children of Charles I. *Fitzwilliam Museum, Cambridge. The Duke of Gloucester on the right.*

Illus. 10. Unknown artist. Henry Duke of Gloucester(?) Collection of Earl Fitzwilliam, Milton, Peterborough. So inscribed but identification doubtful.

The identification of the Mellon youth as William II would probably have remained unquestioned had it not been for Miss Margaret Toynbee. She found a copy of the Washington portrait at Milton, one of two estates owned by Earl Fitzwilliam, a descendant of the Earl of Strafford, whose property after several centuries he inherited (illus. 10). On this painting there is an old inscription reading "Henry Duke of Glocster 3rd sonn to Kg Charles ye 1st."[10] The inscription has been accepted as accurate without further inquiry. I believe I am the first person to examine it critically.

The inscription cannot be earlier than 1689, many years after Gloucester's death, which took place in 1660. This is proven by the fact that numerous other pictures in the collection of Lord Fitz-

Illus. 11. "William of Nassau; to the Waste copied by Hesket." Wentworth Woodhouse. Collection of Earl Fitzwilliam. Published for the first time.

Illus. 12. Unknown artist. Frederick Henry of Nassau. Wentworth Woodhouse. Collection of Earl Fitzwilliam. Published for the first time.

william, those at Wentworth Woodhouse and those now moved to his second estate at Milton, are inscribed apparently at the same time with the same yellow paint and in the same handwriting (illus. 6, 11, and 12). On one portrait, that of William II as a mature man, there is a reference to William III as "Present Kg of England" (illus. 6). These inscriptions therefore must have been written during the reign of William III, 1689-1702, probably by the executors of the second Earl of Strafford when an inventory was required.

Strafford's will of 1695, the year he died, is preserved in the Sheffield City Library. It lists nearly all the pictures he possessed, those at Wentworth Woodhouse and those transferred more recently to Milton. But it is significant that this testament does not mention a portrait of Henry Duke of Gloucester. William II is mentioned, probably a reference to illustration 6. The portraits listed are easily identified and bear inscriptions in yellow paint. But the unknown scrivener, who painted these identifying names, made several errors, one of which must have embarrassed the first Earl of Strafford's ghost. The cataloger confused Lucy Percy, Countess of Carlysle, reputedly his lordship's mistress, with his wife Lady Arabella. One imagines the benighted iconographer must have had a cold reception in the next world from these ladies and from the Earl himself!

Since Strafford's list of 1695 does not mention a portrait of Henry Duke of Gloucester, the major evidence for this identification is the inscription on the copy at Milton. Country house inscriptions are notoriously unreliable. Is this one better than others? What were the cataloger's opportunities for accurate information when he could not depend on the Strafford testament?

The background of the portraits at Wentworth Woodhouse makes this particular inscription especially dubious.[11] Consider for a moment the difficulties facing the cataloger. When the inscriptions were written neither the second Earl nor his first wife were alive.[12] His second wife, a Frenchwoman, had been married only a year when she became a widow. She found herself at Wentworth Woodhouse surrounded by scores of portraits with no labels. How could she have possibly known whom they represented? The Strafford title, in abeyance for eleven years, finally passed to a distant cousin, who spent his life in the army. There was probably no one to advise the nameless cataloger. All he could do was depend on Strafford's will and, when a picture was not listed in it, make up his own identification.

This may have been what happened. The writer with his pot of yellow paint busily inscribing portrait after portrait suddenly comes on the likeness of a boy, which is not listed in the testament. With nothing to help him he decides he must use his deductive reasoning, if he is to complete his inventory. Although no Sherlock Holmes, he nevertheless notices that the portrait offers two clues: one, a ribbon which he connects with the Order of the Garter; two, a baton which he recognizes as a sign of high military rank. He thinks naturally of the Stuarts. He knows the features of Charles II and James II as kings. He had no idea of what they looked like as boys, but he may have remembered that James II had blue eyes, which ruled him out. Charles II, when he grew up, looked so different that he put him aside. But what about their younger brother, Henry Duke of Gloucester? Thirty years after his death few people knew what he looked like, especially during his adolescence spent in Cromwell's custody. An admirable choice this cataloger may have thought. Today we know Henry's youthful appearance. There are the portraits at Petworth (illus. 7), Hampton Court (illus. 8), and the Fitzwilliam Museum, Cambridge (illus. 9), all identified authentically. They are remarkably alike. Henry had a round, puffy face, not at all like the long, narrow face of the Mellon youth. But the cataloger had never been at Petworth or Hampton Court. Having made his choice, he wrote on the canvas with his yellow paint a name recent scholars have accepted dogmatically.

Bearing all this in mind, confidence in the inscription must diminish. Does it still offer enough evidence to upset a tradition going back at least two centuries that the original is a portrait of William II?[13] Or is it better evidence than that the other two copies are of Charles II, for which there is also a tradition? Charles II resembles more closely the Mellon youth than does the Duke of Gloucester. Later Charles came to look like a dissipated spaniel, but in childhood he was quite a handsome boy with brown eyes and curly hair. If painted by Van Dyck his appearance was doubtless further improved (illus. 13).

The principal evidence against the Mellon portrait representing the Duke of Gloucester is the date and nature of the sitter's clothes. I am not an authority on Stuart dress, but the experts I have consulted place the costume earlier than 1650. This would exclude Henry of Gloucester, who was in the custody of Cromwell until 1653. It was not till then that he was given the Garter by his brother, Charles II. Two of the leading authorities on British clothes of this period are Mr John Nevinson and Miss Janet Arnold. I consulted them both. Mr Nevinson pointed out that the metal-braid and striped sleeves of the coat can be seen in portraits by Dobson "mostly painted in Oxford in 1644." This he believes is the correct date for the portrait, but an earlier date is possible, whereas a dating as late as 1653 is hardly likely. Mr R. E. Hutchison, Keeper of the Scottish National Portrait Gallery, after consultation with his staff, has concluded that 1653 is definitely too late a date. Miss Arnold has pointed to a number of portraits all from the 1640s with marked similarity of costume. She too thinks the 1650s too late for this attire. Although, I repeat, I am inexperienced in the clothing worn in Stuart times, I have looked at innumerable photographs of portraits of the 1640s and '50s. Among these the style of dress that I believe most closely resembles the armor and doublet worn by the Washington sitter is shown in a portrait identified as Colonel John Russell, attributed to John Hayls, and now dated circa 1645 (illus. 14). Previously it was thought to be of Lord Brooke, in accordance with yet another unreliable inscription in the left-hand corner, which dates it 1642. To me the evidence of this picture and of others seems, on balance, to place the Washington portrait in the

Illus. 13. David des Granges. Charles II as a Young Man. *Ham House. Victoria and Albert Museum.*

257

Illus. 14. John Hayls. Colonel John Russell. *The Trustees of the Warwick Castle Resettlement.*

early 1640s as Gluck and Burchard thought, who were after all authorities on seventeenth-century dress, rather than as late as 1653. This conclusion also arises from my belief, which I shall discuss, that the portrait is probably by Van Dyck although worked on in his studio, as was customary with all his paintings at the end of his life.

Moreover, a further problem about the clothes in the Mellon painting suggests itself. Gloucester was sent to France by Cromwell so that he could be with his mother. He did not escape or fight his way to the sea. He probably left England wearing civilian clothes. He must have received his military attire on arrival. Why then should a royal prince be portrayed wearing clothes experts agree were fashionable ten years earlier? Surely in an official portrait he would not have wanted to appear dowdy. Also he holds a general's baton in his right hand. Yet he had never seen action in any battle and he was not at that time an army commander. Being a prince he could of course dress himself up, but the baton is hard to explain. William II, on the other hand, had been made a general at the age of four and thus had the right to hold a symbol of his high military rank. Having been with the Dutch army much of his life, it is not surprising that he would wear armor. Moreover, his whole costume fits the dates 1640–1645, when he was the right age to be the youth in the Mellon portrait.

The clothes, too, make Charles II a most likely choice, as do other factors in his life. First, two of the copies, those of Lord Bristol and Mrs. Baden Powell, were traditionally so identified. Second, born in 1630 Charles II was made a Knight of the Garter in 1638. Third, he was also at an early age the commander of his father's troops. Fourth, as a child he was frequently painted by Van Dyck, and it may have been he that is referred to in Jane Drummond's letter. Fifth, at Wentworth Woodhouse there are two portraits of Charles II, both showing him as a mature man. He was greatly admired by the second Earl of Strafford, whose attainder he reversed. One of his portraits at Wentworth Woodhouse is an oval and is the same size as the Milton copy. Perhaps the second Earl of Strafford wanted to show Charles as the monarch and also as a youth, hanging the two portraits as pendants. And sixth, there was one particular reason for the Straffords to want a portrait of Charles not only as a man but also as a boy. When he was only eleven the young Prince of Wales carried his father's request to Parliament for the reprieve for the first Earl of Strafford, the King's

*Illus. 15. Adriaen Hanneman.*William III, Prince of Orange as a Child. *The Rijksmuseum, Amsterdam.*

friend and councillor, then under sentence of execution. With so many reasons to think that the Mellon portrait might be Charles II, why has this identification been ignored? The principal reason is the king's later looks. His saturnine, dissolute appearance seems to rule him out. Perhaps it does. But one must remember that as a boy in the portrait at Ham House (illus. 13) he looks not unlike the Mellon youth. The life he led of such utter dissipation could have entirely changed his features.

I have not discussed the change of attribution of the Mellon painting from Van Dyck to Hanneman. My own field is Italian art, and I am reluctant to make a judgment between two Flemish artists. But having scrutinized paintings all my life, I have developed what I believe to be a sense of quality. Illustration 15 is a likeness of William III painted in 1654 by Hanneman. Assuming the Mellon youth to be the Duke of Gloucester, he must have been portrayed around the same time. It seems to me the quality of the portrait by Hanneman is so inferior to the work of the artist who painted the Mellon portrait that I find it difficult to believe both are by the same person. But such a belief presents no problem to those who reject the attribution of the Washington picture to Van Dyck. I urge the reader to compare the hands in the two pictures (illus. 1 and 15). In the Washington portrait they are fully modeled and articulated. In the Amsterdam painting they are the appendages of a doll. The Mellon boy exists as volume; the Rijksmuseum child could easily be a cutout. One has substance and is firmly planted on the ground; the other floats decoratively across the canvas. The National Gallery of Art picture seems to me to be by a superior master; the picture in Holland by contrast suggests a competent face painter with some sense of decoration. I find it hard to believe that an artist painting two pictures at virtually the same time could have executed one with such skill and the other with such ineptness. But matters of connoisseurship are always debatable, and I am not familiar enough with the work of Hanneman to know whether he could rise to the level of quality apparent in the Mellon painting. Gluck and Burchard evidently thought not, and I am inclined to side with them. In a study of Italian art the differences I have mentioned would indicate distinct artists, but in Flemish painting they may be meaningless.

To sum up, if I were to make book on the identification and attribution of the portrait in the National Gallery of Art (knowing full well that it is unbecoming for an ex–museum director to suggest odds like a bookmaker) I would risk even money that the sitter is William II; I would only give short odds to anyone clever enough to bet he is Charles II; and I would give very long odds to those so rash as to believe he is Henry Duke of Gloucester. Again it seems to me that an attribution to Van Dyck is at least an even money bet; to Hanneman three to two against; and to the rest of the field (all other painters), very long odds indeed. But this is an exercise in futility. With our present information such wagers will never be settled. The Mellon painting may always remain a mystery. But if the traditional "William II" is to be rejected, if two copies designated Charles II are to be ignored, if the attribution to Van Dyck is to be repudiated, where are we? What kind of an honest label should a museum place on such a puzzling picture? I would suggest "*A Young Prince* by Sir Anthony Van Dyck or a Follower, probably Adriaen Hanneman." This leaves the question open. It seems to me dishonest to pretend to a nonexistent certitude.

NOTES

[1]Heinrich von Bruhl (1700–1763) was prime minister and chief of the Saxon Court during the thirty-year reign of Frederick Augustus II, Elector of Saxony, who was also King Augustus III of Poland. Augustus III, like his father Augustus II, was a lavish patron of art and learning and greatly beautified his capital, Dresden. Von Bruhl, while buying works of art for him in tremendous quantity (more than 700 paintings were purchased in one particular year), also took the opportunity to enrich his own collection. He used the representatives of the Saxon Court in all the principal cities of Europe to scout out works of art which might be coming on the market. Those he bought for the king formed the nucleus of the Dresden Gallery.

[2]In the catalog of the Hermitage Gallery are the following references: Baron B de Koehne (in consultation with Thore-Burger and Paul Lacroix), *Hermitage*, 1870, ‡ 611, as Van Dyck, *William II of Nassau*. Andrei Ivonovish Somov, *Catalogue de la Galerie des Tableaux*, Hermitage, 1901, pp. 73–74, ‡ 611 as Van Dyck, *William II of Nassau*. Baron Nicholas Wrangell, *Les Chefs-d'Oeuvre de la Galerie de Tableaux De L'Ermitage Imperial a St. Petersbourg*, 1909. Plate 147 as Adriaen Hanneman, *William II of Nassau* (formerly attributed to Anthony Van Dyck).

[3]The full text was reprinted by Henri Hymans, "Les Dernieres Annees de Van Dyck," *Gazette des Beaux-Arts*, 36 (Nov. 1887), 439.

[4]The full text and literal translation of the letter follow:
"Monsieur,
    Je me tiens grandement vostre obligee de la peine qu'il vous a pleu prendre de m'escrire et encore plus, que me jugiez capable de vous prendre service en ce Pays. Je vous supplie de croire que je m'y emploierai avec toute sorte d'affection. Je n'eusse pas ete si longtemps sans vous escrire, n'eust ete que j'ay crue que mes

lettres vour seroyent plus agreables, si elles estoient si heureuses d'accompagner le portrait de son Altesse Royale. Mais le malheur m'en a tant voulu que monsieur Van Dyck a presque toujours este malade, depuis votre depart de ce Pays, tellement que je n'ay pu avoir le portrait qu'il faisoit (de, pour) monsieur le prince jusqu'a ceste heure. Mais il a promis asseurement a la Reyne qu'il auroit le vostre prest, dans huict jours, et qu'il desiroit le porter lui-mesme avec un autre qu'il faisoit pour madame la princesse d'Auranges.

Il est resolu de partir dans dix ou douze jours de ce pays pour le plus tard: Et en passant par l'Hollande, il vous donnera le portrait de Madame. J'espere que ceste verite m'excusera de ce que j'ay este si longtemps sans avoir faict response a vostre lettre et a m'acquitter de ma promesse.

Croyez, monsieur, que je puis manquer de pouvoir, mais jamais de volonte, en toutes occasions, de vous tesmoigner que je suis,

Monsieur,

Vostre humble et obeissante servante
JANE ROXBROUGH
De Richmont, ce 13ᵉ d'aoust 1641."

Sir,

I am very much obliged to you for the pains you took to write to me, and even more, for judging me capable of being of service to you in this country. I beg you to believe that I will occupy myself with it with great devotion. I would not have waited so long to write to you, had I not believed that my letters would be more agreeable to you, were they so fortunate as to accompany the portrait of (His, Her) Royal Highness. But by great ill fortune Van Dyck has been almost always sick, since your departure from this country, so much so that I could not have the portrait which he was making (of, for) the prince until, now. But he has definitely promised the Queen that he will have yours ready in eight days, and that he wishes to take it himself with another which he was making for Madame the Princess of Orange.

He has decided to leave this country at the latest in ten or twelve days: and in passing through Holland, he will give you the portrait of Madame. I hope that this fact will excuse me for having waited for so long without replying to your letter and keeping my promise.

Believe me sir, I may lack the power, but never the desire, on every occasion to prove myself,

Your humble and obedient servant,
JANE ROXBROUGH

⁵Margaret R. Toynbee, letter in *Burlington Magazine*, October 1943, p. 257.

⁶Leo van Puyvelde, letter in ibid., p. 258.

⁷Gustav Gluck, *Van Dyck, des Meisters Gemalde*, (Klassiker der Kunst), New York, 1931, p. 577, ‡ 506. The note in the English edition reads:

"This extremely attractive and beautifully composed portrait, which was traditionally always referred to as representing the young William II of Orange (see . . . The Marriage Portrait), and which was considered one of the outstanding late works of Van Dyck, has been attributed by Cust, p. 154, to Adriaen Hanneman. Cust came to the conclusion that it represents the *son* of this Prince, later King William III of England (1650-1702). But the comparison suggested by Cust with a portrait of William III in Hampton Court, inscribed with the name of Hanneman and the date 1664, does not substantiate this theory: neither the identity of the subject (a slight similarity of the features can be explained by the father-son relationship; the similarity of the pose, by the influence of Van Dyck) nor the sameness of the style can be sustained. The collar of the Leningrad portrait belongs to the period around 1641, that of the Hampton Court portrait to 1664. Because of these considerations, for which I have to thank the perspicacity of Ludwig Burchard, who has seen the original in Leningrad, this portrait must be recognised as one of the very last works by Van Dyck, and actually of William II. Further-more, Van Dyck had painted and sketched this same prince in earliest youth, along with the portraits of his parents, in 1628 in the Hague: examples in full length and in long dress, with a dog at his side, are in the Damenstift (Ladies' Home) Mosigkau at Dessau, in the collection of the Earl of Hallwyl in Stockholm, and formerly with Colnaghi in London; a copy in the Rudolphinum in Prague; a drawing for a different composition in the British Museum in London (Hind 39, sketch for an oil at Petworth); a portrait at half-length mentioned in a bill of sale of Charles I dated August 8, 1632 (Carpenter, p. 71)."

[8]Count von Bruhl evidently intended to publish a catalog of his entire collec-tion, but only Volume I is to be found in the libraries of the British Museum and the Victoria and Albert, leading one to suppose that further volumes were never issued. Unfortunately the Mellon-Hermitage portrait is not listed in the first volume.

[9]Much importance is given by those opposed to the identification of the Mellon youth as William II to the cleft chin in other portraits of the stadtholder. This feature, however, is not apparent in his likeness in Amsterdam (illus. 2). On the other hand, in the Petworth portrait of the children of Charles II, the child on the left, the Duke of Gloucester, has an obvious cleft in his chin, which, if one accepts this argument, should exclude him as the model for the Mellon portrait (illus. 7). But this cleft disappears in later portraits, and one must conclude that artists when painting children overlooked such peculiarities. I have omitted from discussion a portrait at Hampstead Marshall, a National Trust property, which is said to have a resemblance to the Mellon youth. Its identification as Gloucester seems to me extremely dubious for the following reasons:

a. The sitter does not resemble the certain portraits of this obscure prince (illus. 7, 8, 9). The dimples and fleshy appearance are missing and the nose is upturned rather than aquiline.

b. As the Craven pictures to a great extent came from Lord Craven's closest friend, Elizabeth of Bohemia, it is more than likely that the portrait represents one of her sons.

c. The theory that the painting portrays Gloucester is based largely on the emblem of Saint George and the Dragon which he wears. It is assumed therefore that the sitter was a Knight of the Garter and must have been a Stuart prince; and since the portrait does not resemble Charles II or James II, it follows that it must be their brother, Henry. But this is an unconvincing deduction. First, some experts on heraldry do not believe that the insignia worn this way has anything to do with the Garter. Second, if it has, Elizabeth's son, Charles Louis, Elector Palatine, received the Garter at sixteen, the right age for the youth in the portrait.

d. But accepting that it is Gloucester dressed up to take part in a masque, it must have been painted between 1653, when he arrived in Holland, and the Stuart Restoration. Yet during that period his aunt, Elizabeth of Bohemia, was almost penniless, and Henry of Gloucester was spending most of his time with his brother, Charles II, in Germany or fighting as a mercenary. In these years of poverty and strife how unlikely that he would have been painted in fancy dress.

[10]Margaret R. Toynbee, "Adrian Hanneman and the English Court in Exile," *Burlington Magazine*, March 1950, p. 76. At the time Miss Toynbee saw the copy it was at Wentworth Woodhouse; it is now at Milton, a second estate of Earl Fitzwilliam. See also A. Staring, "Willem II of III of wie?", *Oud-Holland*, 1956, vol. LXXI, pp. 153-161.

[11]Country house inscriptions are notorious for their fanciful identifications, and there is no reason to believe that "Henry Duke of Glocster" is more reliable than many. Indeed the history of the Strafford paintings makes unreliability in this case more than probable. Most of the portraits came into the family at various times through Henrietta Maria Stanley, the first wife of the second Earl of Strafford. They were given to her by her mother, the wife of the seventh Earl of Derby, according to Lord Fitzwilliam. Why the paintings did not remain with the Derbys is a mystery, for under primogeniture daughters have few rights of inheritance. Perhaps Charlotte de la Tremouille, Countess of Derby, gave them to Lady Henrietta because she wanted her ancestors kept separate from those of her husband. She was proud of her ancestry, particularly her connection with the Oranges. She had portraits of her grandfather, William the Silent (illus. 11), his son, Frederick Henry (illus. 12), and her cousin, William II (illus. 6). All are mentioned in the Strafford will and are here published for the first time. What more likely than that she would want another likeness of cousin William, as a boy? The original, if of William II, was probably at The Hague; and she would have asked her cousin, by then stadtholder, to have a replica of his youthful likeness painted for her. Lady Henrietta, her daughter, who would have known the identity of this boy, died in 1685 before the inscriptions were written on the pictures. The Earl himself died in 1695, and it is entirely possible that no one knew the identity of the youth whose portrait had been copied, for though the faces of famous men are generally recognized, what they looked like as children is often confused. That the copy, along with a few other pictures, was not listed in Strafford's testament is unfortunate for this would have solved all problems. But the close connection between the second Earl's first wife and the family of the Oranges makes it more likely that there should be two portraits of a cousin, William II, one as a man and one as a boy, than that there should be a likeness of the youngest of the sons of Charles I, the obscure Duke of Gloucester. And if it is Henry Duke of Gloucester why choose to copy a portrait showing him as an adolescent?

[12]The confusion between the first Lord Strafford's wife and his probable mistress proves two things: one, that the cataloger must have been ignorant of the Strafford family and the first Earl's friendships or love affairs; second, that the inscriptions were not put on during the lifetime of the second Earl, who would doubtless have corrected so embarrassing an error.

[13]The principal argument against the traditional identification as William II, apart from the inscription, is the blue sash. Miss Toynbee believes this to be the Garter Ribbon, and those who have confidence in the inscription and consider the portrait to be of the Duke of Gloucester agree. The sash is the right color and worn in the right way. William II, born May 27, 1626, was not given this order until he was seventeen, possibly too old an age to be the boy in the Mellon portrait. It occurred to me, however, that scarves were worn by Dutch officers in the seventeenth century, and I asked the opinion of Dr. van de Watering of the Rijksbureau Voor Kunsthistorische Documentatie and he kindly replied, "It seems to be possible that the ribbon seen on the portrait is an officer's ribbon and not the ribbon belonging to the Order of the Garter." I then wrote Sir Anthony Wagner, Garter King of Arms, the final authority on the Order of the Garter, and

asked whether one could be sure that the ribbon in the Mellon painting indicated that the sitter was a Knight of that Order. His reply was, "All I can say . . . is that I should not be positive that the ribbon depicted indicates with certainty that the subject was a Knight of the Garter." To be quite sure one would need to see the emblem as well, he pointed out. Thus it would seem that using the evidence of the blue scarf to dispose of the William II identification is at best moot. Moreover, assuming it is the Garter Ribbon Charles I may have promised it to his son-in-law at the time of his marriage and might have permitted him to be painted wearing it before the formal investiture, which was delayed by the Civil War. The nomination actually took place at Oxford on 2 March 1644/45, and because of the general disruption of the country the Garter and George had to be sent to William in Holland. This was done on 4 March.

A FRAGONARD LANDSCAPE AFTER JACOB VAN RUISDAEL'S "WOODED LANDSCAPE WITH A POND"

Seymour Slive

Fogg Art Museum, Harvard University

I WISH I WERE ABLE to express my enormous admiration and gratitude to Franklin Murphy with a fine work of art instead of some remarks about one. My consolation is the hope that comments which aim to shed a bit of light on a painting and the working method of an outstanding artist may interest him.

Every student of Fragonard's *oeuvre* knows that he painted a group of landscapes *dans le goût hollandais*. Those who have studied them naturally have asked: were any done after identifiable seventeenth-century Dutch landscapes?

To the best of my knowledge no one has been able to give a positive response to this query. Georges Wildenstein, for example, does not identify one in the corpus of Fragonard's paintings he published in 1960.[1] Richard Carpenter, who completed his study of the artist's Dutch sources in 1955, searched for a connection between Fragonard's landscapes and those done by seventeenth-century Dutch artists. He reported: "I have not been able to uncover one convincing example of the direct derivation of a Fragonard landscape from a Dutch landscape. Nor have I found any record of a Fragonard copy in any medium of a Dutch landscape."[2] Jacques Wilhelm, whose analysis of Fragonard's landscapes done in the Dutch manner appeared in 1948,[3] answered the question with a resounding "No." He argues that every single one of Fragonard's "realistic landscapes" was the result of the artist's study of nature, not Dutch painting. According to Wilhelm, in Fragonard's landscapes "constructed like those of the Dutch masters . . . there is . . . not a tree, not a rock, bush, puddle, not an ox nor a herd of sheep that has not been seen in nature by the artist."[4]

Clearly the close connection between Fragonard's *The Pond* (illus. 1), now at the Kimbell Art Museum, Fort Worth, Texas,[5] and Jacob van Ruisdael's landscape of the same subject (illus. 2), formerly in the collection of H. L. Larsen, New York, and now untraceable,[6] was unknown to recent students of Fragonard's landscapes. Juxtaposition of these two paintings establishes that at least one of Fragonard's landscapes *dans la manière hollandaise* is a creative copy after a work by the greatest Dutch landscape painter of the seventeenth century.

For the Kimbell painting Fragonard chose as his model a small landscape done by Ruisdael in the late 1640s when the young artist concentrated on humble views seen close-up of ponds, tangled thickets and sandy dunes near his native town of Haarlem. The loving attention to detail and rather heavy granular paint in Ruisdael's landscape is characteristic of his early phase. Fragonard copied the work, but not slavishly. He has almost doubled the size of the original and in his hands the landscape has become sunnier and Ruisdael's tall tree has been stripped of much of its dense foliage exposing paradigmatic rococo branches. His touch is much livelier and more liquid than Ruisdael's and his staffage more anecdotal: a barking dog and two young washerwomen, one with her skirt tucked up above her knees, have been added.

Unless Fragonard's early biographer Le Carpentier had a fundamentally different conception from ours of a deceptive copy, the Kimbell painting could not have been the kind he had in mind when he wrote: "On l'a vu souvent imiter Ruysdaël et d'autres peintres de cette école à tromper."[7] Although the painting clearly is derived from the Ruisdael, it is an unmistakable Fragonard.

Fragonard's variation on Ruisdael made its first appearance in the literature when it was catalogued for the sale, de M. ★ ★ ★ [Le Roy de Senneville], Paris, 5 *sqq.* April 1780, no. 49 (bought in):

> Un paysage touffu d'arbres, à la gauche duquel monte un chemin sur un terrain elevé & sabloneux, qui paroît conduire a l'entrée d'un bois épais sur le devant, on voir deux jeunes femmes qui lavent du linge dans un étang & à la droite, un chien qui poursuit des canards. Ce morceau, fait au premier coup, est un ressouvenir juste pour l'effet, du tableau de Ruisdael de M. Lempereur, & qui par la touche facile & spirituelle, devient original.
>
> Hauteur 24 pouces, Largeur 26. T.

A. J. Paillet, the author of Senneville's 1780 sale catalogue was well informed.[8] He was able to tell his readers that Fragonard's painting was reminiscent of a Ruisdael in Lempereur's collection. He was quite right. The early Ruisdael landscape that served as Fragonard's model was in Lempereur's collection before it was offered at his sale at Paris in 1773.[9]

The impact of seventeenth-century Dutch art on Fragonard has been discussed often, and much ink has been spilled over the question of whether he made firsthand contact and copied works by masters of the heroic age of Dutch painting during the course of a trip to the Netherlands. One thing, however, is incontestable: the great vogue that seventeenth-century Dutch painters had with Parisian collectors in Fragonard's time gave him ample opportunity to study and copy Dutch paintings without leaving Paris. Best known are his copies of Rembrandt's *Danaë* and *Holy Family* which were made when the originals were in the collection of Crozat de Thiers in Paris before they were acquired by Catherine II for the Hermitage in 1772.[10] Paillet's reference to the relationship of Fragonard's landscape to the Ruisdael in Lempereur's collection suggests that it, too, was a copy painted in Paris. There is a tantalizing reference to yet another candidate: when Fragonard's *Windmill*, now untraceable, appeared in the sale, Widow Le Bas de Courmont, 26 May 1795, no. 29, it was described as "after Ruysdael."[11]

An additional point regarding the history of Ruisdael's *Wooded Landscape with a Pond* and its connection with Fragonard's copies after Netherlandish pictures is worth noting. When it appeared in the sale of the painter J. A. Gros (died 1789; father of Baron A. J. Gros, principal painter of Napoleon's military history), Paris, 14 April 1778, it was sold along with Fragonard's drawing after Jordaen's *Apotheosis of Prince Frederick Henry of Orange-Nassau*, now in

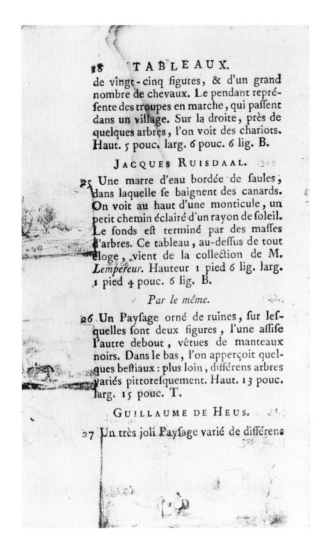

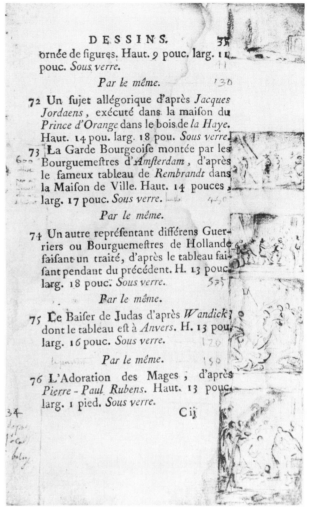

Illus. 3. Gabriel de Saint-Aubin, three drawings on a page of a sale catalogue of J. -A. Gros, 1778. No. 25 is a drawing after Wooded Landscape with a Pond by Ruisdael. No. 26 is a drawing after an unidentified landscape by Ruisdael.

Illus. 4. Gabriel de Saint-Aubin, four drawings on a page of a sale catalogue of J. -A. Gros, 1778. No. 73 is a sketch after Fragonard's copy of Rembrandt's Night Watch. No. 74 is a sketch after Fragonard's copy of Bartholomeus van der Helst's Celebration of the Peace of Münster, which the compiler of the sale catalogue erroneously attributed to Rembrandt.

a private collection, Paris; his copy of Rembrandt's *Night Watch*, whereabouts unknown; and his sketch after Bartholomeus van der Helst's *Celebration of the Peace of Münster in the Headquarters of the St. George Civic Guard Company of Amsterdam* (wrongly catalogued as a copy after Rembrandt), whereabouts unknown.[12] Gabriel de Saint-Aubin made thumbnail sketches in his copy of the Gros sale catalogue of the Ruisdael that served as the model for the Fragonard landscape now at the Kimbell and of another Ruisdael landscape that has not been identified (illus. 3, nos. 25, 26; respectively). Saint-Aubin did not sketch Fragonard's copy after the Jordaens (no. 72), but his tiny chalk *aides-mémoire* after Fragonard's drawings of the Rembrandt and van der Helst are unmistakable (illus. 4, nos. 73, 74; respectively).[13]

In Fragonard's day the three paintings he copied were considered among the most notable seventeenth-century paintings in Holland. Indeed, most visitors ranked van der Helst's group portrait higher than the *Night Watch*. Sir Joshua Reynolds was so disappointed with the latter when he saw it during a visit to Amsterdam in 1781, that he doubted Rembrandt had painted the picture: ". . . it seemed to me to have more of the yellow manner of Boll."[14]

Since the famous Jordaens, Rembrandt, and van der Helst paintings never left Holland, the possibility that Fragonard made his drawings of them during the course of a trip to the Netherlands must be considered. On the other hand, there is no documentary evidence that he ever made the trip. Until some proof is found, the possibility that he made these copies from other copies while working in Paris (or elsewhere) cannot be excluded, and his visit to Holland remains a hypothetical journey.

POSTSCRIPT

While this essay was in press the second Ruisdael landscape copied by Saint-Aubin reappeared in the art market (illus. 5; Saint-Aubin's drawing is reproduced illus. 3, no. 26). The unsigned painting (canvas, 36 × 41 cm.) was with a Dutch dealer and is now in a private collection in The Netherlands. Perhaps the landscape is identical with Hofstede de Groot, p. 323, nos. 767c and 767f; it may have appeared in the Paillet sale, Paris, 9 April 1793, no. 46 (4,000 francs, Constantin).

Illus. 5. Landscape with Ruins, *Jacob van Ruisdael. Oil on canvas, 36 × 41 cm. Private collection, The Netherlands.*

[1] Georges Wildenstein, *The Paintings of Fragonard* (New York, 1960).

[2] Richard Carpenter, "Dutch Sources of the Art of J. H. Fragonard," Ph.D. diss., Harvard University, (Cambridge, Mass., 1955), p. 147.

[3] Jacques Wilhelm, "Fragonard as a Painter of Realistic Landscape," *The Art Quarterly*, XI (1948), 297 ff.

[4] Ibid., p. 298.

[5] Inv. no. 68.3. Oil on canvas, 65.2 x 73.1 cm. Wildenstein, p. 241, no. 185. For provenance and bibliographical references see *The Kimbell Art Museum, Catalogue*, 1972, pp. 109–110; the compiler of the catalogue entry erroneously states the landscape is painted in the manner of Salomon van Ruysdael.

[6] Oil on panel, 36.5 x 46.5 cm. Monogrammed, lower left.

Provenance: Sale, Lempereur, Paris, 24 May 1773 (800 francs); sale, J. A. Gros, Paris (Lebrun), 13 *sqq.* April 1778, no. 25 (1,300 francs); sale, [Tronchin], Paris (Lebrun), 12-15 January 1780, no. 61 (1,305 francs); sale [Lebrun and other dealers], Paris (Lebrun), 11 December 1780, no. 53 (1,200 francs, Vincent); sale, Godefroy, Paris (Lebrun), 25 April and 15-19 November 1785, no. 22 (1,300 francs); sale, Madame Bandeville, Paris (Remy), 3 December 1787, no. 35 (601 francs); sale, V[ieux]V[illier], Paris (Lebrun), 18 February 1788, no. 25 (1,700 francs, Damon); Jeremiah Harman, London by 1835; sale, Jeremiah Harman, London, 17 May 1844, no. 48 (£378, Burland); dealer C. Benedict, Berlin, ca. 1928; dealer H. Schaeffer, Berlin, ca. 1934; H. L. Larsen, The Hague by 1936-1937; sale, the late H. L. Larsen, New York (Parke Bernet), 6 November 1947, no. 27 ($4,000).

Exhibitions: London, Vermeer Gallery, 1936; The Hague, Gemeente Museum, "Oude Kunst uit Haagsch ·Bezit," 1936-1937, no. 164 (H. L. Larsen).

Bibliography: John Smith, *A Catalogue Raisonné of the Works of the Most Eminent Dutch, Flemish and French Painters*, Vol. VI (London, 1835), p. 16, no. 27; Charles Blanc, *Le Trésor de La Curiosité tiré de Catalogues de Vente*, Vol. I (1857), p. 437; C. Hofstede de Groot, *Beschreibendes und kritisches Verzeichnis der Werke der hervorragendsten holländischen Maler des XVII. Jahrhunderts*, Vol. IV (1911), p. 166, no. 560.

[7] Cited in Roger Portalis, "La Collection Walferdin et ses Fragonard," *Gazette des Beaux-Arts*, XXI (1880), 303, as written by Le Carpentier in 1808. In Roger Portalis, *Honoré Fragonard: sa vie et son oeuvre* (Paris, 1889), p. 126, the date is given as 1821. I have not been able to locate either the 1808 or the 1821 publication.

[8] For more on the activities of François Le Roy de Senneville as a collector, see Yves Durand, *Les Fermiers Géneraux au XVIIIᵉ Siècle* (Paris, 1971), 457 f., 501 f. I am grateful to Eunice Williams for this reference. Wilhelm (pp. 300, 303) was aware of Paillet's remarks that appeared in the Senneville catalogue regarding the Fragonard landscape and its relation to Ruisdael. He wrongly identified the Fragonard painting as *The Pond*, private collection (canvas, 38 x 46 cm.; Wildenstein, p. 233, no. 163, repr.). Since the relationship between *The Pond* and Ruisdael's landscapes is not very close, Wilhelm could use it to help clinch his erroneous thesis that all of Fragonard's landscapes painted in the Dutch manner were done after nature.

[9] The provenance of the painting is cited in n. 6 above.

[10] See Wildenstein, p. 191, nos. 3 and 7.

NOTES

[11]Ibid., p. 241, no. 181. There are also a couple of unpublished references in eighteenth-century sale catalogues to untraceable landscapes by Ruisdael with figures added by Fragonard. Whether these attributions were correct is, of course, unknown: sale, C[lesne], Paris (Paillet), 4 December 1786, no. 16; sale, [Sobert or Saubert and Desmarest], Paris (Paillet), 17 March 1789, no. 39. For the record, it should also be noted that Ruisdael's *Storm on the Dunes*, John G. Johnson Collection, Philadelphia (*Catalogue*, 1972, p. 77, no. 567) is possibly identical with Smith, *A Catalogue Raisonné of the Works of the Most Eminent Dutch, Flemish and French Painters*, Supplement, vol. IX (London, 1842), p. 710, no. 89; in Smith's opinion, the figures in it were added by "a skilful modern hand." The Johnson painting possibly appeared in the sale, Baron Delessert, Paris, 1846, no. 153, and possibly in the sale, Baron Delessert, Paris, 17 March 1869, no. 79; the compilers of these sales catalogues attributed the figures in the landscape to Fragonard. Hofstede de Groot (p. 152, no. 515), whose description of the staffage evidently was inaccurate (see *Johnson Catalogue*, 1972, p. 77, no. 567), also attributed the figures to Fragonard. Valentiner ascribed the figures to Prudhon (*Johnson Catalogue*, Vol. II, 1913, p. 124). Today the question of the authorship of the figures in the Johnson painting is academic; apart from a tiny one on the top of a high dune, they came away when the painting was cleaned in 1941.

[12]Fragonard's three copies are catalogued in A. Ananoff, *L'Oeuvre dessiné de Jean-Honoré Fragonard (1732-1806)*, Vol. I (Paris, 1961), p. 480, fig. 165; Vol. IV (1970), p. 202, nos. 2594, 2595, respectively. Ananoff, following the error made by the compiler of the Gros catalogue, wrongly calls Fragonard's copy after van der Helst a copy after Rembrandt; attention was called to this error in the Gros catalogue by Portalis "Collection Walferdin et ses Fragonard," pp. 303–304. Convincing evidence that Jordaen's painting was intended to be viewed as the apotheosis of Prince Fredrick Henry and not as the "triumph" of the prince, as it has been traditionally described, is given by William S. Heckscher, "Sturm und Drang: Conjectures on the Origin of a Phrase," *Simiolus*, I (1966-1967), 101 n. 8.

[13]For an edited facsimile of the catalogue see Émile Dacier, *Catalogues de Ventes et Livrets de Salons illustrés par Gabriel de Saint-Aubin*, Vol. VII, *Vente J. -A. Gros, 1778* (Paris, 1913).

[14]Sir Joshua Reynolds, "A Journey to Flanders and Holland in the Year 1781," in *The Literary Works of Sir Joshua Reynolds*, ed. by Henry William Beechy, Vol. II (London, 1890), p. 197.

IL "RITRATTO SCHULENBURG" DI GIAN ANTONIO GUARDI

Terisio Pignatti

Università di Venezia

Il *Ritratto del Maresciallo Schulenburg*, oggi esposto nel Museo del Settecento Veneziano a Cà Rezzonico, è una di quelle pitture che sembrano straordinariamente determinate per occupare un posto rilevante nella memoria di chi le osserva anche per breve tempo.[1] Nel formato un po' maggiore del naturale così come nella posa imperativa e magniloquente, nel rilievo delle luci balenanti così come nei colori densi e fermentanti, impreziositi da ori e velluti, il personaggio mi impressionò fortemente sin da quando lo vidi per la prima volta nella collezione del mio vecchio amico avvocato Ruggero Sonino a Venezia. Non mi meravigliò che nel 1952 il più grande conoscitore dei Guardi, il professor Antonio Morassi, lo attribuisse al suo prediletto Gian Antonio (fratello del vedutista Francesco), a quei tempi sottovalutato dalla critica.[2] Tenevo in grandissimo conto il più anziano dei Guardi, e fui subito persuaso della attribuzione, che allora poteva apparire quanto meno arrischiata (se non petulante). Mi adoperai perciò in ogni modo per acquisire il ritratto alle nostre collezioni civiche, dove fortunatamente entrò appunto nel 1955. Torna grato ora, che rispetto a quelle collezioni non mi compete altro che un titolo di Direttore Emerito, ritornare al ritratto del Maresciallo salvatore di Venezia nel 1716, nella occasione che si celebra oggi la attività generosa e geniale di un altro "salvatore di Venezia," l'amico dr. Franklin D. Murphy, cui è dedicato il presente saggio.

Johan Mathias von der Schulenburg nacque a Emden presso Magdeburg nel 1661, ed iniziò la sua brillante carriera militare al servizio di Casa Savoia, poi dei Duchi di Sassonia, quindi fu con gli Asburgo come comandante delle fanterie del Principe Eugenio di Savoia. Fu questo grande Generale che lo inviò alla Repubblica di Venezia per assumere la difesa di Corfù contro i Turchi: una strenua battaglia conclusa vittoriosamente nel 1716, che fruttò allo Schulenburg il titolo di salvatore di Venezia consacrato da monumenti a Corfù e all'Arsenale.[3] Ritiratosi dal servizio, a partire dal 1724 raccolse nel palazzo Loredan a San Vio una straordinaria collezione di pitture, in cui figuravano tutti i maggiori contemporanei. Singolare fu la sua abitudine di assumere stabilmente dei pittori stipendiati, fra i quali Pittoni, Piazzetta, Pitteri e Simonini. Vi primeggiarono i fratelli Guardi, con Gian Antonio che appare nei libri-cassa pressocchè continuamente fra il 1730 e il 1745. Oltre che a funzioni di restauratori e di periti, questi pittori furono impiegati come copisti. In particolare ciò riguardò i Guardi, che sin dall'inizio si erano dedicati a tale attività per scopo di lucro, ma anche forse per un caratteristico disinteresse per la ricerca icono-

Illus. 1. G. A. Guardi, Ritratto del Maresciallo Schulenburg. *Venezia, Ca' Rezzonico.*

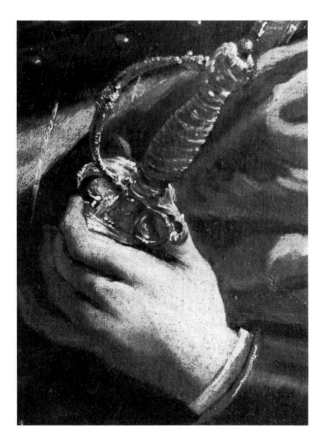

Illus. 2. G. A. Guardi, Ritratto del Maresciallo Schulenburg *(particolare). Venezia, Ca' Rezzonico.*

Illus. 3. G. A. Guardi, Ritratto del Maresciallo Schulenburg *(particolare). Venezia, Ca' Rezzonico.*

grafica, riservando tutto il loro genio alla realizzazione pittorica, nei modi del più scintillante Rococò.

Molte di codeste copie furono eseguite proprio da Gian Antonio. Ad esempio, negli anni fra il 1737 e il 1742 i "ritratti" del Maresciallo Schulenburg commissionatigli e pagati sono venti: essi servivano per regali che il vanitoso soldato faceva a parenti, ammiratrici, amici illustri, principi in tutta Europa. Allo stesso tempo, lo Schulenburg faceva copiare per proprio diletto i ritratti di altri personaggi famosi, per adornare le sale di Cà Loredan. Gli inventari della collezione, riscoperti dal Morassi presso gli eredi a Hehlen[4] permettono di identificare alcuni importanti gruppi, tuttora esistenti in quella galleria: cinque ritratti di principi di Casa d'Austria, sei di principi della casa regnante di Spagna, e numerosi altri. E' singolare la circostanza che nessuno di quei personaggi era noto direttamente ai Guardi: in molti casi, ne era però identificabile la fonte. Il Morassi infatti riconosce i modelli nelle pitture del Van Loo, Rigaud, Largillière, Van Schuppen, eccetera.[5]

Illus. 4. J. Van Schuppen, Ritratto del Principe Eugenio. *Amsterdam, Rijksmuseum.*

In codesto momento particolarissimo della attività di Gian Antonio Guardi—che in seguito svilupperà ben altra originalità creativa—cade anche il ritratto del Maresciallo Schulenburg conservato a Cà Rezzonico. Già il Morassi[6] ne identificava la fonte probabile in un originale "francese, tipo Largillière, o meglio Van Schuppen." Considerata la famigliarità con il Principe Eugenio, il Morassi ritenne anzi di poter indicare come modello della tela il *ritratto a cavallo del Principe Eugenio,* della Pinacoteca Sabauda di Torino, dipinto appunto dal Van Schuppen, del quale avrebbe ripreso "l'atteggiamento e lo spirito."[7] In verità, il ritratto Schulenburg riproduce quasi alla lettera posa e misure di un altro dipinto del

Illus. 5. G. A. Guardi, Ritratto di Don Filippo di Spagna. *Hehlen, Collezione Schulenburg.*

Van Schuppen, e cioè il *ritratto a mezzo busto del Principe Eugenio,* che si conserva al Rijksmuseum di Amsterdam (A. 373, cm. 147 x 119).[8]

Il confronto fra il modello del Van Schuppen (inciso da Bernhard Picart nel 1718 e noto quindi al Guardi forse per quella via) e il ritratto veneziano sembrano confermare la identità della composizione. La figura è vista di 3/4, allo stesso modo; simile è l'andamento delle braccia e l'angolazione dello sguardo; del tutto simili sono anche gli sfondi con una battaglia di cavalleria incor-

niciata dal braccio destro del personaggio; mentre un albero a larghi fogliami bilancia la scena sul lato opposto. Le differenze sono invece sensibili nei volti, che appartengono a due persone diverse. Quella del dipinto veneziano spicca per la eccezionale, immediata vitalità.

Non mi pare dubbio, pertanto, che mentre il dipinto del Van Schuppen rappresenta il Principe Eugenio, quello di Venezia sia invece il ritratto dello Schulenburg. Che sia dipinto da Gian Antonio Guardi, è provato ad evidenza dal confronto con i numerosi altri ritratti documentati dal libro-cassa, fra il quarto e il quinto decennio. Ad esempio, il giovane *Don Filippo di Spagna*, oggi degli eredi Schulenburg, pagato a Gian Antonio nel 1741, appare addirittura sovrapponibile, nel fastoso trattamento delle sete della bandoliera, nell'elmo piumoso, nell'impasto sciolto e frizzante delle superfici, nello sfondo dai toni sfocati e plumbei.

Un'ultima osservazione si riferisce alla identificazione del per-

Illus. 6. F. Rusca-M. Pitteri, Ritratto del Maresciallo Schulenburg *(stampa).*

Illus. 7. G. B. Piazzetta, Ritratto del Maresciallo Schulenburg *(disegno). Collezione dell'Art Institute di Chicago.*

sonaggio che è certo lo Schulenburg, per il confronto con i numerosi ritratti che ce ne sono giunti, eseguiti anche da diversi artisti. Una *stampa del Pitteri* del 1735, tratta da un dipinto del Rusca, presenta il Maresciallo con un aspetto assai prestante: non si direbbe davvero che potesse avere a quel tempo già 74 anni! Come già annotammo nel 1960,[9] il ritratto di Cà Rezzonico è databile sul 1730, cioè quando il Maresciallo era circa settantenne (ma come d'uso lo ringiovanisce alquanto). Decisamente più tardi sembrano invece i due *ritratti a disegno, del Piazzetta,* noti nelle collezioni del Castello Sforzesco a Milano e in quella Schulenburg in Germania (passato ora all'Art Institute di Chicago). Faremmo qualche riserva sulla identificazione del primo (che peraltro la Precerutti Garberi e in genere la letteratura gli danno);[10] stupendo e certamente identificabile è il foglio di Chicago, che mostra un Generale pateticamente invecchiato, con l'occhio un pò spento e le carni appassite, anche se le labbra contratte e la posa marziale del capo ben ricordano il suo inflessibile carattere. Poichè sembra che il disegno di Chicago sia identificabile con un foglio pagato 7 zecchini al Piazzetta, secondo i libri dell'archivio Schulenburg,[11] ecco dunque stabilito un *antequem* che confermerebbe la nostra datazione della tela di Cà Rezzonico intorno al 1730.

Erano quelli i primi anni del servizio di Gian Antonio presso il suo nobile protettore: e sono le sue vere sembianze, quelle mostrate dalla tela di Cà Rezzonico, riprese dal vero e non ricopiate—come poi altre volte—da opere altrui. Ciò dà ancora maggior valore a quest'opera singolarissima nella storia artistica del nostro pittore.

NOTE

[1] T. Pignatti, *Il Museo Correr di Venezia* (Venezia, 1960), p. 105. Inv. 2187.

[2] A. Morassi, "Settecento inedito," *Arte Veneta*, 6 (1952), 85–98.

[3] A. Morassi, "Antonio Guardi ai servigi del Feldmaresciallo Schulenburg," *Emporium*, 131, 784 (4/1960), 147–164, 785 (5/1960), 199–212.

[4] Ibid., passim.

[5] A. Morassi, *Guardi* (Venezia, 1973), pp. 59 e segg.

[6] Morassi, "Antonio Guardi" (1960), pp. 200–203.

[7] Morassi, *Guardi*, (1973), p. 55.

[8] Ringrazio cordialmente il pittore Nat Leeb, che nel 1979 volle parteciparmi queste notizie con molta generosità, indicandomi anche la pittura di Amsterdam, e suggerendo che la tela di Ca' Rezzonico rappresentasse il Principe Eugenio. Il Leeb non escludeva però che l'autore del nostro dipinto fosse il Guardi. Ringrazio anche la Direzione del Museo che mi ha fornito le foto.

[9] Pignatti, *Il Museo Correr di Venezia* (1960), p. 108.

[10] M. Precerutti Garberi, *G. B. Piazzetta e l'Accademia* (Milano, 1971), n. 3.

[11] Ibid.

AGGIUNTE AL CATALOGO DI ANTONIO GUARDI "COPISTA"

Francesco Valcanover
Soprintendente ai Beni Artistici e Storici di Venezia

Illus. 1. Antonio Guardi, S. Giovanni Battista. Dublin, National
Gallery of Ireland.

Illus. 2. Tiziano. S. Giovanni Battista. Venezia, Gallerie dell'Accademia.

NELL'ARTICOLO fondamentale per la ricostruzione dell'attività di Antonio Guardi al servizio di Giovanni Matteo von der Schulemburg,[1] comandante delle truppe veneziane di terra nei primi decenni del Settecento, Antonio Morassi offre molte notizie sulla copia tratta dall'artista dal "S. Giovanni Battista" di Tiziano, in origine conservato nella chiesa veneziana di S. Maria Maggiore ed oggi alle Gallerie dell'Accademia. La copia, già iniziata nel novembre 1738, era ultimata nel febbraio del 1739 poichè il 12 di quel mese Antonio Guardi riceveva il saldo definitivo. Che si trattasse di un'opera di particolare importanza lo si ricava, secondo il Morassi, dalla durata del lavoro, dal costo di 24 ducati e dalla stima di 100 ducati contenuta nell'inventario manoscritto della Galleria Schulemburg. Il dipinto, ereditato da Federico Adolfo, nipote dello Schulemburg, ed inviato in Germania il 24 marzo 1741 con la dodicesima spedizione della Galleria Schulemburg, non è più ricordato in alcun elenco o inventario e quindi è considerato scomparso dal Morassi. Fortunatamente la tela (illus. 1) esiste ancora ed è conservata nella National Gallery of Ireland di Dublino.[2] Le sue misure, di m. 1,64 x 1,28, sono relativamente di poco inferiori a quelle del prototipo tizianesco (illus. 2), che misura m. 2,01 x 1,34. Antonio Guardi, nella impaginazione della figura, nell'agnello e nei particolari dello sfondo paesistico, si attiene all'originale di Tiziano. Ma profondamente personale ne è la interpretazione stilistica. La soda pienezza plastica del "S. Giovanni Battista," con la quale Tiziano sembra porsi in gara con Michelangelo nel momento di più dichiarata crisi manieristica, muta nella "copia" del Guardi senior in un morbido e macchiato pittoricismo, creato dal rapido fraseggio di pennellate incrociate, al quale è estraneo ogni contorno, ogni disegno preciso. Per questo magistrale gioco di tocco e per l'effervescente andamento del chiaroscuro la figura del Battista sembra allungarsi e come atteggiarsi in una mossa di balletto. Non meno risolto nel trasparente impasto del colore franto dal colpeggiare franco del pennello in brillii improvvisi di luce è il fondale paesistico che traspone su di un piano di frizzante decorativismo di gusto rococò il testo tizianesco così densamente "naturalistico."

La nuova opera di Antonio Guardi tratta dall'anonimato è di notevole importanza essendo un altro termine di paragone cronologicamente sicuro per la ricostruzione dell'attività dell'artista sullo scorcio del quarto decennio del Settecento, di cui si conoscono altre prove di certa datazione eseguite anch'esse per lo Schulemburg: la copia del 1738 del Museo di Halle (Saale) di una "Ultima

Cena" di Sebastiano Ricci[3] e le due copie del 1739 di collezione privata di Milano della "Fortezza" e della "Temperanza" di scuola tintorettesca della chiesa veneziana della Madonna dell'Orto.[4] Il gruppo di dipinti si caratterizza per la morbida densità della struttura pittorica, ancora non sfatta nella diafana ed impalpabile luminosità delle opere tarde. E questo momento di stile si ritrova nella paletta della chiesa parrocchiale di Vigo d'Anaunia[5] e nell' "Ultima Cena" della Collezione Stramezzi di Milano[6] che quindi non devono valicare di molto la fine del quarto decennio del Settecento.

NOTE

[1]A. Morassi, "Antonio Guardi ai servigi del Feldmaresciallo Schulenburg," *Emporium*, 131, 784, 154–155.

[2]Ringrazio Michael Wynne di avermi concesso la pubblicazione in questa sede del dipinto e ricordo che Egli aveva ben compreso l'importanza dell'opera.

[3]A. Morassi, *Antonio e Francesco Guardi* (Alfieri, Venezia, s.d.), I, 313; II, fig. 37.

[4]*Ibid.*, I, 330; II, fig. 136 e 137.

[5]*Ibid.*, I, 318; II, fig. 61.

[6]*Ibid.*, I, 313; II, fig. 35.

PARS PRO TOTO
HANDS AND FEET AS SCULPTURAL SUBJECTS BEFORE RODIN

H. W. Janson

New York University

RODIN'S OEUVRE includes a number of hands, single or paired, which he treated as self-contained works. The earliest, such as the *Clenched Left Hand* (illus. 1), date from about 1885 and seem to be by-products of the artist's studies for *The Burghers of Calais*. What this group has in common is a concentration on the expressive potential of the male hand as a conveyor of extreme states of emotional tension. A second group, dating from around the turn of the century, includes *The Hand of God* (illus. 2), perhaps the best-known example, c.1895; *The Devil's Hand*; and *The Industrial Hand*. Their common denominator is the hand as a creative instrument. These hands, too, are emphatically masculine, and the small figures held by *The Hand of God* and *The Devil's Hand* suggest that they are really the hands of the divine (or demonic) sculptor whose power to breathe life into dead unshaped matter is only a single step beyond Rodin's own. That such an analogy, or near identity, was indeed thought of by Rodin himself, or at least among his close associates, is indicated by a pastiche, a life cast of Rodin's right hand taken some weeks before his death in 1917 by Paul Cruet, a member of his studio, into which Cruet has inserted one of the artist's small female torsos.

Meanwhile, between 1908 and 1910, Rodin had produced another group of works in which he explored the symbolic meaning of hands. In *The Cathedral*, two female right hands are grouped so as to enclose a lozenge-shaped empty space suggestive of a Gothic arch. Its male counterpart is *The Secret*, exhibited in 1910 as *Hands Holding the Sacred Tablets*. Another pair of hands, one male, one female, emerges from a block; Georges Grappe calls them *Hands of Lovers*, and their relationship does indeed recall the many troubled lovers in Rodin's earlier work. Finally, there is *The Hand from the Tomb* (illus. 3), a single male hand thrusting upward from a draped rectangular block with an uninscribed tablet on its front.

Unlike Rodin's torsos, whose origin and significance have been explored in recent years,[1] these hands have attracted little analytic attention. John L. Tancock, in his scholarly catalogue of the Rodin Museum in Philadelphia, offers the most extensive study of the subject so far, citing the traditional image of the Hand of God, a drawing of a hand by Victor Hugo, and Eadweard Muybridge's photographs of hands in motion.[2] Significant as these sources are, they suggest neither the full range of the iconographic traditions behind Rodin's hands nor their sculptural antecedents. The subject

Ilus. 1. Auguste Rodin, Clenched Left Hand. *Bronze, c. 1885. Private collection. Courtesy Albert Elsen.*

Facing page

Illus. 2. Auguste Rodin, The Hand of God. *Marble, c. 1895. Musée Rodin, Paris. Courtesy Foto Marburg.*

is in fact so rich that this essay can do no more than suggest its many ramifications.

The Hand of God as a *pars pro toto*, as the single, and sufficient, anthropomorphic feature of the Deity, owes its origin to the cult of the sun god Aten introduced by Akhenaten about 1360 B.C. In numerous images dating from that pharaoh's reign, we see him adoring the sun disk, each of whose rays terminates in a hand. In Assyria, as seen in a relief in the British Museum (illus. 4), these multiple hands are reduced to two, reaching down from a radiant disk or cloud in the sky. It is this Mesopotamian tradition that accounts for the Judeo-Christian Hand of God thrusting into the picture space from above, which makes its earliest known appearance about A.D. 250 in the wall paintings of the synagogue at Dura-Europos. Each of these hands seems to represent a specific divine

Illus. 4. Assyria, "Broken Obelisk,"
c. 1100 B.C. British Museum, Lon-
don. Reproduced by permission.

Illus. 5. The Vision of Ezekiel,
detail. Wall painting from the Syn-
agogue at Dura-Europos, c. A.D. 250.
Museum, Damascus. Yale University
Art Gallery, Dura-Europos Collec-
tion.

Illus. 6. Egypt, Torso (Ex-Voto). *Limestone, Third Century* B.C. *Private Collection, Courtesy L'Ibia Gallery, New York.*

command, so that some of these murals, containing more than one biblical episode, show several Hands of God (illus. 5).[3] While such literal-mindedness is rare, The Hand of God became a ubiquitous feature of Early Christian and Medieval art. The tradition is so well known that we need not review it here.

Classical antiquity contributed little to our subject. There are large numbers of isolated hands and feet, as well as other organs, deposited in temples as ex-votos; they are mostly of terracotta and betray no artistic ambition.[4] We also find occasional rhytons in the shape of feet (illus. 7) and numerous hands, often of bronze, linked with magic practices.[5] These, too, are aesthetically negligible, although of great interest to historians of religion. Still, they may stand in some sort of ancestral relationship with the hand- (or more usually arm-) and foot-shaped reliquaries of the Middle Ages. Many of them are splendid products of the goldsmith's art and can claim to be the earliest aesthetically ambitious self-contained sculptural images of hands and feet, but they are also unmistakably containers, hence of very limited expressive potential.

In Renaissance art, the Hand of God reaching down out of the clouds was replaced by the image of the Lord, in the shape of a majestic old man, moving through the sky, as in Ghiberti's *Gates of Paradise* or in the Sistine Ceiling. It survived, however, in emblem books, which also contain various nondivine hands, often derived from the study of hieroglyphics and other occult signs. We now also meet the first systematic studies of hands as instruments of a "language of gestures," related to the revived interest in physiognomics and chiromancy. John Bulwer's *Chirologia* (London, 1644) is typical of this genre. The title page defines the subject of the treatise as "the natural language of the hand," which the author terms "the chiefest instrument of eloquence." We can hardly begrudge him his self-chosen title of *Philochirosophus.* The plates, each with forty or more images of hand gestures, constitute a veritable dictionary of manual eloquence.

It is not until the mid-eighteenth century, however, that we encounter the earliest sculptures of hands made for aesthetic reasons as works complete in themselves. They are six terracotta hands, three male and three female, by François Roubiliac in the Victoria and Albert Museum (illus. 8, 9). The cuts above the wrists are carefully smoothed and the details are finely finished, so that these objects could not be bozzetti or studies. Nor are they related to the hands of any of Roubiliac's known statues. A look at the

female hands makes it obvious that these pieces are not life casts of actual hands, since they are clearly stylized in conformity with the Baroque ideal of the sensuously beautiful female hand. For what purpose, if any, were they made? Nothing is known about them except that they were given to the Museum in 1944 by the daughter of the Victorian painter Edward Henry Corbould, who had acquired them at some point in his career. The sale catalogue of Roubiliac's collection in May, 1762, lists four lots, of twelve hands each, under "Sundries in Plaister."[6] Conceivably, some or all of these hands were by Roubiliac, rather than plaster casts of hands of classical statues, and some of them may have been of terracotta rather than plaster. If so, the six hands now in the Victoria and Albert Museum remained in the artist's studio until his death. That

Illus. 8. François Roubiliac, Female Left Hand. Terracotta, c. 1750. Victoria and Albert Museum, London (Crown Copyright). Reproduced by permission.

Illus. 9. François Roubiliac, Female Left Hand. *Terracotta, c. 1750. Victoria and Albert Museum, London (Crown Copyright). Reproduced by permission.*

they are indeed by Roubiliac may be regarded as certain on grounds of style. The most plausible answer to our question, then, is that they were made as models to be copied by Roubiliac's students.

It is likely that ever since the later sixteenth century many artists' workshops included collections of plaster or terracotta heads, hands, feet, and torsos as study objects to be copied by apprentices. These *disjecta membra* were portions of famous classical or recent statues cut apart for convenience. That this practice does indeed go back to the late Cinquecento is proved by a considerable number of terracotta hands, feet, legs, and torsos that used to be regarded as studies by Michelangelo but are now recognized as reduced copies after details of the master's best-known works, produced as exercises or for study by apprentices. The largest group of them can be traced back to the collection of the Nuremberg patrician Paul von Praun, who probably acquired them around 1600 in Bologna, where he spent many years of his life. Some of the Praun terracottas have ended up in the Victoria and Albert Museum, where they are catalogued as "after Michelangelo" without attri-

Illus. 10. Vincenzo Vela, The Art-ist's Right Hand. *Marble, c. 1850-1860. Museo Vela, Ligornetto (Ticino). Photo H. W. Janson.*

bution to any specific maker. Their age, as I have been kindly informed by the staff, is indeed roughly four hundred years, according to thermoluminescence tests. All of the Praun terracottas are directly related to parts of well-known statues by Michelangelo, so closely, in fact, that they cannot possibly be studies for these statues. One of them has a metal peg attached to it for convenient suspension on a string or nail. What differentiates the Roubiliac hands from these earlier pieces is that they are original productions, homemade paradigms, as it were, rather than copies of "classics."

Roubiliac's hands had no immediate successors. Neoclassical sculptors shunned the self-contained fragment, except of course for the bust, which was sanctioned by ancient precedent. Romanticism, in contrast, reveled in sculptured hands, investing them with every kind of high sentiment.[7] The hands of great individuals, especially artists and poets, were thought as meaningful as the face in revealing the unique personality of genius. Among the most famous examples are the clasped hands of Robert and Elizabeth Browning by the American sculptress Harriet Hosmer, based on a life cast made in 1853, which became a symbol of the ideal marriage of these two poetic souls. The right hand of the Italian sculptor Pietro Tenerani was portrayed in 1852 by his pupil Amadori.[8] Soon after, the Swiss sculptor Vincenzo Vela carved a "double portrait" of himself and his wife (illus. 10, 11): his own right hand,

Illus. 11. Vincenzo Vela, The Left Hand of Mrs. Vela. *Marble, c. 1850-1860. Museo Vela, Ligornetto (Ticino). Photo H. W. Janson.*

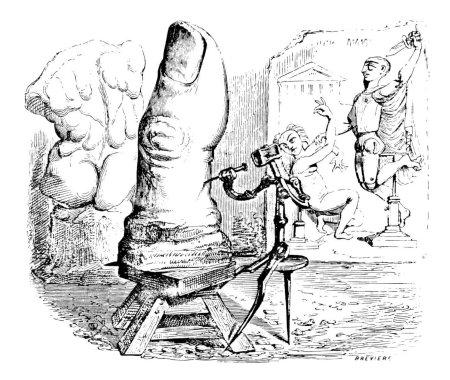

Illus. 12. Grandville, The Finger of God, *from* Un autre monde. *1844. Photo H. W. Janson.*

Illus. 13. Hiram Powers, Loulie's Hand. *Plaster, c. 1840. National Collection of Fine Arts, Washington, D.C. Photo H. W. Janson.*

holding a modeling tool, and her left, displaying a cameo of her husband along with a pen, a ball of thread, and a pair of scissors. Examples such as these could be multiplied ad infinitum, from the 1830s to the end of the century.[9] The mania was caricatured by Grandville in 1844 in one of his illustrations for *Un autre monde,* which shows a gigantic sculptured thumb with the title *The Finger of God* (illus. 12). But Romantic hands did not necessarily have to stand for individual genius or character. Hiram Powers' *Loulie's Hand* (illus. 13), the hand of his baby daughter framed by a cuff of flower petals, could be widely admired as embodying the miracle of birth and childhood.[10] Elegant anonymous women's hands were popular as flower vases or paperweights, emblems of femininity. More rarely, a woman's foot could serve the same purpose, although here a sharper distinction must be drawn between the impersonal perfection of the feet of classical Venuses, casts of which were widely reproduced,[11] and sculptured "portraits" of female feet from life, intimate mementos of love frowned upon by Victorian prudery. The highly individual marble foot preserved in a country house near Dublin, carved (after a life cast?) by the Irish sculptor John Hogan, is of the latter kind (illus. 14). Still more redolent with erotic appeal is an exceptionally graceful terracotta foot at Compiègne (illus. 15), said to be that of a famous French actress of the 1850s. With its turban above the ankle, its string of pearls, and the bit of flowery lawn on which it rests, it represents the perfect *pars pro toto* of an odalisque.

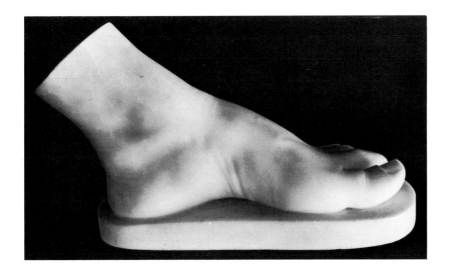

Illus. 14. John Hogan, Left Foot of Lady Cloncurry. *Marble, 1841. Lyons House, County Dublin. Photo H. W. Janson.*

Illus. 15. Anonymous, Female Right Foot. *Terracotta, c. 1860. Chateau, Compiègne. Photo H. W. Janson.*

Illus. 16. Steeple of the First Presbyterian Church, completed 1859. Port Gibson, Mississippi. Photo H. W. Janson.

Grandville's *Finger of God* has no counterpart in the sculpture of the period, but the Hand of God made a surprising appearance in the American South in the second half of the century as the crowning feature of church steeples, replacing the traditional cross. One exists in Port Gibson, Mississippi (illus. 16). The building was completed in 1859, and the gigantic hand was carved soon after by a local craftsman. This wooden hand, twelve feet tall and overlaid with gold leaf, had so deteriorated by the end of the century that it had to be replaced by a gilt metal hand. While Port Gibson prides itself on its steeple hand as unique, there must have been quite a number of such hands. Another specimen, of wood and of more modest size—it is only 50" tall—exists in Georgia, from the now destroyed Presbyterian church in the little town of Midway. Since the Port Gibson hand also crowns the steeple of a Presbyterian church, such hands may have been a local Presbyterian tradition.

But we are straying too far afield. Let us return to France, and to the most spectacular and artistically ambitious antecedent for Rodin's earliest hand sculptures such as the *Clenched Left Hand* (illus. 1). It is, somewhat unexpectedly, the work of Frédéric-Auguste Bartholdi, the sculptor of the Statue of Liberty. He was Alsatian but an ardent Francophile. Out of sheer patriotism he designed in 1872, immediately after the Franco-Prussian War, a memorial to two members of the *garde nationale* from his hometown, Colmar, who had been killed while resisting the invaders. The monument was placed in the municipal cemetery, some distance from the center of town, and successfully hidden from the Nazis during World War II. Its main elements consist of a headstone with a suitable inscription and two horizontal slabs, one of which is being lifted by a ghostly bronze hand; the right arm has already pushed through the crack and is vainly reaching for a saber that remains beyond its grasp (illus. 17). That hand, although far more realistic in detail, is a close match for Rodin's excessively strained hands of 1885.

Did Rodin know the Colmar memorial? Bartholdi showed the model for it in the Paris Salon of 1898, in time for Rodin to have seen it before he designed his own *Hand from the Tomb* (illus. 3). But how accessible was it during the intervening years since 1872? Presumably, any visitor could see it in Bartholdi's studio, although there is no record of any link between Rodin and Bartholdi. There remains a third possibility: the model for the Colmar memorial could have been discussed, and quite possibly reproduced, in the

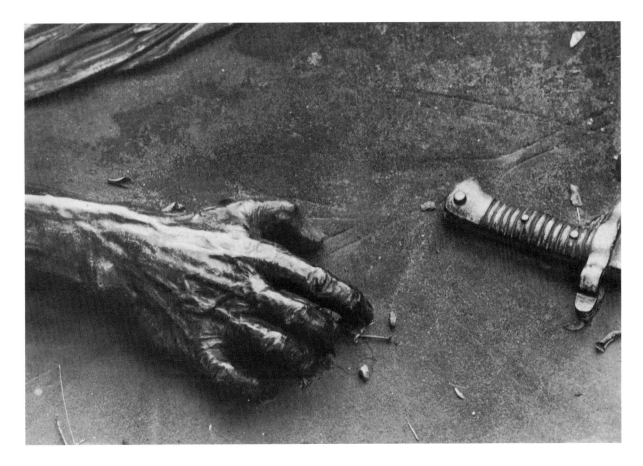

press between 1872 and 1898. If that had happened before the early 1880s—unfortunately, there is no way to verify this hypothesis without sifting a huge mass of material—Rodin would almost surely have been aware of it, since he was a voracious reader of newspapers and journals.[12] Whether or not Bartholdi helped to inspire Rodin's *Clenched Left Hand*, it is difficult to conceive of *The Hand from the Tomb* without the influence of the Colmar memorial.

NOTES

[1]See especially Albert Elsen, *The Partial Figure in Modern Sculpture from Rodin to 1969*, Exhibition Catalogue, Baltimore Museum of Art (Baltimore, Md., 1969), pp. 16 ff.

[2]John L. Tancock, *The Sculpture of Auguste Rodin* (Philadelphia, 1976), pp. 616–638. For the Hand of God, Rodin's own view and the responses of contemporary critics, see Ruth Butler, "Religious Sculpture in Post-Christian France," in *The Romantics to Rodin: French Nineteenth-Century Sculpture from North American Collections*, ed. Peter Fusco and H. W. Janson, Exhibition Catalogue, Los Angeles County Museum of Art, (Los Angeles, Calif., 1980), pp. 346 f.

[3]A possible intermediate stage between the Assyrian type and Dura-Europos is the cult of Sabathius, whose symbol was a hand; see H. P. L'Orange, *Studies on the Iconography of Cosmic Kingship in the Ancient World* (Oslo, 1953).

[4]Egyptian ex-votos of the late Pharaonic and early Ptolemaic periods (the custom does not appear to have existed earlier) are of limestone and some are of remarkable quality. Interestingly enough, they may include torsos (illus. 6), presumably as thanks offerings for the curing of ills of the body as distinguished from those of the head or the extremities. See C. C. Edgar, *Sculptor's Studies and Unfinished Works* (Catalogue général des antiquités egyptiennes du Caire) (Cairo, 1906) for material of this kind. The rough surface of the example here reproduced does not indicate that the piece was left unfinished but only that it lacks the final polish, which apparently was not thought necessary for ex-votos. I owe my acquaintance with Egyptian ex-votos to the kindness of my friend and colleague, Bernard V. Bothmer.

[5]Many of the latter were linked with the cult of Sabathius; see n. 3 above.

[6]I am indebted to Charles Avery and Ronald Lightbown of the Victoria and Albert Museum staff for the information reported here on the Roubiliac terracotta hands.

[7]See Donald M. Reynolds, "The 'Unveiled Soul': Hiram Powers' Embodiment of the Ideal," *The Art Bulletin* 59 (1977): 402 f.

[8]I owe my acquaintance with this piece to the kindness of its owner, William Gerdts.

[9]A large group of bronze hands was included in the sale of the Dodge Collection at Sotheby's, New York, in 1975. Two surgeons in the New York area have been collecting such hands for their medical as well as their aesthetic interest.

[10]See Reynolds, "The 'Unveiled Soul'."

[11]Lady Morgan, in 1821, refers to the foot of the Venus de'Medici as "a monument in itself" (ibid.).

[12]For Rodin's alertness to writings on art of every sort, see Ruth Butler, *Rodin in Perspective*, Artists in Perspective (Englewood Cliffs, N.J.: Spectrum Books, Prentice-Hall, Inc., 1980), pp. 1–31.

Author's Note. An earlier version of this essay was presented at the annual meeting of the College Art Association of America in Los Angeles, February 3-5, 1977.

CLAUDE BUCK AND THE INTROSPECTIVES

Charles C. Eldredge
The University of Kansas

Illus. 1. Claude Buck, Self Portrait, *ca. 1910, oil on canvas. Collection Mrs. Benjamin D. Kopman, Haddam, Connecticut.*

ON THE SECOND OF April, 1917, President Woodrow Wilson addressed the joint Congress which he had called into extraordinary session. The President advised "that the Congress declare the recent course of the Imperial German Government to be in fact nothing less than war against the government and people of the United States and that it formally accept the status of belligerent which has thus been thrust upon it . . ." Wilson made his recommendation "with a profound sense of the solemn and even tragical character of the step I am taking and of the grave responsibilities which it involves . . ." He warned the nation that "there are, it may be, months of fiery trial and sacrifice ahead of us. It is a fearful thing to lead this great peaceful people into war, into the most terrible and disastrous of all wars, civilization itself seeming to be in the balance." But, the United States must "do these things, these deeply momentous things" in order that "the world . . . be made safe for democracy."[1]

While Wilson was making his memorable address, another, less noted event was taking place in New York City, an occurrence which, like so many others that day, was to be overshadowed and ultimately overwhelmed by world war. On April 2, 1917, the Knoedler Galleries opened a special exhibition of "Imaginative Paintings by Thirty Young Artists," a show intended to introduce new talent to the American art audience. Under the rubric of imaginative, the thirty painters were joined in an effort to highlight the subjectivist tendency in modern art. Theirs was a pictorial protest "against superficial surface art, however excellent the craftsmanship, and a plea for art which expresses insight, feeling, imagination."[2] The interest in such qualities was occasioned by the artists' "romantic and idealistic character—because, in the face of present world calamities . . . the note of idealism . . . is the most important contribution the American artist can make to the public."[3]

Unfortunately for the artists and their public, the idealistic contributions were overlooked in the war fever that followed President Wilson's declaration. The war to make the world "safe for democracy" had a phenomenal impact on society, deeply affecting not only American art but all aspects of national life. In the altered America which emerged from the war, the "imaginative" painters were no longer to have a collective identity or influence. A few—notably the Zorachs, William and Marguerite—achieved note in subsequent careers, but generally not with the motifs nor even the mediums introduced at Knoedler's. Most went on to obscurity, victims of a changing environment and aesthetics in the years following World War I. What ever happened to Sulamith Sokolsky, Fred J. Wehrle, or Mary Bayne Bugbird? Where are the later works of Paulet Thevenay, Thomas Carilear Cole, and Olive Rush? And what became of the self-designated "Introspective Painters"— Claude Buck, Abraham Harriton, Benjamin D. Kopman, and Jennings Tofel—the quartet around whom the Knoedler exhibition was organized?

The Introspectives' relative obscurity today can be traced in part to the social and artistic upheavals that attended American entry into world war, cutting off opportunities for their youthful promise. The foursome centered on the gregarious Buck and his future brother-in-law, Kopman. Tofel was the theorist of the group, the most given to reflection upon their chosen pursuit of subjective imagery.[4] It was he who authored the Introspective manifesto which was published in conjunction with the Knoedler exhibition. Harriton, who had with Buck and Kopman been a student at the National Academy of Design, did not long continue his association with the group following their introduction at Knoedler's, after which he endured a fifteen-year hiatus before his first one-man show.

Buck's career is characteristic of many of his generation, and well represents the particular goals and fate of the Introspectives. Charles Claude Buck was born July 3, 1890, in New York City. His father, William Robert Buck, was a photographer and carver, who named his son after the French landscapist, Claude Lorrain. He encouraged his children's interest in art and offered young Claude his first instruction. When only eight years old, Buck applied to General Cesnola, director of the Metropolitan Museum, for permission to copy in the galleries. The precocious youth was denied a permit because of his age, but with persistence and family contacts was finally granted permission to copy when he was eleven. For the next three years he worked regularly in the Metropolitan galleries, copying practically every great painting in the collection. The affection for the Old Masters which Buck developed at that early age remained with him throughout his long career.[5]

The artist's formal training commenced with his admission to the National Academy of Design at age fourteen. There, he initially studied still life painting with Emil Carlsen, who especially favored his talented student. He subsequently pursued figure study with George deForest Brush, and also took instruction in sculpture, etching and portraiture, winning many prizes in student competitions. Buck remained at the Academy for eight years, and during that time came to know well many of the leading academicians. Francis C. Jones and his brother, H. Bolton Jones, befriended him and welcomed him to their studios. Kenyon Cox in particular favored Buck and invited him to spend a summer at his country home, where he and Cox's son, Allyn, became close friends. In short, Buck excelled in his student role, earning the acclaim and respect of his teachers and fellow students alike. A fragment of an early self-portrait suggests something of the artist's Byronic appearance and debonair manner at that age (illus. 1).

The successful student's transition to professional career was not, however, entirely a smooth one. Buck initially had difficulty interesting dealers in his distinctive compositions, many of which were suggestive of the Renaissance models which he continued to admire. What art dealers there were in New York preferred the original Old Masters to modern variants on them, and those few brave gallery owners who advanced the cause of modern and American art, such as Alfred Stieglitz, did not encourage Buck. Thus, it was not on the basis of his favorite religious and allegorical subjects that Buck supported himself, but rather by his portrait commissions. He produced numerous and competent life-sized paintings (for $5 to $15 each, including frames), while privately pursuing his other artistic interests. The frustration that attended this commerical work was considerable, and the artist turned with increased interest to evocative literary motifs and complex allegorical schemes which, although finding no exhibitors, provided an outlet for his fertile imagination.

Buck's fascination with imaginative themes extended from his National Academy days to the mid-1920s, and was most pronounced in the period from *circa* 1914 to 1921. His subjects were generally invested with a strongly evocative and moody quality, reflecting a predilection for the imaginative literature which he read extensively during this period. Blake and Poe, Dante and Shakespeare, the Bible, Byron, Shelley and Keats, Baudelaire—all were familiar to and admired by Claude Buck, and from such diverse sources he drew motifs for his paintings and drawings.

Most of Buck's early oil paintings (other than the commissioned portraits) were small in size. They were often marked by subdued tonalities, probably inspired by the heavily varnished Old Masters he admired, but were relieved by brilliant highlights of jeweled color. Unity of effect was achieved by generalizations of form and by an atmospheric haziness which pervaded many compositions; this last device suggests Buck's allegiance to Leonardo and his *sfumato* technique. Buck was primarily a figurative artist, and often concentrated on the nude, particularly the female. His figures were distinctively and gracefully elongated, a trademark suggestive of sources as disparate as the School of Fontainebleau, the pre-Raphaelite Brotherhood, Arthur B. Davies and Ivan Meštrović. The painter especially admired the Yugoslav sculptor who had "rejuvenated by exaggeration the long-lost principle known as movement in form, used as an emotional force."[6]

Buck's concentration upon emotional force led him to decry the efforts of the so-called realists whose art, he thought, "must be judged only by how well it performs its function. At best, the purely realistic picture is a technical performance, for which we must admire the skill of the artist more than the picture."[7] He believed that "the poetry of a picture means more . . . than the imitation or even the representation of nature . . . We have had no dearth of prose painters painting prose stories and prose histories; what the world needs most, tho, is poet painters! Painters of lyrics and epics."[8]

With Tofel and the other Introspectives, Buck believed that "a work of art shall be abstracted from nature, and in the confines of its frame, shall live in its own complete life, requiring no commentaries, no exterior exegesis. . . . It shall suggest more than relate, for suggestion is the depth beyond the depth—the gauntlet to the imagination of the observer, that disturbs and quickens his susceptibilities." Furthermore, a work of art "shall be subdued in tone. Sunlight hatches no profound thoughts. It shall surprise and inspire, it shall soothe and exalt, and lift the behold from the dust of the earth, even if only for a moment. For such moments are the perfect life, the life beautiful and sublime."[9]

With such elevated sentiments did the Introspectives introduce their work in 1917. The first showing of the quartet's work opened in Mrs. Harry Payne Whitney's Studio on March 20, 1917, several weeks prior to the Knoedler show. It was Buck who had sought Mrs. Whitney's interest and patronage for the group; with the assistance of The Friends of the Young Artists, an organization in which the noted patroness had a decided interest, he prevailed upon Mrs. Whitney to sponsor their first showing. Buck also induced Van Deering Perrine to join in the exhibition, as Mrs. Whitney required that the Introspectives must include at least one well-known artist in the show; ultimately three other artists, the painters Jacque R. Chesno and Felix Russmann and the wood-carver Robert Laurent, accepted invitations to participate in the Whitney Studio showing.

To that exhibition Buck contributed twenty-eight pictures, mostly works done in the preceding two years.[10] In addition to portraits of his wife, of Kopman, and of himself, he exhibited paintings drawn from Biblical themes (*Adam and Eve*, 1915; *Hagar at the Well*; *Creation of Man*; *Ruth*) and literary or legendary sources (*Salome*, 1917; *Death and the Girl*, 1917). Other works had titles suggestive of idyll, reverie, and allegory (*Poet Shepherd* and *Poet Shepherdess*; *Moonlight Fantasy*; *Il Pensero*, 1915, *L'Allegro*, 1915, and *Death*, 1913).

Buck's subjects and their distinctive handling, as well as the artist's pronouncements and those of his colleagues, demonstrate the Introspectives' descent from the lineage of Poe and Blake, Ryder and Moreau, and other visionaries of an earlier epoch. The emphasis upon the artwork's suggestive powers aligns the Introspectives particularly with the Symbolist mood of the turn of the century. This affinity is not surprising in view of the Symbolists' impact upon American thought and art during Buck's formative years.

The fabled Armory Show of 1913 introduced American audiences to large numbers of European modernists. Although that exhibition's impact has been sometimes overestimated in subsequent accounts, it does nevertheless provide one important landmark in histories of twentieth-century American art. While much attention was paid to the innovative cubists, and commentaries on "explosions in shingle factories" prevailed, the Armory Show actually gave greater proportional representation to artists of other persuasions. The exhibition's large showings of Redon, Gauguin, Moreau and other European Symbolists—particularly from the French school—made available examples of their work which had never before been available here in such numbers. From these encounters American artists might have drawn a general iconography of Symbolist painting. The reliance upon figurative themes that often emphasized feminine subjects; the preponderant concern for topics of mortality and life cycles; the interest in analogical

Illus. 2. Claude Buck, Death, *1913, watrcolor on paper. Collection Mrs. Benjamin D. Kopman, Haddam, Connecticut.*

relationships between figures and a variety of nonhuman subjects—in short, an entire vocabulary of subjectivist response to man's condition in the modern world appeared in the work of younger American artists in the years immediately preceding World War I.

Claude Buck and his Introspective colleagues represent the culmination of efforts to codify this subjectivist view of the world. Their 1917 manifesto declared that modernism had served its purpose in revitalizing art, but faulted the modernists for being sensational and not profound. Jennings Tofel lamented the backsliding of art into "the hands of intellectual blacksmiths . . . whose art is the art of illustration—the journalism of art, the occurrences of the day, the things of the day." The Introspectives' credo, which called for a new poet-painter, drew heavily upon the precedent of French Symbolist thought, particularly on Baudelaire and Mallarmé. "There are no rules laid down for the constituents of this Introspective group to obey. They agree, however, on the principles of beauty, order and the faculties of imagination and fancy."[11] Like the Symbolists, Claude Buck believed in art "as echo of the human voice within, an intensification of the spiritual and physical life of nature." With the Introspectives he sought to "reconcile the individual with the universal."[12] Such expressions led some critics to characterize Buck and his fellow artists as "leaning toward the transcendental."[13]

The poetic visions of Edgar Allen Poe had been influential in the formation of the Symbolist aesthetics in Europe. Baudelaire's discovery of the American writer in 1847 and his subsequent translation of his verse had been an event of signal importance in the evolution of the Symbolist spirit. In Poe's writing, as defined by one nineteenth-century biographer, "everything was subordinate to sound. But his poetry, as it places us under the spell of the senses, enables us to enter, through their reaction upon the spirit, his indefinable mood. . . ."[14] This quality, which constituted the primary basis of Poe's attraction for the Symbolists, also appealed to Buck. He admired the Southern poet as "the first human being to play great emotional symphonies on the full keyboard of human sensations. He did not reject any sensation a human being could feel, but found them all valuable to better reveal his conception of beauty."[15]

Buck shared several of Poe's thematic obsessions. For instance, Buck's *Death* (illus. 2), a 1913 watercolor included in the Whitney Studio exhibition, parallels one of the poet's major concerns. In his attraction to such a motif, Buck was representative of an attitude especially prevalent in the difficult years surrounding World War I. Speaking of American literature, Matthew Josephson later observed: "In a large measure the strain of morbidity in Hawthorne and Poe seems to have been handed on. The obsession with evil, early sorrow and death, appears astonishingly native to the American muse. . . ."[16] So too in painting, especially Claude Buck's, was death a recurrent theme. The small watercolor is executed in brilliant hues; these belie the ghastly theme, and also suggest an affinity with the palette of the Symbolist master, Gustave Moreau. Buck's Grim Reaper has undergone a gender change, and is here presented as a comely maiden holding her skeletal attribute. In this choice Buck reflect's his generation's interest in the female as symbol of varied moods and qualities.

Another of the Symbolist's morbid subjects, the enchanting and murderous Salome who so fascinated Moreau, was also painted by Buck (illus. 3). His small panel shows the nude woman holding the Baptist's head on the charger, while parading gracefully and seductively before a seated crowd. *Salome* was also exhibited at the Whitney show, as was *Death and the Girl* of 1917 (illus. 4). That small painting incorporated many of the motifs which were favored by European Symbolists, particularly the more decadent: dead woman, nude, before a still water, with peacocks and symbolic blossoms in the foreground. The death-and-maiden theme was a traditional one in European art, especially for Northern artists, and had been essayed frequently from the sixteenth century onward. In Buck's hands, however, the painting took on new symbolic overtones. Painted as it was on the eve of American entry into the horrors of international warfare, is it possible that the maiden expiring on the shore represents not a single casualty, but civilization itself, whose perils President Wilson had announced?

Such evocative themes as Buck and the Introspectives treated met with a sympathetic response of the part of some New York critics. Generally they recognized the works' derivation from earlier sources—"apparently their effort is to return to the golden age of painting, extending from Botticelli down to the time of the so-called men of 1830 . . ."[17]—and their paintings were welcomed as evidence of "a more serious tendency" than the "sensational art productions and 'stunts' such as the patient and generous-minded public" had been offered by the "moderns" in the years immediately preceding.[18] "Much in art is flippant," wrote one reviewer.

Illus. 3. Claude Buck, Salome, *1917, oil on plywood. Private collection.*

"For this exhibition it can be said that it is serious. Whatever lack of joy there may be in this world, seriousness remains a commendable quality."[19] Among the Introspective paintings at the Whitney Studio, it was Buck who "perhaps realiz[ed] his ideas of paintings and style of olden times best . . ." with his amalgam of Botticelli, the Old Masters, and the Greek classics.[20] While admitting that "he is extraordinarily uneven," another critic noted that "it is not long before we discern . . . that at his best—and this is in his small pictures, like his *Adam and Eve* and *Death of the Girl*— that he has a surpassing gift for line and composition and that he has already given us utterly exquisite productions."[21]

Among those attracted to Buck's work was the Chicago art dealer, James W. Young. He bought five of Buck's small paintings for $50 each; en route back to Chicago he sold two of the pictures in Cleveland for $250 each, and the remaining three were quickly acquired by Chicago collectors. At Young's request Buck dispatched more paintings, all similarly imaginative compositions of

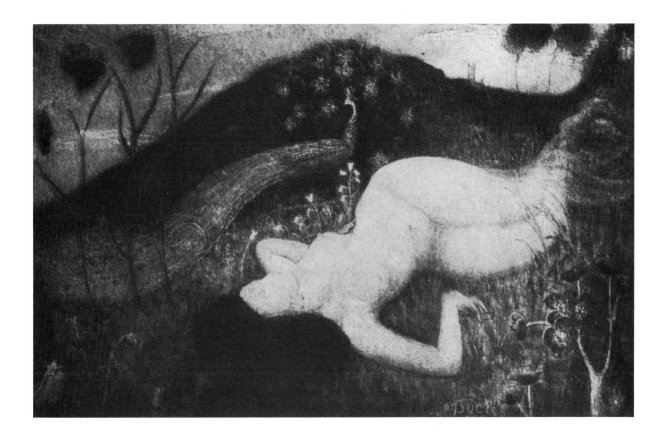

Illus. 4. Claude Buck, Death and the Girl, *1917. Location unknown.*

small scale, and they too sold quickly. Encouraged by this response, Buck determined to move to Chicago since his income was from there, and to dispense with the commissioned portraiture which still was the basis for his New York income. His new association with Young was a happy one, and the dealer sent him the entire proceeds of some sales to finance the artist's move to Illinois.

In March, 1918, Buck's work was shown at Young's Art Galleries. In introducing Buck's work to the Chicago audience, Young acclaimed his "dignified" compositions and praised "this talented young man's knowledge of art terms [which] corresponds with his lofty viewpoint."[22] Local viewers agreed with Buck's new dealer, and repeated the commendation for the painter's poetic themes. "[T]his young painter not only paints well, but has something to say . . . what he has to say is said not in prose but in poetry. It is a relief," concluded one commentator, "to find a young painter of such great talent and such a high view point as Buck."[23]

The Young's Gallery show concentrated upon the imaginative

paintings that had first drawn the dealer's attention. Included were more Poe images, such as one from *Ulalume*, as well as figurative paintings and the "little dream pictures, such as have been purchased by musicians. . . ."[24] Young showed as well the work of Felix Russmann and Benjamin Kopman, two of Buck's Introspective co-exhibitors. Buck's Chicago success inspired his friends to move to Chicago also, and by 1919 the three Introspectives had neighboring studios in the city; within a year they had moved to the hill country just outside of Chicago, where they formed the nucleus of an Introspective art colony—"a smaller 'Brown county' region and more accessible than the Indiana happy valley for busy Chicago men. These young men have their studio homes in Palos Park and find materials for painting in the forest preserve and surrounding country."[25] Local reviewers welcomed their appearance upon the Chicago scene and praised the trio as "strongly individual and inclined to clash with the conservatives."[26]

While the Introspectives provided a catalyst for some, their work was not immediately accepted by the established academicians in Chicago. Although Buck managed to have two pictures included in the 1920 exhibition of area artists at the Art Institute of Chicago, they were carefully placed in the galleries. According to Henriette Weber, a sympathetic local critic, "the few irregulars are tucked away . . . where they will be the least disturbing to the complacency of the jury, in those cases where they have managed to hit the bell. And so we find Claude Buck's two pictures hung where they will cause the least flutter, he is 'so different, you know,' and Russmann's *Moonlight* you have to fish for before you discover it."[27]

While Buck might have been "tucked away" at the Art Institute in January, by April, 1920, he was in full view at the Thurber Art Galleries. The Chicago dealer featured the young Introspective's paintings in a one-man show which occasioned Miss Weber's observation that "The censor of our civic aesthetics has evidently been asleep during the past few days while covering that part of his beat that takes him along East Washington Street. For otherwise how could *Eve*, as she is revealed in a large canvas in an art gallery window there have remained so unmolested as a center of attraction?"[28] The Thurber show was the largest that Buck had had to date, including sixty-five paintings ranging from imaginative compositions to portraits of family and friends. In his foreword to the exhibition catalog Buck reiterated the basic Introspective principles first enunciated at the Whitney Studio and Knoedler Gallery exhibitions. He expressed his admiration for earlier "poet painters,"

those "lonely spirits scattered through the entire trend of the world's art"—Giorgione, El Greco, Rembrandt, Millet, Monticelli, and the Americans, Fuller, Ryder, and Blakelock. "Solitary figures in their age, whose work casts its glory over the world, and their life its gloom—quiet dreamers of profound understanding! Their work is the crown of art, their sincerity and their beauty of feeling, examples to emulate. They are as wonderful as the great universal epics and the lyrics of Shakespeare."[29]

The effect of the Thurber exhibition made one reviewer think that she was "living back in the days of Rossetti, Blake, and Watts, those famous English painters about whom hover[s] such a romantic atmosphere." Like theirs, Buck's themes, drawn from literature, poetry, and the Bible, emphasized concerns remote from those of the resurgent realists. Buck's *Island of Death, Conqueror Worm* (illus. 5), *A Dream within a Dream,* or *Love and Mystery*—"How different from the prosy *Across the Street, Woman Reading, The Road* and *Winter Snows,* which are characteristic titles of the works of most of our present day painters! Realism, dashing technique and sunlight are not the things which Mr. Buck is seeking to express. . . . Mr. Buck is attempting to bring back to art something of the spiritual quantities that we have lost in our scramble for brilliant technique."[30] Or, in the words of another commentator, "it's painting the unseeable that is Buck's strong point. . . ."[31]

Buck's exhibition at the Thurber Art Galleries demonstrated

Illus. 5. Claude Buck, The Conqueror Worm, *1920, oil on canvas. Spencer Museum of Art, The University of Kansas, Gift of Mrs. Claude Buck.*

again his continuing fascination with Edgar Allan Poe's work. He looked to the poet's gruesome verses and tales as the inspiration for essays on ideal beauty, exercises made effective through contrast. "Contrast has been used in many effective ways in painting, music, literature and architecture to reveal the beautiful," he explained. "The beauty of a curved line is revealed by a straight line. . . . Beauty of color is revealed by gray, black, white, brown and gold. . . . Discord has been used to reveal magnificent harmonies in music. Goya, Beardsley, Rembrandt and Durer have used ugliness to enhance their pictures." Thus, in turing to *Ulalume, Lenore, The Masque of the Red Death*, or *The Conqueror Worm*, ". . . I have tried to do what Poe did so wonderfully. Beauty was my intention, and ugliness was used to reveal beauty."[32]

Based on the successes of the Thurber and Young gallery shows, Buck and the Introspectives of Palos Park drew into their orbit a number of more adventuresome young artists, who came to constitute a short-lived Chicago branch of the Introspectives. Raymond Jonson is perhaps the best known of the new recruits, but a number of other Chicago secessionists participated as well. The Chicago Introspectives made their formal bow at the Arts Club in May, 1921. Buck and Kopman were rejoined for this show by Jennings Tofel; also exhibiting at the Arts Club were Jonson and George Constant, Bert Elliott, Anders Haugseth, Gerritt St. Clair, George Rich, Anthony Angarola, Rudolph Weisenborn, Karl Mattern, and (surprisingly) the academic George Eggers from the Art Institute. According to press reports the show proved "to be one of the most interesting events of the year" and it was notable for being "the first exhibition at the Arts Club at which interest in the pictures surpassed the interest in the social side and the tea!"[33] The veteran subjectivists, Buck and Kopman, were praised as "the most expert and advanced in the art of introspecting. Turning to literature and the Old Masters for his inspiration Mr. Buck produces an art which generally has little in common with modern art either in feeling or treatment."[34]

Buck's quest for ideal beauty did indeed lead him away from the emerging concerns for postwar American artists. One visitor to the Arts Club show noted that group's efforts at accommodation of tradition and modernism. "There must always be explorers," preached Katharine Roberts, "unless we are to deteriorate and ultimately perish of inbreeding and stagnation. If the theories of the more radical seem to lead them too far into the mystic realism of the unknown and, to many, incomprehensible, there are also those explorers who keep a tighter rein on their adventuresome spirits and guide us to regions equally new and quite understandable. We are always endeavoring to strike a balance and, at the same time, to find the sane way to fuller truth and beauty. The Introspectives are trying for that very thing."[35]

Yet in the altered artistic environment of America in the 1920s, the public's taste for poet-painters was less pronounced than in the stressful years before and during World War I. The first wave of modernist experimentation retreated shortly after 1918, to be replaced by a period of more "realist" concentration upon objective themes, frequently drawn from native sources. Cubist fracture yielded to more decorative abstractions. Abstraction itself gave way in many quarters to realism and reportage. Precision in technique, be it Charles Sheeler's or Luigi Lucioni's, gained a new premium, predominating for a time over the more expressive stroke and content of prewar painting. And Introspective dreams were replaced by American scenes.

In Chicago, Claude Buck was not immune to such alterations in taste and style. Portraiture, which had been a recurrent exercise for him from the start, regained its importance in the mid-1920s, an interest reawakened by painting his wife and children. Concurrently he turned new attention to topical themes, and about 1923 became particularly concerned with the life of the urban poor; this led to a series of genre paintings of life among the lowly, a subject that sometimes had Biblical overtones but rarely recaptured the elusive mood and mystery of his earlier religious scenes. His first trip to Europe, in 1927-28, introduced him in great numbers to the Old Masters whose paintings he had admired at the Metropolitan Museum three decades earlier. In Germany, for instance, he was attracted anew to Dürer's work and admired the aritst's schematic system of the "Golden Section," which he saw as derived from Leonardo. Just as Buck had earlier been drawn to Jay Hambridge's Dynamic Symmetry, so too did he now try to emulate Dürer's scheme. What resulted was a figurative style of new chasteness and precision; but, as one contemporary noted, "it is a question . . . whether what has been gained in a plastic and compositional way here has not been lost in sustained emotion."[36]

If the emotional power, the poetry, was sacrificed, the technical finesse did earn new acclaim from Chicago traditionalists. In the 1929 Art Institute exhibition of Artists of Chicago and Vicinity, the same show in which Buck's work had been "tucked away" nine years earlier, he was awarded the John C. Shaffer Prize for his *Mother and Children*. Another family portrait was awarded a $300 prize in the Chicago Galleries association competitive exhibition in 1927. In 1932, Buck won the First Mr. and Mrs. Frank G. Logan Medal, also at the Institute's Chicago area show, for his *Girl Reading*.

Over the years, Buck taught at the Art Institute of Chicago, at the Chicago Academy of Fine Arts, and elsewhere. Occasionally he painted imaginative compositions, but these never again recaptured the single attention or interest they had claimed during the Introspective era. A large one-man exhibition of the artist's work at the Grand Central Galleries in New York in 1940, Buck's first major showing there since the Whitney and Knoedler debuts in 1917, was notable for the diversity of styles, subjects and techniques that the painter displayed. In reviewing the show, Edward Alden Jewell noted that "a visitor . . . might well be pardoned . . . in supposing this to be not a one-man show but a group show, so various and often contradictory are the various styles vouchsafed. It is curious indeed to find an artist, within so short a span of time, exposing, as it were, so many style 'entities'."[37]

In 1943, Buck moved to California, initially to the art colony at Santa Cruz and ultimately to Santa Barbara, where he died August 4, 1974. The last painting on which he worked, a monochrome which was left unfinished at his death, was on an imaginative theme. At the close of his life, as he had done intermittently for half a century, Claude Buck returned to the evocative motifs and suggestive subjects that had marked his introduction in 1917. It is perhaps moot as to whether, without the coincidence of American involvement in world war and the changes it brought, Buck and the Introspectives might have had a larger impact on American art generally. But their collaborative experiment does provide a neglected chapter in the history of American romanticism and points out, once again, the mutability of artistic fortunes.

[1] Woodrow Wilson's speech for declaration of war against Germany, delivered at joint session of the two Houses of Congress, April 2, 1917 (U.S. 65th Congress, 1st Session, *Senate Doc. 5*).

[2] Edith W. Powell, "The Introspectives," *International Studio*, 61:242 (April, 1917), xcii.

[3] Winifred Ward, quoted in ibid.

[4] See the Tofel Papers, especially his correspondence with Benjamin D. Kopman, on deposit at the Yiva Institute for Jewish Research, New York, N.Y.

[5] Information on Buck's boyhood was kindly provided by his wife, Leslie Buck, by his sister, Grace Buck Kopman, and by his niece, Diana Kopman Link. Reflecting upon his study and admiration for the Old Masters, Buck once wrote: "If I ever paint as well as De Vinci (*sic*) I will be the first painter who ever did. Angelo equalled his drawing only—Raphael only his composition—Titian only his color—and Rembrandt only his shadows. De Vinci equalled all these men in all these things." Claude Buck to William Robert Buck, November 27, 1940; letter in possession of Mrs. Benjamin D. Kopman.

[6] Claude Buck, "Foreword," in catalog for his exhibition at Thurber Art Galleries, Chicago, 1920; copy from artist's scrapbook, courtesy Mrs. Claude Buck (hereafter, Buck Scrapbook).

[7] Claude Buck, "What Is Art?" *Palos in Autumn* (Palos Park, Il.), 2 (1923), 3.

[8] Buck, "Foreword" to Thurber Art Galleries catalog, Buck Scrapbook.

[9] *Imaginative Paintings by Thirty Young Artists of New York City* (New York: Knoedler Galleries, 1917), [1].

[10] The published catalog lists only 19 paintings; however, the artist's personal copy of the publication includes in his own hand a list of another nine works which were uncataloged; Buck Scrapbook.

[11] Jennings Tofel, Introspective Manifesto, quoted in Powell, p. xcii.

[12] Unidentified newspaper clipping, Chicago, *circa* 1921, Buck Scrapbook.

[13] Evelyn Marie Stuart, "Chicago," *American Art News*, 19:31 (May 14, 1921), 10, review of Introspectives' exhibition at Chicago Arts Club.

[14] Edmund Chase Stedman, "Edgar Allan Poe," *Scribner's Monthly*, 20 (May, 1880), 117.

[15] Buck, quoted in untitled clipping, Chicago *Post*, 1924, Buck Scrapbook.

[16] Matthew Josephson, *Portrait of the Artist as American* (New York: Octagon Books, 1964; first published 1930), p. xviii.

[17] "Glowing Exhibits in Art Galleries," unidentified newspaper clipping, New York, March (?), 1917, Buck Scrapbook.

[18] "Art and Artists," *The Globe and Commercial Advertiser* (New York), October 30, 1917, Buck Scrapbook.

NOTES

[19]Review of Whitney Studio exhibition, New York *Herald*, March 25, 1917, Buck Scrapbook.

[20]"Glowing Exhibits in Art Galleries."

[21]Powell, p. xciii.

[22]Unidentified magazine clipping (from Young's Art Galleries?), Chicago, 1918; copy in vertical files, FA/PG Library, Smithsonian Institution, Washington, D.C.

[23]"Annual Exhibition of American Paintings at the Art Institute," *The Shopper's Blue Book of Chicago* (Chicago, 1919), p. 2.

[24]"Three Young Artists at Young's Gallery," unidentified clipping from *American Art News*, Buck Scrapbook.

[25]"Palos Park Painters," unidentified newspaper clipping, Buck Scrapbook.

[26]Henriette Weber, "Art: Bellows Causes Flutter," undated clipping from Chicago *Herald and Examiner*, Buck Scrapbook.

[27]Henriette Weber, "Art," undated clipping from Chicago *Herald and Examiner*, 1920, review of 24th Annual Exhibition by Artists of Chicago and Vicinity, Buck Scrapbook.

[28]Henriette Weber, "Calude Buck Painting the Unseeable," April 18, 1920, unidentified newspaper clipping; courtesy Mrs. Benjamin D. Kopman (hereafter, Kopman Scrapbook).

[29]Buck, "Foreword" to Thurber Art Galleries catalog, in Buck Scrapbook.

[30]Marguerite B. Williams, "Exhibition by Buck," undated clipping from Chicago *Daily News*, 1920, Buck Scrapbook.

[31]Weber, "Claude Buck Painting the Unseeable."

[32]Unidentified newspaper clipping, Chicago, 1924, Buck Scrapbook.

[33]Stuart, "Chicago," p. 10.

[34]Marguerite Williams, " 'Introspectives' Put Art Circles in Whirl," Chicago *Daily News*, May 12, 1921, Buck Scrapbook.

[35]Katharine Eggleston Roberts, "Introspectives Challenge Chicago Critics," unidentified magazine clipping, June 1921, Buck Scrapbook.

[36]Marguerite B. Williams, "Here and There in the World of Art," undated clipping from Chicago *Daily News*, *circa* 1928, Kopman Scrapbook.

[37]Edward Alden Jewell, "Claude Buck Gives One-Man Art Show," New York *Times*, December 10, 1940, Kopman Scrapbook.

The text was set in Bembo by Graphic Typesetting Service. The book was printed on Cameo dull, 80 lb., by Printers Incorporated, and bound in Roxite C cloth by Stauffer Edition Binding Co. The endpapers are Americana Text, 80 lb. Larry du Pont designed the format and, assisted by Cheryl Lobenburg, prepared the pages for reproduction. Teresa Joseph, UCLA Latin American Center, coordinated the project assisted by Carol Leyba, UCLA Institute of Archaeology. Kim Lockard, UCLA Publication Services, supervised production.

DATE

DEMCO, INC. 38-2931